THE
IRRATIONAL KNOT

THE SECOND NOVEL OF HIS NONAGE

GEORGE BERNARD SHAW

1st WORLD
LIBRARY
Literary Society

The Irrational Knot

George Bernard Shaw

© 1st World Library, 2007
PO Box 2211
Fairfield, IA 52556
www.1stworldlibrary.com
First Edition

LCCN: 2007920676

Softcover ISBN: 978-1-4218-3958-5
Hardcover ISBN: 978-1-4218-3858-8
eBook ISBN: 978-1-4218-4058-1

Purchase *"The Irrational Knot"*
as a traditional bound book at:
www.1stWorldLibrary.com/purchase.asp?ISBN=978-1-4218-3958-5

1st World Library is a literary, educational organization
dedicated to:

- Creating a free internet library of downloadable ebooks

- Hosting writing competitions and offering book
  publishing scholarships.

Interested in more 1st World Library books?
contact: literacy@1stworldlibrary.com
Check us out at: www.1stworldlibrary.com

1ˢᵗ World Library Literary Society

Giving Back to the World

"If you want to work on the core problem, it's early school literacy."

- James Barksdale, former CEO of Netscape

"No skill is more crucial to the future of a child, or to a democratic and prosperous society, than literacy."

- Los Angeles Times

Literacy... means far more than learning how to read and write... The aim is to transmit... knowledge and promote social participation."

- UNESCO

"Literacy is not a luxury, it is a right and a responsibility. If our world is to meet the challenges of the twenty-first century we must harness the energy and creativity of all our citizens."

- President Bill Clinton

"Parents should be encouraged to read to their children, and teachers should be equipped with all available techniques for teaching literacy, so the varying needs and capacities of individual kids can be taken into account."

- Hugh Mackay

PREFACE TO THE AMERICAN EDITION OF 1905

This novel was written in the year 1880, only a few years after I had exported myself from Dublin to London in a condition of extreme rawness and inexperience concerning the specifically English side of the life with which the book pretends to deal. Everybody wrote novels then. It was my second attempt; and it shared the fate of my first. That is to say, nobody would publish it, though I tried all the London publishers and some American ones. And I should not greatly blame them if I could feel sure that it was the book's faults and not its qualities that repelled them.

I have narrated elsewhere how in the course of time the rejected MS. became Mrs. Annie Besant's excuse for lending me her ever helping hand by publishing it as a serial in a little propagandist magazine of hers. That was how it got loose beyond all possibility of recapture. It is out of my power now to stand between it and the American public: all I can do is to rescue it from unauthorized mutilations and make the best of a jejune job.

At present, of course, I am not the author of The Irrational Knot. Physiologists inform us that the substance of our bodies (and consequently of our souls) is shed and renewed at such a rate that no part of us lasts longer than eight years: I am therefore not now in any atom of me the person who wrote The Irrational Knot in 1880. The last of that author perished in 1888; and two of his successors have since joined the majority. Fourth of his line, I cannot be expected to take any very lively interest in the novels of my literary great-grand-father. Even my personal recollections of him are becoming vague and overlaid with those most misleading of all traditions, the traditions founded on the lies a man tells, and at last comes to believe, about himself *to* himself. Certain things, however, I remember very well. For instance, I am significantly clear as to the price of the paper on which I wrote The Irrational Knot. It was cheap—a white demy of unpretentious quality—so that sixpennorth lasted a long time. My daily allowance of composition was five pages of this demy in quarto; and I held my natural laziness sternly to that task day in, day out, to the end. I remember also that Bizet's Carmen being then new in London, I used it as a safety-valve for my romantic impulses. When I was tired of the sordid realism of Whatshisname (I have sent my only copy of The Irrational Knot to the printers, and cannot remember the name of my hero) I went to the piano and forgot him in the glamorous society of Carmen and her crimson toreador and yellow dragoon. Not that Bizet's music could infatuate me as it infatuated Nietzsche. Nursed on greater masters, I thought less of him than he deserved; but the Carmen music was—in places—exquisite of its kind, and could enchant a man like me, romantic enough to have come to the end of romance before I began to create in art for myself.

When I say that *I* did and felt these things, I mean, of course, that the predecessor whose name I bear did and felt them. The I of to-day is (? am) cool towards Carmen; and Carmen, I regret to say, does not take the slightest interest in him (? me). And now enough of this juggling with past and present Shaws. The grammatical complications of being a first person and several extinct third persons at the same moment are so frightful that I must return to the ordinary misusage, and ask the reader to make the necessary corrections in his or her own mind.

This book is not wholly a compound of intuition and ignorance. Take for example the profession of my hero, an Irish-American electrical engineer. That was by no means a

George Bernard Shaw

flight of fancy. For you must not suppose, because I am a man of letters, that I never tried to earn an honest living. I began trying to commit that sin against my nature when I was fifteen, and persevered, from youthful timidity and diffidence, until I was twenty-three. My last attempt was in 1879, when a company was formed in London to exploit an ingenious invention by Mr. Thomas Alva Edison—a much too ingenious invention as it proved, being nothing less than a telephone of such stentorian efficiency that it bellowed your most private communications all over the house instead of whispering them with some sort of discretion. This was not what the British stockbroker wanted; so the company was soon merged in the National Telephone Company, after making a place for itself in the history of literature, quite unintentionally, by providing me with a job. Whilst the Edison Telephone Company lasted, it crowded the basement of a huge pile of offices in Queen Victoria Street with American artificers. These deluded and romantic men gave me a glimpse of the skilled proletariat of the United States. They sang obsolete sentimental songs with genuine emotion; and their language was frightful even to an Irishman. They worked with a ferocious energy which was out of all proportion to the actual result achieved. Indomitably resolved to assert their republican manhood by taking no orders from a tall-hatted Englishman whose stiff politeness covered his conviction that they were, relatively to himself, inferior and common persons, they insisted on being slave-driven with genuine American oaths by a genuine free and equal American foreman. They utterly despised the artfully slow British workman who did as little for his wages as he possibly could; never hurried himself; and had a deep reverence for anyone whose pocket could be tapped by respectful behavior. Need I add that they were contemptuously wondered at by this same British workman as a parcel of outlandish adult boys, who sweated themselves for their employer's benefit instead of looking after their own interests? They adored Mr. Edison as the greatest man of all time in every possible department of science, art and philosophy, and execrated Mr. Graham Bell, the inventor of the rival telephone, as his Satanic adversary; but each of them had (or pretended to have) on the brink of completion, an improvement on the telephone, usually a new transmitter. They were free-souled creatures, excellent company: sensitive, cheerful, and profane; liars, braggarts, and hustlers; with an air of making slow old England hum which never left them even when, as often happened, they were wrestling with difficulties of their own making, or struggling in no-thoroughfares from which they had to be retrieved like strayed sheep by English-men without imagination enough to go wrong.

In this environment I remained for some months. As I was interested in physics and had read Tyndall and Helmholtz, besides having learnt something in Ireland through a fortunate friendship with a cousin of Mr. Graham Bell who was also a chemist and physicist, I was, I believe, the only person in the entire establishment who knew the current scientific explanation of telephony; and as I soon struck up a friendship with our official lecturer, a Colchester man whose strong point was pre-scientific agriculture, I often discharged his duties for him in a manner which, I am persuaded, laid the foundation of Mr. Edison's London reputation: my sole reward being my boyish delight in the half-concealed incredulity of our visitors (who were convinced by the hoarsely startling utterances of the telephone that the speaker, alleged by me to be twenty miles away, was really using a speaking-trumpet in the next room), and their obvious uncertainty, when the demonstration was over, as to whether they ought to tip me or not: a question they either decided in the negative or never decided at all; for I never got anything.

So much for my electrical engineer! To get him into contact with fashionable society before he became famous was also a problem easily solved. I knew of three English peers who actually preferred physical laboratories to stables, and scientific experts to gamekeepers: in fact, one of the experts was a friend of mine. And I knew from personal experience that if science brings men of all ranks into contact, art, especially music, does the same for men and women. An electrician who can play an accompaniment can go anywhere and know anybody. As far as

George Bernard Shaw

mere access and acquaintance go there are no class barriers for him. My difficulty was not to get my hero into society, but to give any sort of plausibility to my picture of society when I got him into it. I lacked the touch of the literary diner-out; and I had, as the reader will probably find to his cost, the classical tradition which makes all the persons in a novel, except the comically vernacular ones, or the speakers of phonetically spelt dialect, utter themselves in the formal phrases and studied syntax of eighteenth century rhetoric. In short, I wrote in the style of Scott and Dickens; and as fashionable society then spoke and behaved, as it still does, in no style at all, my transcriptions of Oxford and Mayfair may nowadays suggest an unaccountable and ludicrous ignorance of a very superficial and accessible code of manners. I was not, however, so ignorant as might have been inferred at that time from my somewhat desperate financial condition.

I had, to begin with, a sort of backstairs knowledge; for in my teens I struggled for life in the office of an Irish gentleman who acted as land agent and private banker for many persons of distinction. Now it is possible for a London author to dine out in the highest circles for twenty years without learning as much about the human frailties of his hosts as the family solicitor or (in Ireland) the family land agent learns in twenty days; and some of this knowledge inevitably reaches his clerks, especially the clerk who keeps the cash, which was my particular department. He learns, if capable of the lesson, that the aristocratic profession has as few geniuses as any other profession; so that if you want a peerage of more than, say, half a dozen members, you must fill it up with many common persons, and even with some deplorably mean ones. For "service is no inheritance" either in the kitchen or the House of Lords; and the case presented by Mr. Barrie in his play of The Admirable Crichton, where the butler is the man of quality, and his master, the Earl, the man of rank, is no fantasy, but a quite common occurrence, and indeed to some extent an inevitable one, because the English are extremely particular in selecting their butlers, whilst they do not select their barons at all, taking them as the accident of birth sends them. The consequences include much ironic comedy. For instance, we have in England a curious belief in first rate people, meaning all the people we do not know; and this consoles us for the undeniable secondrateness of the people we do know, besides saving the credit of aristocracy as an institution. The unmet aristocrat is devoutly believed in; but he is always round the corner, never at hand. That *the* smart set exists; that there is above and beyond that smart set a class so blue of blood and exquisite in nature that it looks down even on the King with haughty condescension; that scepticism on these points is one of the stigmata of plebeian baseness: all these imaginings are so common here that they constitute the real popular sociology of England as much as an unlimited credulity as to vaccination constitutes the real popular science of England. It is, of course, a timid superstition. A British peer or peeress who happens by chance to be genuinely noble is just as isolated at court as Goethe would have been among all the other grandsons of publicans, if they had formed a distinct class in Frankfurt or Weimar. This I knew very well when I wrote my novels; and if, as I suspect, I failed to create a convincingly verisimilar atmosphere of aristocracy, it was not because I had any illusions or ignorances as to the common humanity of the peerage, and not because I gave literary style to its conversation, but because, as I had never had any money, I was foolishly indifferent to it, and so, having blinded myself to its enormous importance, necessarily missed the point of view, and with it the whole moral basis, of the class which rightly values money, and plenty of it, as the first condition of a bearable life.

Money is indeed the most important thing in the world; and all sound and successful personal and national morality should have this fact for its basis. Every teacher or twaddler who denies it or suppresses it, is an enemy of life. Money controls morality; and what makes the United States of America look so foolish even in foolish Europe is that they are always in a state of flurried concern and violent interference with morality, whereas they throw their money into the street to be scrambled for, and presently find that their cash reserves are not in their

George Bernard Shaw

own hands, but in the pockets of a few millionaires who, bewildered by their luck, and unspeakably incapable of making any truly economic use of it, endeavor to "do good" with it by letting themselves be fleeced by philanthropic committee men, building contractors, librarians and professors, in the name of education, science, art and what not; so that sensible people exhale relievedly when the pious millionaire dies, and his heirs, demoralized by being brought up on his outrageous income, begin the socially beneficent work of scattering his fortune through the channels of the trades that flourish by riotous living.

This, as I have said, I did not then understand; for I knew money only by the want of it. Ireland is a poor country; and my father was a poor man in a poor country. By this I do not mean that he was hungry and homeless, a hewer of wood and a drawer of water. My friend Mr. James Huneker, a man of gorgeous imagination and incorrigible romanticism, has described me to the American public as a peasant lad who has raised himself, as all American presidents are assumed to have raised themselves, from the humblest departments of manual labor to the loftiest eminence. James flatters me. Had I been born a peasant, I should now be a tramp. My notion of my father's income is even vaguer than his own was—and that is saying a good deal—but he always had an income of at least three figures (four, if you count in dollars instead of pounds); and what made him poor was that he conceived himself as born to a social position which even in Ireland could have been maintained in dignified comfort only on twice or thrice what he had. And he married on that assumption. Fortunately for me, social opportunity is not always to be measured by income. There is an important economic factor, first analyzed by an American economist (General Walker), and called rent of ability. Now this rent, when the ability is of the artistic or political sort, is often paid in kind. For example, a London possessor of such ability may, with barely enough money to maintain a furnished bedroom and a single presentable suit of clothes, see everything worth seeing that a millionaire can see, and know everybody worth knowing that he can know. Long before I reached this point myself, a very trifling accomplishment gave me glimpses of the sort of fashionable life a peasant never sees. Thus I remember one evening during the novel-writing period when nobody would pay a farthing for a stroke of my pen, walking along Sloane Street in that blessed shield of literary shabbiness, evening dress. A man accosted me with an eloquent appeal for help, ending with the assurance that he had not a penny in the world. I replied, with exact truth, "Neither have I." He thanked me civilly, and went away, apparently not in the least surprised, leaving me to ask myself why I did not turn beggar too, since I felt sure that a man who did it as well as he, must be in comfortable circumstances.

Another reminiscence. A little past midnight, in the same costume, I was turning from Piccadilly into Bond Street, when a lady of the pavement, out of luck that evening so far, confided to me that the last bus for Brompton had passed, and that she should be grateful to any gentleman who would give her a lift in a hansom. My old-fashioned Irish gallantry had not then been worn off by age and England: besides, as a novelist who could find no publisher, I was touched by the similarity of our trades and predicaments. I excused myself very politely on the ground that my wife (invented for the occasion) was waiting for me at home, and that I felt sure so attractive a lady would have no difficulty in finding another escort. Unfortunately this speech made so favorable an impression on her that she immediately took my arm and declared her willingness to go anywhere with me, on the flattering ground that I was a perfect gentleman. In vain did I try to persuade her that in coming up Bond Street and deserting Piccadilly, she was throwing away her last chance of a hansom: she attached herself so devotedly to me that I could not without actual violence shake her off. At last I made a stand at the end of Old Bond Street. I took out my purse; opened it; and held it upside down. Her countenance fell, poor girl! She turned on her heel with a melancholy flirt of her skirt, and vanished.

Now on both these occasions I had been in the company of

George Bernard Shaw

people who spent at least as much in a week as I did in a year. Why was I, a penniless and unknown young man, admitted there? Simply because, though I was an execrable pianist, and never improved until the happy invention of the pianola made a Paderewski of me, I could play a simple accompaniment at sight more congenially to a singer than most amateurs. It is true that the musical side of London society, with its streak of Bohemianism, and its necessary toleration of foreign ways and professional manners, is far less typically English than the sporting side or the political side or the Philistine side; so much so, indeed, that people may and do pass their lives in it without ever discovering what English plutocracy in the mass is really like: still, if you wander in it nocturnally for a fitful year or so as I did, with empty pockets and an utter impossibility of approaching it by daylight (owing to the deplorable decay of the morning wardrobe), you have something more actual to go on than the hallucinations of a peasant lad setting his foot manfully on the lowest rung of the social ladder. I never climbed any ladder: I have achieved eminence by sheer gravitation; and I hereby warn all peasant lads not to be duped by my pretended example into regarding their present servitude as a practicable first step to a celebrity so dazzling that its subject cannot even suppress his own bad novels.

Conceive me then at the writing of The Irrational Knot as a person neither belonging to the world I describe nor wholly ignorant of it, and on certain points quite incapable of conceiving it intuitively. A whole world of art which did not exist for it lay open to me. I was familiar with the greatest in that world: mighty poets, painters, and musicians were my intimates. I found the world of artificial greatness founded on convention and money so repugnant and contemptible by comparison that I had no sympathetic understanding of it. People are fond of blaming valets because no man is a hero to his valet. But it is equally true that no man is a valet to his hero; and the hero, consequently, is apt to blunder very ludicrously about valets, through judging them from an irrelevant standard of heroism: heroism, remember, having its faults as well as its qualities. I, always on the heroic plane imaginatively, had two disgusting faults which I did not recognize as faults because I could not help them. I was poor and (by day) shabby. I therefore tolerated the gross error that poverty, though an inconvenience and a trial, is not a sin and a disgrace; and I stood for my self-respect on the things I had: probity, ability, knowledge of art, laboriousness, and whatever else came cheaply to me. Because I could walk into Hampton Court Palace and the National Gallery (on free days) and enjoy Mantegna and Michael Angelo whilst millionaires were yawning miserably over inept gluttonies; because I could suffer more by hearing a movement of Beethoven's Ninth Symphony taken at a wrong tempo than a duchess by losing a diamond necklace, I was indifferent to the repulsive fact that if I had fallen in love with the duchess I did not possess a morning suit in which I could reasonably have expected her to touch me with the furthest protended pair of tongs; and I did not see that to remedy this I should have been prepared to wade through seas of other people's blood. Indeed it is this perception which constitutes an aristocracy nowadays. It is the secret of all our governing classes, which consist finally of people who, though perfectly prepared to be generous, humane, cultured, philanthropic, public spirited and personally charming in the second instance, are unalterably resolved, in the first, to have money enough for a handsome and delicate life, and will, in pursuit of that money, batter in the doors of their fellow men, sell them up, sweat them in fetid dens, shoot, stab, hang, imprison, sink, burn and destroy them in the name of law and order. And this shews their fundamental sanity and rightmindedness; for a sufficient income is indispensable to the practice of virtue; and the man who will let any unselfish consideration stand between him and its attainment is a weakling, a dupe and a predestined slave. If I could convince our impecunious mobs of this, the world would be reformed before the end of the week; for the sluggards who are content to be wealthy without working and the dastards who are content to work without being wealthy, together with all the pseudo-moralists and ethicists and cowardice mongers generally, would be exterminated without shrift, to the unutterable enlargement of life and ennoblement of humanity. We might even make some

George Bernard Shaw

beginnings of civilization under such happy circumstances.

In the days of The Irrational Knot I had not learnt this lesson; consequently I did not understand the British peerage, just as I did not understand that glorious and beautiful phenomenon, the "heartless" rich American woman, who so thoroughly and admirably understands that conscience is a luxury, and should be indulged in only when the vital needs of life have been abundantly satisfied. The instinct which has led the British peerage to fortify itself by American alliances is healthy and well inspired. Thanks to it, we shall still have a few people to maintain the tradition of a handsome, free, proud, costly life, whilst the craven mass of us are keeping up our starveling pretence that it is more important to be good than to be rich, and piously cheating, robbing, and murdering one another by doing our duty as policemen, soldiers, bailiffs, jurymen, turnkeys, hangmen, tradesmen, and curates, at the command of those who know that the golden grapes are *not* sour. Why, good heavens! we shall all pretend that this straightforward truth of mine is mere Swiftian satire, because it would require a little courage to take it seriously and either act on it or make me drink the hemlock for uttering it.

There was the less excuse for my blindness because I was at that very moment laying the foundations of my high fortune by the most ruthless disregard of all the quack duties which lead the peasant lad of fiction to the White House, and harness the real peasant boy to the plough until he is finally swept, as rubbish, into the workhouse. I was an ablebodied and able-minded young man in the strength of my youth; and my family, then heavily embarrassed, needed my help urgently. That I should have chosen to be a burden to them instead was, according to all the conventions of peasant lad fiction, mons-trous. Well, without a blush I embraced the monstrosity. I did not throw myself into the struggle for life: I threw my mother into it. I was not a staff to my father's old age: I hung on to his coat tails. His reward was to live just long enough to read a review of one of these silly novels written in an obscure journal by a personal friend of my own (now eminent in literature as

Mr. John Mackinnon Robertson) prefiguring me to some extent as a considerable author. I think, myself, that this was a handsome reward, far better worth having than a nice pension from a dutiful son struggling slavishly for his parent's bread in some sordid trade. Handsome or not, it was the only return he ever had for the little pension he contrived to export from Ireland for his family. My mother reinforced it by drudging in her elder years at the art of music which she had followed in her prime freely for love. I only helped to spend it. People wondered at my heartlessness: one young and romantic lady had the courage to remonstrate openly and indignantly with me, "for the which" as Pepys said of the shipwright's wife who refused his advances, "I did respect her." Callous as Comus to moral babble, I steadily wrote my five pages a day and made a man of myself (at my mother's expense) instead of a slave. And I protest that I will not suffer James Huneker or any romanticist to pass me off as a peasant boy qualifying for a chapter in Smiles's Self Help, or a good son supporting a helpless mother, instead of a stupendously selfish artist leaning with the full weight of his hungry body on an energetic and capable woman. No, James: such lies are not only unnecessary, but fearfully depressing and fundamentally immoral, besides being hardly fair to the supposed peasant lad's parents. My mother worked for my living instead of preaching that it was my duty to work for hers: therefore take off your hat to her, and blush.[A]

It is now open to anyone who pleases to read The Irrational Knot. I do not recommend him to; but it is possible that the same mysterious force which drove me through the labor of writing it may have had some purpose which will sustain others through the labor of reading it, and even reward them with some ghastly enjoyment of it. For my own part I cannot stand it. It is to me only one of the heaps of spoiled material that all apprenticeship involves. I consent to its publication because I remember that British colonel who called on Beethoven when the elderly composer was working at his posthumous quartets, and offered him a commission for a work in the style of his jejune septet. Beethoven drove the Colonel out of the house with objurgation. I think that was uncivil. There is a time for the septet, and a time for the posthumous quartets. It is true that if a man called on me now and asked me to write something like The Irrational Knot I should have to exercise great self-control. But there are people who read Man and Superman, and then tell me (actually to my face) that I have never done anything so good as Cashel Byron's Profession. After this, there may be a public for even The Irrational Knot; so let it go.

LONDON, *May* 26, 1905.

[Footnote A: James, having read the above in proof, now protests he never called me a peasant lad: that being a decoration by the sub-editor. The expression he used was "a poor lad." This is what James calls tact. After all, there is something pastoral, elemental, well aerated, about a peasant lad. But a mere poor lad! really, James, *really*—!!!]

P.S.—Since writing the above I have looked through the proof-sheets of this book, and found, with some access of respect for my youth, that it is a fiction of the first order. By this I do not mean that it is a masterpiece in that order, or even a pleasant example of it, but simply that, such as it is, it is one of those fictions in which the morality is original and not readymade. Now this quality is the true diagnostic of the first order in literature, and indeed in all the arts, including the art of life. It is, for example, the distinction that sets Shakespear's Hamlet above his other plays, and that sets Ibsen's work as a whole above Shakespear's work as a whole. Shakespear's morality is a mere reach-me-down; and because Hamlet does not feel comfortable in it, and struggles against the misfit, he suggests something better, futile as his struggle is, and incompetent as Shakespear shews himself in his effort to think out the revolt of his feeling against readymade morality. Ibsen's morality is original all through: he knows well that the men in the street have no use for principles, because they can neither understand nor apply them; and that what they can understand and apply are arbitrary rules of conduct, often frightfully destructive and inhuman, but at least definite rules enabling the common stupid man to know where he stands and what he may do and not do without getting into trouble. Now to all writers of the first order, these rules, and the need for them produced by the moral and intellectual incompetence of the ordinary human animal, are no more invariably beneficial and respectable than the sunlight which ripens the wheat in Sussex and leaves the desert deadly in Sahara, making the cheeks of the ploughman's child rosy in the morning and striking the ploughman brainsick or dead in the afternoon; no more inspired (and no less) than the religion of the Andaman islanders; as much in need of frequent throwing away and replacement as the community's boots. By writers of the second order the readymade morality is accepted as the basis of all moral judgment and criticism of the characters they portray, even when their genius forces them to represent their most attractive heroes and heroines as violating the readymade code in all directions. Far be it from me to pretend that the first order is more readable than the second! Shakespear, Scott, Dickens, Dumas *pere* are not, to say the least, less readable than Euripides and Ibsen. Nor is the first order always more constructive; for Byron, Oscar Wilde, and Larochefoucauld did not get further in positive philosophy than Ruskin and Carlyle, though they could snuff Ruskin's Seven Lamps with their fingers without flinching. Still, the first order remains the first order and the second the second for all that: no man who shuts his eyes and opens his mouth when religion and morality are offered to him on a long spoon can share the same Parnassian bench with those who make an original contribution to religion and morality, were it only a criticism.

Therefore on coming back to this Irrational Knot as a stranger after 25 years, I am proud to find that its morality is not readymade. The drunken prima donna of a bygone type of musical burlesque is not depicted as an immoral person, but as a person with a morality of her own, no worse in its way than the morality of her highly respectable wine merchant in *its* way. The sociology of the successful inventor is his own sociology too; and it is by his originality in this respect that he

George Bernard Shaw

passes irresistibly through all the readymade prejudices that are set up to bar his promotion. And the heroine, nice, amiable, benevolent, and anxious to please and behave well, but hopelessly secondhand in her morals and nicenesses, and conesquently without any real moral force now that the threat of hell has lost its terrors for her, is left destitute among the failures which are so puzzling to thoughtless people. "I cannot understand why she is so unlucky: she is such a nice woman!": that is the formula. As if people with any force in them ever were altogether nice!

And so I claim the first order for this jejune exploit of mine, and invite you to note that the final chapter, so remote from Scott and Dickens and so close to Ibsen, was written years before Ibsen came to my knowledge, thus proving that the revolt of the Life Force against readymade morality in the nineteenth century was not the work of a Norwegian microbe, but would have worked itself into expression in English literature had Norway never existed. In fact, when Miss Lord's translation of A Doll's House appeared in the eighteen-eighties, and so excited some of my Socialist friends that they got up a private reading of it in which I was cast for the part of Krogstad, its novelty as a morally original study of a marriage did not stagger me as it staggered Europe. I had made a morally original study of a marriage myself, and made it, too, without any melodramatic forgeries, spinal diseases, and suicides, though I had to confess to a study of dipsomania. At all events, I chattered and ate caramels in the back drawing-room (our green-room) whilst Eleanor Marx, as Nora, brought Helmer to book at the other side of the folding doors. Indeed I concerned myself very little about Ibsen until, later on, William Archer translated Peer Gynt to me *viva voce*, when the magic of the great poet opened my eyes in a flash to the importance of the social philosopher.

I seriously suggest that The Irrational Knot may be regarded as an early attempt on the part of the Life Force to write A Doll's House in English by the instrumentality of a very immature writer aged 24. And though I say it that should not, the choice was not such a bad shot for a stupid instinctive force that has to work and become conscious of itself by means of human brains. If we could only realize that though the Life Force supplies us with its own purpose, it has no other brains to work with than those it has painfully and imperfectly evolved in our heads, the peoples of the earth would learn some pity for their gods; and we should have a religion that would not be contradicted at every turn by the thing that is giving the lie to the thing that ought to be.

WELWYN, *Sunday, June* 25, 1905.

BOOK I

CHAPTER I

At seven o'clock on a fine evening in April the gas had just been lighted in a room on the first floor of a house in York Road, Lambeth. A man, recently washed and brushed, stood on the hearthrug before a pier glass, arranging a white necktie, part of his evening dress. He was about thirty, well grown, and fully developed muscularly. There was no cloud of vice or trouble upon him: he was concentrated and calm, making no tentative movements of any sort (even a white tie did not puzzle him into fumbling), but acting with a certainty of aim and consequent economy of force, dreadful to the irresolute. His face was brown, but his auburn hair classed him as a fair man.

The apartment, a drawing-room with two windows, was dusty and untidy. The paint and wall paper had not been renewed for years; nor did the pianette, which stood near the fireplace, seem to have been closed during that time; for the interior was dusty, and the inner end of every key begrimed. On a table between the windows were some tea things, with a heap of milliner's materials, and a brass candlestick which had been pushed back to make room for a partially unfolded cloth. There was a second table near the door, crowded with coils, batteries, a galvanometer, and other electrical apparatus. The mantelpiece was littered with dusty letters, and two trays of Doulton ware which ornamented it were filled with accounts, scraps of twine, buttons, and rusty keys.

A shifting, rustling sound, as of somebody dressing, which had been audible for some minutes through the folding doors, now ceased, and a handsome young woman entered. She had thick black hair, fine dark eyes, an oval face, a clear olive complexion, and an elastic figure. She was incompletely attired in a petticoat that did not hide her ankles, and stays of bright red silk with white laces and seams. Quite unconcerned at the presence of the man, she poured out a cup of tea; carried it to the mantelpiece; and began to arrange her hair before the glass. He, without looking round, completed the arrangement of his tie, looked at it earnestly for a moment, and said, "Have you got a pin about you?"

"There is one in the pincushion on my table," she said; "but I think it's a black one. I dont know where the deuce all the pins go to." Then, casting off the subject, she whistled a long and florid cadenza, and added, by way of instrumental interlude, a remarkably close imitation of a violoncello. Meanwhile the man went into her room for the pin. On his return she suddenly became curious, and said, "Where are you going tonight, if one may ask?"

"I am going out."

She looked at him for a moment, and turned contemptuously to the mirror, saying, "Thank you. Sorry to be inquisitive."

"I am going to sing for the Countess of Carbury at a concert at Wandsworth."

"Sing! You! The Countess of Barbury! Does she live at Wandsworth?"

"No. She lives in Park Lane."

"Oh! I beg her pardon." The man made no comment on this; and she, after looking doubtfully at him to assure herself that he was in earnest, continued, "How does the Countess of Whatshername come to know *you*, pray?"

George Bernard Shaw

"Why not?"

A long pause ensued. Then she said: "Stuff!", but without conviction. Her exclamation had no apparent effect on him until he had buttoned his waistcoat and arranged his watch-chain. Then he glanced at a sheet of pink paper which lay on the mantelpiece. She snatched it at once; opened it; stared incredulously at it; and said, "Pink paper, and scalloped edges! How filthily vulgar! I thought she was not much of a Countess! Ahem! 'Music for the People. Parnassus Society. A concert will be given at the Town Hall, Wandsworth, on Tuesday, the 25th April, by the Countess of Carbury, assisted by the following ladies and gentlemen. Miss Elinor McQuinch'— what a name! 'Miss Marian Lind'—who's Miss Marian Lind?"

"How should I know?"

"I only thought, as she is a pal of the Countess, that you would most likely be intimate with her. 'Mrs. Leith Fairfax.' There is a Mrs. Leith Fairfax who writes novels, and very rotten novels they are, too. Who are the gentlemen? 'Mr. Marmaduke Lind'—brother to Miss Marian, I suppose. 'Mr. Edward Conolly'—save the mark! they must have been rather hard up for gentlemen when they put *you* down as one. The Conolly family is looking up at last. Hm! nearly a dozen altogether. 'Tickets will be distributed to the families of working men by the Rev. George Lind'—pity they didnt engage Jenny Lind on purpose to sing with you. 'A limited number of front seats at one shilling. Please turn over. Part I. Symphony in F: Haydn. Arranged for four English concertinas by Julius Baker. Mr. Julius Baker; Master Julius Abt Baker; Miss Lisette Baker (aged 8); and Miss Totty Baker (aged 6-1/2)'. Good Lord! 'Song: Rose softly blooming: Spohr. Miss Marian Lind.' I wonder whether she can sing! 'Polonaise in A flat major: Chopin'— what rot! As if working people cared about Chopin! Miss Elinor McQuinch is a fool, I see. 'Song: The Valley: Gounod.' Of course: I knew you would try that. Oho! Here's something sensible at last. 'Nigger melody. Uncle Ned. Mr. Marmaduke Lind, accompanied by himself on the banjo.'

Dum, drum. Dum, drum. Dum, drum. Dum—
'And there was an ole nigga; and his name was Uncle Ned;
An' him dead long ago, long ago.
An' he had no hair on the top of his head
In the place where the wool ought to grow,'

Mr. Marmaduke Lind will get a double *encore*; and no one will take the least notice of you or the others. 'Recitation. The Faithful Soul. Adelaide Proctor. Mrs. Leith Fairfax.' Well, this certainly is a blessed attempt to amuse Wandsworth. *Another* reading by the Rev.—"

Here Conolly, who had been putting on his overcoat, picked the program deftly from his sister's fingers, and left the room. She, after damning him very heartily, returned to the glass, and continued dressing, taking her tea at intervals until she was ready to go out, when she sent for a cab, and bade the driver convey her to the Bijou Theatre, Soho.

Conolly, on arriving at the Wandsworth Town Hall, was directed to a committee room, which served as green-room on this occasion. He was greeted by a clean shaven young clergyman who protested that he was glad to see him there, but did not offer his hand. Conolly thanked him briefly, and went without further ceremony to the table, and was about to place his hat and overcoat on a heap of similar garments, when, observing that there were some hooks along the wall, he immediately crossed over and hung up his things on them, thereby producing an underbred effect of being more prudent and observant than the rest. Then he looked at his program, and calculated how soon his turn to sing would come. Then he unrolled his music, and placed two copies of Le Vallon ready to his hand upon the table. Having made these arrangements with a self-possession that quite disconcerted the clergyman, he turned to examine the rest of the company.

His first glance was arrested by the beauty of a young lady with light brown hair and gentle grey eyes, who sat near the fire. Beside her, on a lower chair, was a small, lean, and very restless young woman with keen dark eyes staring defiantly from a worn face. These two were attended by a jovial young gentleman with curly auburn hair, who was twanging a banjo, and occasionally provoking an exclamation of annoyance from the restless girl by requesting her opinion of his progress in tuning the instrument. Near them stood a tall man, dark and handsome. He seemed unused to his present circumstances, and contemptuous, not of the company nor the object for which they were assembled, but in the abstract, as if habitual contempt were part of his nature.

The clergyman, who had just conducted to the platform an elderly professor in a shabby frock coat, followed by three well-washed children, each of whom carried a concertina, now returned and sat down beside a middle-aged lady, who made herself conspicuous by using a gold framed eyeglass so as to convey an impression that she was an exceedingly keen observer.

"It is fortunate that the evening is so fine," said the clergyman to her.

"Yes, is it not, Mr. Lind?"

"My throat is always affected by bad weather, Mrs. Leith Fairfax. I shall be so handicapped by the inevitable comparison of my elocution with yours, that I am glad the weather is favorable to me, though the comparison is not."

"No," said Mrs. Fairfax, with decision. "I am not in the least an orator. I can repeat a poem: that is all. Oh! I hope I have not broken my glasses." They had slipped from her nose to the floor. Conolly picked them up and straightened them with one turn of his fingers.

"No harm done, madam," said he, with a certain elocutionary correctness, and rather in the strong voice of the workshop than the subdued one of the drawing-room, handing the glasses to her ceremoniously as he spoke.

"Thank you. You are very kind, very kind indeed."

Conolly bowed, and turned again toward the other group.

"Who is that?" whispered Mrs. Fairfax to the clergyman.

"Some young man who attracted the attention of the Countess by his singing. He is only a workman."

"Indeed! Where did she hear him sing?"

"In her son's laboratory, I believe. He came there to put up some electrical machinery, and sang into a telephone for their amusement. You know how fond Lord Jasper is of mechanics. Jasper declares that he is a genius as an electrician. Indeed it was he, rather than the Countess, who thought of getting him to sing for us."

"How very interesting! I saw that he was clever when he spoke to me. There is so much in trifles—in byplay, Mr. Lind. Now, his manner of picking up my glass had his entire history in it. You will also see it in the solid development of his head. That young man deserves to be encouraged."

"You are very generous, Mrs. Leith Fairfax. It would not be well to encourage him too much, however. You must recollect that he is not used to society. Injudicious encouragement might perhaps lead him to forget his real place in it."

"I do not agree with you, Mr. Lind. You do not read human nature as I do. You know that I am an expert. I see men as he sees a telegraph instrument, quite uninfluenced by personal feeling."

"True, Mrs. Leith Fairfax. But the heart is deceitful above all things and des—at least I should say—er. That is, you will admit that the finest perception may err in its estimate of the inscrutable work of the Almighty."

"Doubtless. But really, Mr. Lind, human beings are *so* shallow! I assure you there is nothing at all inscrutable about them to a trained analyst of character. It may be a gift, perhaps; but people's minds are to me only little machines made up of superficial motives."

"I say," said the young gentleman with the banjo, interrupting them: "have you got a copy of 'Rose softly blooming' there?"

"I!" said Mrs. Fairfax. "No, certainly not."

"Then it's all up with the concert. We have forgotten Marian's music; and there is nothing for Nelly—I beg pardon, I mean Miss McQuinch—to play from. She is above playing by ear."

"I *cannot* play by ear," said the restless young lady, angrily.

"If you will sing 'Coal black Rose' instead, Marian, I can accompany you on the banjo, and back you up in the chorus. The Wandsworthers—if they survive the concertinas—will applaud the change as one man."

"It is so unkind to joke about it," said the beautiful young lady. "What shall I do? If somebody will vamp an accompaniment, I can get on very well without any music. But if I try to play for myself I shall break down."

Conolly here stepped aside, and beckoned to the clergyman.

"That young man wants to speak to you," whispered Mrs. Fairfax.

"Oh, indeed. Thank you," said the Rev. Mr. Lind, stiffly. "I suppose I had better see what he requires."

"I suppose you had," said Mrs. Fairfax, with some impatience.

"I dont wish to intrude where I have no business," said Conolly quietly to the clergyman; "but I can play that lady's accompaniment, if she will allow me."

The clergyman was too much afraid of Conolly by this time—he did not know why—to demur. "I am sure she will not object," he said, pretending to be relieved by the offer. "Your services will be most acceptable. Excuse me for one moment, whilst I inform Miss Lind."

He crossed the room to the lady, and said in a lower tone, "I think I have succeeded in arranging the matter, Marian. That man says he will play for you."

"I hope he *can* play," said Marian doubtfully. "Who is he?"

"It is Conolly. Jasper's man."

Miss Lind's eyes lighted. "Is that he?" she whispered, glancing curiously across the room at him. "Bring him and introduce him to us."

"Is that necessary?" said the tall man, without lowering his voice sufficiently to prevent Conolly from hearing him. The clergyman hesitated.

"It is quite necessary: I do not know what he must think of us already," said Marian, ashamed, and looking apprehensively at Conolly. He was staring with a policemanlike expression at the tall man, who, after a vain attempt to ignore him, had eventually to turn away. The Rev. Mr. Lind then led the electrician forward, and avoided a formal presentation by saying with a simper: "Here is Mr. Conolly, who will extricate us from all our difficulties."

Miss McQuinch nodded. Miss Lind bowed. Marmaduke shook hands good-naturedly, and retired somewhat abashed, thrumming his banjo. Just then a faint sound of clapping was followed by the return of the quartet party, upon which Miss Lind rose and moved hesitatingly toward the platform. The tall man offered his hand.

"Nonsense, Sholto," said she, laughing. "They will expect you to do something if you appear with me."

"Allow *me*, Marian," said the clergyman, as the tall man, offended, bowed and stood aside. She, pretending not to notice her brother, turned toward Conolly, who at once passed the Rev. George, and led her to the platform.

"The original key?" he enquired, as they mounted the steps.

"I dont know," she said, alarmed.

For a moment he was taken aback. Then he said, "What is the highest note you can sing?"

"I can sing A sometimes—only when I am alone. I dare not attempt it before people."

Conolly sat down, knowing now that Miss Lind was a commonplace amateur. He had been contrasting her with his sister, greatly to the disparagement of his home life; and he was disappointed to find the lady break down where the actress would have succeeded so well. Consoling himself with the reflexion that if Miss Lind could not rap out a B flat like Susanna, neither could she rap out an oath, he played the accompaniment much better than Marian sang the song. Meanwhile, Miss McQuinch, listening jealously in the green-room, hated herself for her inferior skill.

"Cool, and reserved, is the modern Benjamin Franklin," observed Marmaduke to her.

"Better a reserved man who can do something than a sulky one who can do nothing," she said, glancing at the tall man, with whom the clergyman was nervously striving to converse.

"Exquisite melody, is it not, Mr. Douglas?" said Mrs. Fairfax, coming to the clergyman's rescue.

"I do not care for music," said Douglas. "I lack the maudlin disposition in which the taste usually thrives."

Miss McQuinch gave an expressive snap, but said nothing; and the conversation dropped until Miss Lind had sung her song, and received a round of respectful but not enthusiastic applause.

"Thank you, Mr. Conolly," she said, as she left the platform. "I am afraid that Spohr's music is too good for the people here. Dont you think so?"

"Not a bit of it," replied Conolly. "There is nothing so very particular in Spohr. But he requires very good singing—better than he is worth."

Miss Lind colored, and returned in silence to her seat beside Miss McQuinch, feeling that she had exposed herself to a remark that no gentleman would have made.

"Now then, Nelly," said Marmaduke: "the parson is going to call time. Keep up your courage. Come, get up, get up."

"Do not be so boisterous, Duke," said Marian. "It is bad enough to have to face an audience without being ridiculed beforehand."

"Marian," said Marmaduke, "if you think Nelly will hammer a love of music into the British workman, you err. Lots of them get their living by hammering, and they will most likely resent feminine competition. Bang! There she goes. Pity the sorrows of a poor old piano, and let us hope its trembling limbs wont come through the floor."

"Really, Marmaduke," said Marian, impatiently, "you are excessively foolish. You are like a boy fresh from school."

Marmaduke, taken aback by her sharp tone, gave a long whispered whistle, and pretended to hide under the table. He had a certain gift of drollery which made it difficult not to laugh even at his most foolish antics, and Marian was giving way in spite of herself when she found Douglas bending over her and saying, in a low voice:

"You are tired of this place. The room is very draughty: I fear it will give you cold. Let me drive you home now. An apology can be made for whatever else you are supposed to do for these people. Let me get your cloak and call a cab."

Marian laughed. "Thank you, Sholto," she said; "but I assure you I am quite happy. Pray do not look offended because I am not so uncomfortable as you think I ought to be."

"I am glad you are happy," said Douglas in his former cold tone. "Perhaps my presence is rather a drawback to your enjoyment than otherwise."

"I told you not to come, Sholto; but you would. Why not adapt yourself to the circumstances, and be agreeable?"

"I am not conscious of being disagreeable."

"I did not mean that. Only I do not like to see you making an enemy of every one in the room, and forcing me to say things that I know must hurt you."

"To the enmity of your new associates I am supremely indifferent, Marian. To that of your old friends I am accustomed. I am not in the mood to be lectured on my behavior at present; besides, the subject is hardly worth pursuing. May I gather from your remarks that I shall gratify you by withdrawing?"

"Yes," said Marian, flushing slightly, and looking steadily at him. Then, controlling her voice with an effort, she added, "Do not try again to browbeat me into telling you a falsehood, Sholto."

Douglas looked at her in surprise. Before he could answer, Miss McQuinch reappeared.

"Well, Nelly," said Marmaduke: "is there any piano left?"

"Not much," she replied, with a sullen laugh. "I never played worse in my life."

"Wrong notes? or deficiency in the sacred fire?"

"Both."

"I believe your song comes next," said the clergyman to Conolly, who had been standing apart, listening to Miss McQuinch's performance.

"Who is to accompany me, sir?"

"Oh—ah—Miss McQuinch will, I am sure," replied the Rev. Mr. Lind, smiling nervously. Conolly looked grave. The young lady referred to closed her lips; frowned; said nothing. Marmaduke chuckled.

"Perhaps you would rather play your own accompaniment," said the clergyman, weakly.

Conolly shook his head decisively, and said, "I can do only one thing at a time, sir."

"Oh, they are not very critical: they are only workmen," said the clergyman, and then reddened deeply as Marmaduke gave him a very perceptible nudge.

"I'll not take advantage of that, as I am only a workman myself," said Conolly. "I had rather leave the song out than accompany myself."

"Pray dont suppose that I wish to be disagreeable, Mr. Lind," said Miss McQuinch, as the company looked doubtfully at her; "but I have disgraced myself too completely to trust my fingers again. I should spoil the song if I played the accompaniment."

"I think you might try, Nell," said Marmaduke, reproachfully.

"I might," retorted Miss McQuinch; "but I wont."

"If somebody doesnt go out and do something, there will be a shindy," said Marmaduke.

Marian hesitated a moment and then rose. "I am a very indifferent player," she said; "but since no better is to be had, I will venture—if Mr. Conolly will trust me."

Conolly bowed.

"If you would rather not," said Miss McQuinch, shamed into remorse, "I will try the accompaniment. But I am sure to play it all wrong."

"I think Miss McQuinch had better play," said Douglas.

Conolly looked at Marian; received a reassuring glance; and went to the platform with her without further ado. She was not a sympathetic accompanist; but, not knowing this, she was not at all put out by it. She felt too that she was, as became a lady, giving the workman a lesson in courtesy which might stand him in stead when he next accompanied "Rose, softly blooming." She was a little taken aback on finding that he not only had a rich baritone voice, but was, as far as she could judge, an accomplished singer.

"Really," she said as they left the platform, "you sing most beautifully."

"One would hardly have expected it," he said, with a smile.

Marian, annoyed at having this side of her compliment

exposed, did not return the smile, and went to her chair in the green-room without taking any further notice of him.

"I congratulate you," said Mrs. Leith Fairfax to Conolly, looking at him, like all the rest except Douglas, with a marked access of interest. "Ah! what wonderful depth there is in Gounod's music!"

He assented politely with a movement of his head.

"I know nothing at all about music," said Mrs. Fairfax.

"Very few people do."

"I mean technically, of course," she said, not quite pleased.

"Of course."

A tremendous burst of applause here followed the conclusion of the first verse of "Uncle Ned."

"*Do* come and listen, Nelly," said Marian, returning to the door. Mrs. Fairfax and Conolly presently went to the door too.

"Would you not like to help in the chorus, Nelly?" said Marian in a low voice, as the audience began to join uproariously in the refrain.

"Not particularly," said Miss McQuinch.

"Sholto," said Marian, "come and share our vulgar joy. We want you to join in the chorus."

"Thank you," said Douglas, "I fear I am too indifferent a vocalist to do justice to the occasion."

"Sing with Mr. Conolly and you cannot go wrong," said Miss McQuinch.

"Hush," said Marian, interposing quickly lest Douglas should retort. "There is the chorus. Shall we really join?"

Conolly struck up the refrain without further hesitation. Marian sang with him. Mrs. Fairfax and the clergyman looked furtively at one another, but forbore to swell the chorus. Miss McQuinch sang a few words in a piercing contralto voice, and then stopped with a gesture of impatience, feeling that she was out of tune. Marian, with only Conolly to keep her in countenance, felt relieved when Marmaduke, thrice encored, entered the room in triumph. Whilst he was being congratulated, Douglas turned to Miss McQuinch, who was pretending to ignore Marmaduke's success.

"I hope, Miss McQuinch," he said in a low tone, "that you will be able to relieve Marian at the piano next time. You know how she dislikes having to play accompaniments for strangers."

"How mean it is of you to be jealous of a plumber!" said Miss McQuinch, with a quick glance at him which she did not dare to sustain, so fiercely did he return it.

When she looked again, he seemed unconscious of her presence, and was buttoning his overcoat.

"Really going at last, Sholto?" said Marian. Douglas bowed.

"I told you you wouldnt be able to stand it, old man," said Marmaduke. "Mrs. Bluestockings wont be pleased with you for not staying to hear her recite." This referred to Mrs. Fairfax, who had just gone upon the platform.

"Good night," said Miss McQuinch, shortly, anxious to test how far he was offended, but unwilling to appear solicitous for a reconciliation.

"Until to-morrow, farewell," he said, approaching Marian, who gave him her hand with a smile: Conolly looking thoughtfully at him meanwhile. He left the room; and so, Mrs.

Fairfax having gone to the platform to recite, quiet prevailed for a few minutes.

"Shall I have the pleasure of playing the accompaniment to your next song?" said Conolly, sitting down near Marian.

"Thank you," said Marian, shrinking a little: "I think Miss McQuinch knows it by heart." Then, still anxious to be affable to the workman, she added, "Lord Jasper says you are a great musician."

"No, I am an electrician. Music is not my business: it is my amusement."

"You have invented something very wonderful, have you not?"

"I have discovered something, and I am trying to invent a means of turning it to account. It will be only a cheap electro-motor if it comes to anything."

"You must explain that to me some day, Mr. Conolly. I'm afraid I don't know what an electro-motor means."

"I ought not to have mentioned it," said Conolly. "It is so constantly in my mind that I am easily led to talk about it. I try to prevent myself, but the very effort makes me think of it more than ever."

"But I like to hear you talk about it," said Marian. "I always try to make people talk shop to me, and of course they always repay me by trying to keep on indifferent topics, of which I know as much—or as little—as they."

"Well, then," said Conolly, "an electro-motor is only an engine for driving machinery, just like a steam engine, except that it is worked by electricity instead of steam. Electric engines are so imperfect now that steam ones come cheaper. The man who finds out how to make the electric engine do what the steam engine now does, and do it cheaper, will make his fortune if he

George Bernard Shaw

has his wits about him. Thats what I am driving at."

Miss Lind, in spite of her sensible views as to talking shop, was not interested in the least. "Indeed!" she said. "How interesting that must be! But how did you find time to become so perfect a musician, and to sing so exquisitely?"

"I picked most of it up when I was a boy. My grandfather was an Irish sailor with such a tremendous voice that a Neapolitan music master brought him out in opera as a *buffo*. When he had roared his voice away, he went into the chorus. My father was reared in Italy, and looked more Italian than most genuine natives. He had no voice; so he became first accompanist, then chorus master, and finally trainer for the operatic stage. He speculated in an American tour; married out there; lost all his money; and came over to England, when I was only twelve, to resume his business at Covent Garden. I stayed in America, and was apprenticed to an electrical engineer. I worked at the bench there for six years."

"I suppose your father taught you to sing."

"No. He never gave me a lesson. The fact is, Miss Lind, he was a capital man to teach stage tricks and traditional renderings of old operas; but only the exceptionally powerful voices survived his method of teaching. He would have finished my career as a singer in two months if he had troubled himself to teach me. Never go to Italy to learn singing."

"I fear you are a cynic. You ought either to believe in your father or else be silent about him."

"Why?"

"Why! Surely we should hide the failings of those we love? I can understand now how your musical and electrical tastes became mixed up; but you should not confuse your duties. But please excuse me:" (Conolly's eyes had opened a little wider) "I am lecturing you, without the least right to. It is a failing of mine which you must not mind."

"Not at all. Youve a right to your opinion. But the world would never get on if every practical man were to stand by his father's mistakes. However, I brought it on myself by telling you a long story. This is the first opportunity I ever had of talking about myself to a lady, and I suppose I have abused it."

Marian laughed. "We had better stop apologizing to one another," she said. "What about the accompaniments to our next songs?"

Meanwhile Marmaduke and Miss McQuinch were becoming curious about Marian and Conolly.

"I say, Nelly," he whispered, "Marian and that young man seem to be getting on uncommonly well together. She looks sentimentally happy, and he seems pleased with himself. Dont you feel jealous?"

"Jealous! Why should I be?"

"Out of pure cussedness. Not that you care for the electric man, but because you hate any one to fall in love with any one else when you are by."

"I wish you would go away."

"Why? Dont you like me?"

"I *loathe* you. Now, perhaps you understand me."

"That's a nice sort of thing to say to a fellow," said Marmaduke, roused. "I have a great mind to bring you to your senses as Douglas does, by not speaking to you for a week."

"I wish you would let me come to my senses by not speaking to me at all."

"Oh! Well, I am off; but mind, Nelly, I am offended. We are no longer on speaking terms. Look as contemptuous as you please: you will be sorry when you think over this. Remember: you said you loathed me."

"So I do," said Elinor, stubbornly.

"Very good," said Marmaduke, turning his back on her. Just then the concertists returned from the platform, and a waiter appeared with refreshments, which the clergyman invited Marmaduke to assist him in dispensing. Conolly, considering the uncorking of bottles of soda water a sufficiently skilled labor to be more interesting than making small talk, went to the table and busied himself with the corkscrew.

"Well, Nelly," said Marian, drawing her chair close to Miss McQuinch, and speaking in a low voice, "what do you think of Jasper's workman?"

"Not much," replied Elinor, shrugging her shoulders. "He is very conceited, and very coarse."

"Do you really think so? I expected to find you delighted with his unconventionality. I thought him rather amusing."

"I thought him extremely aggravating. I hate to have to speak to people of that sort."

"Then you consider him vulgar," said Marian, disappointed.

"N—no. Not vulgarer than anybody else. He couldnt be that."

"Sherry and soda, Marian?" said Marmaduke, approaching.

"No, thank you, Marmaduke. Get Nelly something."

"As Miss McQuinch and I are no longer on speaking terms, I leave her to the care of yonder scientific amateur, who has just refused, on teetotal grounds, to pledge the Rev. George in a glass of eighteen shilling sherry."

"Dont be silly, Marmaduke. Bring Nelly some soda water."

"Do nothing of the sort," said Miss McQuinch.

Marmaduke bowed and retired.

"What is the matter between you and Duke now?" said Marian.

"Nothing. I told him I loathed him."

"Oh! I dont wonder at his being a little huffed. How *can* you say things you dont mean?"

"I do mean them. What with his folly, Sholto's mean conceit, George's hypocrisy, that man's vulgarity, Mrs. Fairfax's affectation, your insufferable amiability, and the dreariness of those concertina people, I feel so wretched that I could find it in my heart to loathe anybody and everybody."

"Nonsense, Nelly! You are only in the blues."

"*Only* in the blues!" said Miss McQuinch sarcastically. "Yes. That is all."

"Take some sherry. It will brighten you up."

"Dutch courage! Thank you: I prefer my present moroseness."

"But you are not morose, Nelly."

"Oh, stuff, Marian! Dont throw away your amiability on me. Here comes your new friend with refreshments. I wonder was he ever a waiter? He looks exactly like one."

After this the conversation flagged. Mrs. Fairfax grew loquacious under the influence of sherry, but presently a reaction set in, and she began to yawn. Miss McQuinch, when her turn came, played worse than before, and the audience, longing for another negro melody, paid little attention to her. Marian sang a religious song, which was received with the respect usually accorded to a dull sermon. The clergyman read a comic essay of his own composition, and Mrs. Fairfax recited an ode to Mazzini. The concertinists played an arrangement of a quartet by Onslow. The working men and women of Wandsworth gaped, and those who sat near the door began to slip out. Even Miss McQuinch pitied them.

"The idea of expecting them to be grateful for an infliction like that!" she said. "What do people of their class care about Onslow's quartets?"

"Do you think that people of any class, high or low, would be gratified by such an entertainment?" said Conolly, with some warmth. No one had sufficient spirit left to reply.

At last the concertinists went home, and the reading drew to a close. Conolly, again accompanied by Marian, sang "Tom Bowling." The audience awoke, cheered the singer heartily, and made him sing again. On his return to the green-room, Miss McQuinch, much affected at the fate of Bowling, and indignant with herself for being so, stared defiantly at Conolly through a film of tears. When Marmaduke went out, the people also were so moved that they were ripe for laughter, and with roars of merriment forced him to sing three songs, in the choruses of which they joined. Eventually the clergyman had to bid them go home, as Mr. Lind had given them all the songs he knew.

"I suppose you will not come with us, Duke," said Marian, when all was over, and they were preparing to leave. "We can drop you at your chambers if you like; but you will have to sit on the box. Mrs. Leith Fairfax, George, Nelly, and I, will be a carriageful."

Marmaduke looked at his watch. "By Jove!" he cried, "it is

only ten. I forgot how early we began to-night. No thank you, Marian: I am not going your way; but you may take the banjo and keep it until I call. Ta ta!"

They all went out together; and the ladies, followed by the clergyman, entered their carriage and drove away, leaving Marmaduke and Conolly standing on the pavement. Having shared the success of the concert, each felt well disposed to the other.

"What direction are you going in?" said Marmaduke.

"Westminster Bridge or thereabouts," replied Conolly. "This place is rather out of the way."

"Have you anything particular to do before you turn in for the night?"

"Nothing at all."

"Then I'll tell you what it is, old man. Lets take a hansom, and drive off to the Bijou. We shall just be in time to see Lalage Virtue in the burlesque; and—look here! I'll introduce you to her: youre just the sort of chap she would like to know. Eh?"

Conolly looked at him, nodded, and burst out laughing. Marmaduke, who had set him down as a cool, undemonstrative man, was surprised at his hilarity for a moment, but presently joined in it. Whilst they were both laughing a hansom appeared, and Conolly, recovering himself, hailed the driver.

"We shall get on together, I see," said Marmaduke, jumping into the cab. "Hallo! The Bijou Theatre, Soho, and drive as fast as you can afford to for half a sovereign."

"Right you are, sir," replied the driver, whipping his horse.

The rattling of the cab silenced Conolly; but his companion

persisted for some time in describing the burlesque to which they were going, and particularly the attractions of Mademoiselle Lalage Virtue, who enacted a principal character therein, and with whom he seemed to be in love. When they alighted at the theatre Marmaduke payed the cabman, and Conolly took advantage of this to enter the theatre and purchase two stall tickets, an arrangement which Lind, suddenly recollecting his new friend's position, disapproved of, but found it useless to protest against. He forgot it on hearing the voice of Lalage Virtue, who was at that moment singing within; and he went to his stall with his eyes turned to the stage, treading on toes and stumbling as children commonly do when they walk in one direction and look in another. An attendant, who seemed to know him, proffered a glass for hire. He took it, and leveled it at Mademoiselle Lalage, who was singing some trivial couplets much better than they deserved. Catching sight of him presently, she greeted him with a flash of her dark eye that made him writhe as though his heart had received a fillip from a ponderable missile. She did not spare these roguish glances. They darted everywhere; and Conolly, looking about him to note their effect, saw rows of callow young faces with parted lips and an expression which seemed to have been caught and fixed at the climax of a blissful chuckle. There were few women in the stalls, and the silly young faces were relieved only by stupid old ones.

The couplets ended amidst great applause. Marmaduke placed his glass on his knees, and, clapping his hands vigorously, turned to his companion with a triumphant smile, mutely inviting him to clamor for a repetition of the air. But Conolly sat motionless, with his arms folded, his cheek flushed, and his brow lowered.

"You dont seem used to this sort of thing," said Lind, somewhat disgusted.

"It was well sung," replied Conolly "—better than most of these blackguards know."

"Then why dont you clap?"

"Because she is not giving herself any trouble. That sort of thing, from a woman of her talent, is too cheap to say 'thank you' for."

Marmaduke looked at him, and began to think that he was a priggish fellow after all. But as the burlesque went on, Mademoiselle Lalage charmed away this disagreeable impression. She warbled in an amorous duet, and then sang the pleasures of champagne; tossing her head; waving a gilt goblet; and, without the least appearance of effort, working hard to captivate those who were to be won by bold smiles and arch glances. She displayed her person less freely than her colleagues, being, not more modest, but more skilful in the art of seduction. The slang that served for dialogue in her part was delivered in all sorts of intonations, now demure and mischievous, anon strident and mock tragic. Marmaduke was delighted.

"What I like about her is that she is such a genuine little lady," he said, as her exit released his attention. "With all her go, she is never a bit vulgar. Off the stage she is just the same. Not a spark of affectation about her. It is all natural."

"You know her, then?" said Conolly.

"I should think I do," replied Marmaduke, energetically. "You have no idea what a rattling sort she is."

"To you, who only see her occasionally, no doubt she gives—as a rattling sort—a heightened charm to the order, the refinement, the—the beauty of the home life which you can enjoy. Excuse my introducing such a subject, Mr. Lind; but would you bring your cousin—the lady who sang to-night at the concert—to see this performance?"

"I would if she asked me to," said Marmaduke, somewhat taken aback.

"No doubt. But should you be surprised if she asked you?"

"Not a bit. Fine ladies are neither such fools nor such angels as you—as some fellows think. Miss Lind's notion is to see everything. And yet she is a thoroughly nice woman too. It is the same with Lalage there. She is not squeamish, and she is full of fun; but she knows as well as anybody how to pull up a man who doesnt behave himself."

"And you actually think that this Lalage Virtue is as respectable a woman as your cousin?"

"Oh, I dont bother myself about it. I shouldnt have thought of comparing them if you hadnt started the idea. Marian's way is not the other one's way, and each of them is all right in her own way. Look here. I'll introduce you to Lalage. We can pick up somebody else to make a party for you, and finish with a supper at Jellicoe's."

"Are you privileged to introduce whom you like to Miss Lalage?"

"Well, as to that, she doesnt stand much on ceremony; but then, you see, that cuts two ways. The mere introducing is no difficulty; but it depends on the man himself whether he gets snubbed afterward or not. By the bye, you must understand, if you dont know it already, that Lalage is as correct in her morals as a bishop's wife. I just tell you, because some fellows seem to think that a woman who goes on the stage leaves her propriety behind as a matter of course. In fact, I rather thought so myself once. Not that you wont find loose women there as well as anywhere else, if you want to. But dont take it for granted, that's all."

"Well," said Conolly, "you may introduce me, and we can consider the supper afterwards. Would it be indiscreet to ask how you obtained your own introduction? You dont, I suppose, move in the same circle as she; and if she is as particular as your own people, she can hardly form promiscuous acquaintanceships."

"A man at the point of death does not stop to think about etiquet. She saved my life."

"Saved your life! That sounds romantic."

"There was precious little romance about it, though I owe my being alive now to her presence of mind. It happened in the rummest way. I was brought behind the scenes one night by a Cambridge chum. We were painting the town a bit red. We were not exactly drunk; but we were not particularly sober either; and I was very green at that time, and made a fool of myself about Lalage: staring; clapping like a madman in the middle of her songs; getting into the way of everybody and everything, and so on. Then a couple of fellows we knew turned up, and we got chatting at the wing with some girls. At last a fellow came in with a bag of cherries; and we began trying that old trick—you know—taking the end of a stalk between your lips and drawing the cherry into the mouth without touching it with your hand, you know. I tried it; and I was just getting the cherry into my mouth when some idiot gave me a drive in the waistcoat. I made a gulp; and the cherry stuck fast in my throat. I began to choke. Nobody knew what to do; and while they were pushing me about, some thinking I was only pretending, the girls beginning to get frightened, and the rest shouting at me to swallow the confounded thing, I was getting black in the face, and my head was bursting: I could see nothing but red spots. It was a near thing, I tell you. Suddenly I got a shake; and then a little fist gave me a stunning thump on the back, that made the cherry bounce out against my palate. I gasped and coughed like a grampus: the stalk was down my throat still. Then the little hand grabbed my throat and made me open my mouth wide; and the cherry was pulled out, stalk and all. It was Lalage who did this while the rest were gaping helplessly. I dont remember what followed. I thought I had fainted; but it appears that I nearly cried, and talked the most awful nonsense to her. I suppose the choking made me hysterical. However, I distinctly recollect the stage manager bullying the girls, and turning us all out. I was very angry with myself for being childish, as they told me I had been; and when I got back to Cambridge I actually took to reading. A few months afterward I made another trip to town, and went behind the scenes again. She recognized me, and chaffed me about the cherry. I jumped at my chance; I improved the acquaintance; and now I know her pretty well."

"You doubt whether any of the ladies that were with us at the concert would have been equally useful in such an emergency?"

"I should think I do doubt it, my boy. Hush! Now that the ballet is over, we are annoying people by talking."

"You are right," replied Conolly. "Aha! Here is Miss Lalage again."

Marmaduke raised his opera-glass to his eyes, eager for another smile from the actress. He seemed about to be gratified; for her glance was travelling toward him along the row of stalls. But it was arrested by Conolly, on whom she looked with perceptible surprise and dismay. Lind, puzzled, turned toward his companion, and found him smiling maliciously at Mademoiselle Lalage, who recovered her vivacity with an effort, and continued her part with more nervousness than he had ever seen her display before.

Shortly before the curtain fell, they left the theatre, and re-entered it by the stage door.

"Queer place, isnt it?" said Lind.

Conolly nodded, but went forward like one well accustomed to the dingy labyrinth of old-fashioned stages. Presently they came upon Lalage. She was much heated by her exertions, thickly painted, and very angry.

"Well?" she said quarrelsomely.

Marmaduke, perceiving that her challenge was not addressed to him, but to Conolly, looked from one to the other, mystified.

"I have come to see you act at last," said Conolly.

"You might have told me you were coming. I could have got you a stall, although I suppose you would have preferred to throw away your money like a fool."

"I must admit, my dear," said Conolly, "that I could have spent it to much greater advantage."

"Indeed! and you!" she said, turning to Lind, whose deepening color betrayed his growing mortification: "what is the matter with *you*?"

"I have played a trick on your friend," said Conolly. "He suggested this visit; and I did not tell him of the relation between us. Finding us on terms of familiarity, if not of affection, he is naturally surprised."

"As I have never tried to meddle with your private affairs," said Marmaduke to Lalage, "I need not apologize for not knowing your husband. But I regret—"

The actress laughed in spite of her vexation. "Why, you silly old thing!" she exclaimed, "he is no more my husband than you are!"

"Oh!" said Marmaduke. "Indeed!"

"I am her brother," said Conolly considerately, stifling a smile.

"Why," said Mademoiselle Lalage fiercely, raising her voice, "what else did you think?"

"Hush," said Conolly, "we are talking too much in this crowd. You had better change your dress, Susanna, and then we can

George Bernard Shaw

settle what to do next."

"You can settle what you please," she replied. "I am going home."

"Mr. Lind has suggested our supping together," said Conolly, observing her curiously.

Susanna looked quickly at them.

"Who is Mr. Lind?" she said.

"Your friend, of course," said Conolly, with an answering flash of intelligence that brought out the resemblance between them startlingly. "Mr. Marmaduke Lind."

Marmaduke became very red as they both waited for him to explain.

"I thought that you would perhaps join us at supper," he said to Susanna.

"Did you?" she said, threateningly. Then she turned her back on him and went to her dressing-room.

"Well, Mr. Lind," said Conolly, "what do you think of Mademoiselle Lalage now?"

"I think her annoyance is very natural," said Marmaduke, gloomily. "No doubt you are right to take care of your sister, but you are very much mistaken if you think I meant to act badly toward her."

"It is no part of my duty to take care of her," said Conolly, seriously. "She is her own guardian, and she has never been encouraged to suppose that her responsibility lies with any one but herself."

"It doesnt matter now," said Marmaduke; "for I intend never

to speak to her again."

Conolly laughed. "However that may turn out," he said, "we are evidently not in the mood for further conviviality, so let us postpone the supper to some other occasion. May I advise you not to wait until Susanna returns. There is no chance of a reconciliation to-night."

"I dont want any reconciliation."

"Of course not; I had forgotten," replied Conolly, placably. "Then I suppose you will go before she has finished dressing."

"I shall go now," said Marmaduke, buttoning his overcoat, and turning away.

"Good-night," said Conolly.

"Good-night," muttered Marmaduke, petulantly, and disappeared.

Conolly waited a moment, so that he might not overtake Lind. He then went for a cab, and waited at the stage door until his sister came down, frowning. She got into the hansom without a word.

"Why dont you have a brougham, instead of going about in cabs?" he said, as they drove away.

"Because I like a hansom better than a brougham; and I had rather pay four shillings a night and travel comfortably, than thirteen and be half suffocated."

"I thought the appearance of—"

"There is no use in your talking to me. I cant hear a word you say going over these stones."

When they were alone together in their drawing-room in

George Bernard Shaw

Lambeth, he, after walking up and down the room a few times, and laughing softly to himself, began to sing the couplets from the burlesque.

"Are you aware," she inquired, "that it is half past twelve, and that the people of the house are trying to sleep."

"True," said he, desisting. "By the bye, I, too, have had my triumphs this evening. I shared the honors of the concert with Master Lind, who was so delighted that he insisted on bringing me off to the Bijou. He loves you to distraction, poor devil!"

"Yes: you made a nice piece of mischief there. Where is he?"

"Gone away in a rage, swearing never to speak to you again."

"Hm! And so his name is Lind, is it?"

"Didnt you know?"

"No, or I should have told you when I read the program this evening. The young villain pretended that his name was Marmaduke Sharp."

"Ah! The name reminds me of one of his cousins, a little spitfire that snaps at every one who presumes to talk to her."

"His cousins! Oh, of course; you met them at the concert. What are they like? Are they swells?"

"Yes, they seem to be. There were only two cousins, Miss McQuinch and a young woman named Marian, blonde and rather good looking. There was a brother of hers there, but he is only a parson, and a tall fellow named Douglas, who made rather a fool of himself. I could not make him out exactly."

"Did they snub you?"

"I don't know. Probably they tried. Are you intimate with

many of our young nobility under assumed names?"

"Steal a few more marches to the Bijou, and perhaps you will find out."

"Good-night! Pardon my abrupt departure, but you are not the very sweetest of Susannas to-night."

"Oh, *good*-night."

"By the bye," said Conolly, returning, "this must be the Mr. Duke Lind who is going to marry Lady Constance Carbury, my noble pupil's sister."

"I am sure it matters very little whom he marries."

"If he will pay us a visit here, and witness the working of perfect frankness without affection, and perfect liberty without refinement, he may find reason to conclude that it matters a good deal. Good-night."

CHAPTER II

Marian Lind lived at Westbourne Terrace, Paddington, with her father, the fourth son of a younger brother of the Earl of Carbury. Mr. Reginald Harrington Lind, at the outset of his career, had no object in life except that of getting through it as easily as possible; and this he understood so little how to achieve that he suffered himself to be married at the age of nineteen to a Lancashire cotton spinner's heiress. She bore him three children, and then eloped with a professor of spiritualism, who deserted her on the eve of her fourth confinement, in the course of which she caught scarlet fever and died. Her child survived, but was sent to a baby farm and starved to death in the usual manner. Her husband, disgusted by her behavior (for she had been introduced by him to many noblemen and gentlemen, his personal friends, some one at least of whom, on the slightest encouragement, would, he felt sure, have taken the place of the foreign charlatan she had disgraced him by preferring), consoled himself for her bad taste by entering into her possessions, which comprised a quantity of new jewellery, new lace, and feminine apparel, and an income of nearly seven thousand pounds a year. After this, he became so welcome in society that he could have boasted with truth at the end of any July that there were few marriageable gentlewomen of twenty-six and upward in London who had not been submitted to his inspection with a view to matrimony. But finding it easy to delegate the care of his children to school principals and hospitable friends, he concluded that he had nothing to gain and much comfort to lose by adding a stepmother to his establishment; and, after some time, it became the custom to say of Mr. Lind that the memory of his first wife kept him single. Thus, whilst his sons were drifting to manhood through Harrow and Cambridge, and his daughter passing from one relative's house to another's on a continual round of visits, sharing such private tuition as the cousins with whom she happened to be staying happened to be receiving just then, he lived at his club and pursued the usual routine of a gentleman-bachelor in London.

In the course of time, Reginald Lind, the eldest child, entered the army, and went to India with his regiment. His brother George, less stolid, weaker, and more studious, preferred the Church. Marian, the youngest, from being constantly in the position of a guest, had early acquired habits of self-control and consideration for others, and escaped the effects, good and evil, of the subjection in which children are held by the direct authority of their parents.

Of the numerous domestic circles of her father's kin, that with which she was the least familiar, because it was the poorest, had sprung from the marriage of one of her father's sisters with a Wiltshire gentleman named Hardy McQuinch, who had a small patrimony, a habit of farming, and a love of hunting. In the estimation of the peasantry, who would not associate lands, horses, and a carriage, with want of money, he was a rich man; but Mrs. McQuinch found it hard to live like a lady on their income, and had worn many lines into her face by constantly and vainly wishing that she could afford to give a ball every season, to get a new carriage, and to appear at church with her daughters in new dresses oftener than twice a year. Her two eldest girls were plump and pleasant, good riders and hearty eaters; and she had reasonable hopes of marrying them to prosperous country gentlemen.

Elinor, her third and only other child, was one of her troubles. At an early age it was her practice, once a week or thereabouts, to disappear in the forenoon; be searched anxiously for all day; and return with a torn frock and dirty face at about six o'clock in the afternoon. She was stubborn, rebellious, and passionate under reproof or chastisement: governesses had left the house because of her; and from one school she had run away, from another eloped with a choir boy who wrote verses. Him she deserted in a fit of jealousy, quarter of an hour after her escape from school. The only one of her tastes that conduced to the peace of the house was for reading; and even this made her mother uneasy; for the books she liked best were fit, in Mrs. McQuinch's opinion, for the bookcase only. Elinor read openly what she could obtain by asking, such as Lamb's Tales from Shakespear, and The Pilgrim's Progress. The Arabian Nights Entertainments were sternly refused her; so she read them by stealth; and from that day there was always a collection of books, borrowed from friends, or filched from the upper shelf in the library, beneath her mattress. Nobody thought of looking there for them; and even if they had, they might have paused to reflect on the consequences of betraying her. Her eldest sister having given her a small workbox on her eleventh birthday, had the present thrown at her head two days later for reporting to her parents that Nelly's fondness for sitting in a certain secluded summer-house was due to her desire to read Lord Byron's poetry unobserved. Miss Lydia's forehead was severely cut; and Elinor, though bitterly remorseful, not only refused to beg pardon for her fault, but shattered every brittle article in the room to which she was confined for her contumacy. The vicar, on being consulted, recommended that she should be well whipped. This counsel was repugnant to Hardy McQuinch, but he gave his wife leave to use her discretion in the matter. The mother thought that the child ought to be beaten into submission; but she was afraid to undertake the task, and only uttered a threat, which was received with stubborn defiance. This was forgotten next day when Elinor, exhausted by a week of remorse, terror, rage, and suspense, became dangerously ill. When she recovered, her parents were more indulgent to her, and were gratified by finding her former passionate resistance replaced by sulky obedience. Five years elapsed, and Elinor began to write fiction. The beginning of a novel, and many incoherent verses imitated from Lara, were discovered by her mother, and burnt by her father. This outrage she never forgave. She was unable

The Irrational Knot   55

to make her resentment felt, for she no longer cared to break glass and china. She feared even to remonstrate lest she should humiliate herself by bursting into tears, as, since her illness, she had been prone to do in the least agitation. So she kept silence, and ceased to speak to either of her parents except when they addressed questions to her. Her father would neither complain of this nor confess the regret he felt for his hasty destruction of her manuscripts; but, whilst he proclaimed that he would burn every scrap of her nonsense that might come into his hands, he took care to be blind when he surprised her with suspicious bundles of foolscap, and snubbed his wife for hinting that Elinor was secretly disobeying him. Meanwhile her silent resentment never softened, and the life of the family was embittered by their consciousness of it. It never occurred to Mrs. McQuinch, an excellent mother to her two eldest daughters, that she was no more fit to have charge of the youngest than a turtle is to rear a young eagle. The discomfort of their relations never shook her faith in their "naturalness." Like her husband and the vicar, she believed that when God sent children he made their parents fit to rule them. And Elinor resented her parents' tyranny, as she felt it to be, without dreaming of making any allowances for their being in a false position towards her.

One morning a letter from London announced that Mr. Lind had taken a house in Westbourne Terrace, and intended to live there permanently with his daughter. Elinor had not come down to breakfast when the post came.

"Yes," said Mrs. McQuinch, when she had communicated the news: "I knew there was something the matter when I saw Reginald's handwriting. It must be fully eighteen months since I heard from him last. I am very glad he has settled Marian in a proper home, instead of living like a bachelor and leaving her to wander about from one house to another. I wish we could have afforded to ask her down here oftener."

"Here is a note from Marian, addressed to Nelly," said Lydia, who had been examining the envelope.

"To Nelly!" said Mrs. McQuinch, vexed. "I think she should have invited one of you first."

"Perhaps it is not an invitation," said Jane.

"What else is it likely to be, child?" said Mrs. McQuinch. Then, as she thought how much pleasanter her home would be without Elinor, she added, "After all, it will do Nelly good to get away from here. She needs change, I think. I wish she would come down. It is too bad of her to be always late like this."

Elinor came in presently, wearing a neglected black gown; her face pale; her eyes surrounded by dark circles; her black hair straggling in wisps over her forehead. Her sisters, dressed twinlike in white muslin and gold lockets, emphasized her by contrast. Being blond and gregarious, they enjoyed the reputation of being pretty and affectionate. They had thriven in the soil that had starved Elinor.

"There's a letter for you from Marian," said Mrs. McQuinch.

"Thanks," said Elinor, indifferently, putting the note into her pocket. She liked Marian's letters, and kept them to read in her hours of solitude.

"What does she say?" said Mrs. McQuinch.

"I have not looked," replied Elinor.

"Well," said Mrs. McQuinch, plaintively, "I wish you *would* look. I want to know whether she says anything about this letter from your uncle Reginald."

Elinor plucked the note from her pocket, tore it open, and read it. Suddenly she set her face to hide some emotion from her family.

"Marian wants me to go and stay with her," she said. "They

have taken a house."

"Poor Marian!" said Jane. "And will you go?"

"I will," said Elinor. "Have you any objection?"

"Oh dear, no," said Jane, smoothly.

"I suppose you will be glad to get away from your home," said Mrs. McQuinch, incontinently.

"Very glad," said Elinor. Mr. McQuinch, hurt, looked at her over his newspaper. Mrs. McQuinch was huffed.

"I dont know what you are to do for clothes," she said, "unless Lydia and Jane are content to wear their last winter's dresses again this year."

The faces of the young ladies elongated. "That's nonsense, mamma," said Lydia. "We cant wear those brown reps again." Women wore reps in those days.

"You need not be alarmed," said Elinor. "I dont want any clothes. I can go as I am."

"You dont know what you are talking about, child," said Mrs. McQuinch.

"A nice figure you would make in uncle Reginald's drawing-room with that dress on!" said Lydia.

"And your hair in that state!" added Jane.

"You should remember that there are others to be considered besides yourself," said Lydia. "How would *you* like *your* guests to look like scarecrows?"

"How could you expect Marian to go about with you, or into the Park? I suppose—"

"Here, here!" said Mr. McQuinch, putting down his paper. "Let us have no more of this. What else do you need in the Park than a riding habit? You have that already. Whatever clothes you want you had better get in London, where you will get the proper things for your money."

"Indeed, Hardy, she is not going to pay a London milliner four prices for things she can get quite as good down here."

"I tell you I dont want anything," said Elinor impatiently. "It will be time enough to begrudge me some decent clothes when I ask for them."

"I dont begrudge—"

Mrs. McQuinch's husband interrupted her. "Thats enough, now, everybody. It's settled that she is to go, as she wants to. I will get her what is necessary. Give me another egg, and talk about something else."

Accordingly, Elinor went to live at Westbourne Terrace. Marian had spent a month of her childhood in Wiltshire, and had made of Elinor an exacting friend, always ready to take offence, and to remain jealous and sulky for days if one of her sisters, or any other little girl, engaged her cousin's attention long. On the other hand, Elinor's attachment was idolatrous in its intensity; and as Marian was sweet-tempered, and more apt to fear that she had disregarded Elinor's feelings than to take offence at her waywardness, their friendship endured after they were parted. Their promises of correspondence were redeemed by Elinor with very long letters at uncertain intervals, and by Marian with shorter epistles notifying all her important movements. Marian, often called upon to defend her cousin from the charge of being a little shrew, was led to dwell upon her better qualities. Elinor found in Marian what she had never found at her own home, a friend, and in her uncle's house a refuge from that of her father, which she hated. She had been Marian's companion for four years when the concert took place at Wandsworth.

Next day they were together in the drawing-room at West-bourne Terrace: Marian writing, Elinor at the pianoforte, working at some technical studies, to which she had been incited by the shortcoming of her performance on the previous night. She stopped on hearing a bell ring.

"What o'clock is it?" she said, after listening a moment. "Surely it is too early for a visit."

"It is only half past two," replied Marian. "I hope it is not anybody. I have not half finished my correspondence."

"If you please, Miss," said a maid, entering, "Mr. Douglas wants to see you, and he wont come up."

"I suppose he expects you to go down and talk to him in the hall," said Elinor.

"He is in the dining-room, and wishes to see you most particular," said the maid.

"Tell him I will come down," said Marian.

"He heard me practising," said Elinor, "that is why he would not come up. I am in disgrace, I suppose."

"Nonsense, Nelly! But indeed I have no doubt he has come to complain of our conduct, since he insists on seeing me alone."

Miss McQuinch looked sceptically at Marian's guileless eyes, but resumed her technical studies without saying anything. Marian went to the dining-room, where she found Douglas standing near the window, tall and handsome, frock coated and groomed to a spotless glossiness that established a sort of relationship between him and the sideboard, the condition of which did credit to Marian's influence over her housemaids. He looked intently at her as she bade him good morning.

"I am afraid I am rather early," he said, half stiffly, halfapologetically.

"Not at all," said Marian.

"I have come to say something which I do not care to keep unsaid longer than I can help; so I thought it better to come when I could hope to find you alone. I hope I have not disturbed you. I have something rather important to say."

"You are the same as one of ourselves, of course, Sholto. But I believe you delight in stiffness and ceremony. Will you not come upstairs?"

"I wish to speak to you privately. First, I have to apologize to you for what passed last night."

"Pray dont, Sholto: it doesnt matter. I am afraid we were rude to you."

"Pardon me. It is I who am in fault. I never before made an apology to any human being; and I should not do so now without a painful conviction that I forgot what I owed to myself."

"Then you ought to be ashamed of yourself—I mean for never having apologized before. I am quite sure you have not got through life without having done at least one or two things that required an apology."

"I am sorry you hold that opinion of me."

"How is Brutus's paw?"

"Brutus!"

"Yes. That abrupt way of changing the subject is what Mrs. Fairfax calls a display of tact. I know it is very annoying; so you may talk about anything you please. But I really want to hear how the poor dog is."

"His paw is nearly healed."

"I'm so glad—poor old dear!"

"You are aware that I did not come here to speak of my mother's dog, Marian?"

"I supposed not," said Marian, with a smile. "But now that you have made your apology, wont you come upstairs? Nelly is there."

"I have something else to say—to you alone, Marian. I entreat you to listen to it seriously." Marian looked as grave as she could. "I confess that in some respects I do not understand you; and before you enter upon another London season, through which I cannot be at your side, I would obtain from you some assurance of the nature of your regard for me. I do not wish to harass you with jealous importunity. You have given me the most unequivocal tokens of a feeling different from that which inspires the ordinary intercourse of a lady and gentleman in society; but of late it has seemed to me that you maintain as little reserve toward other men as toward me. I am not thinking of Marmaduke: he is your cousin. But I observed that even the working man who sang at the concert last night was received—I do not say intentionally—with a cordiality which might have tempted a more humbly disposed person than he seemed to be to forget—" Here Douglas, seeing Marian's bearing change suddenly, hesitated. Her beautiful gray eyes, always pleading for peace like those of a good angel, were now full of reproach; and her mouth, but for those eyes, would have suggested that she was at heart an obstinate woman.

"Sholto," she said, "I dont know what to say to you. If this is jealousy, it may be very flattering; but it is ridiculous. If it is a lecture, seriously intended, it is—it is really most insulting. What do you mean by my having given you unequivocal signs of regard? Of course I think of you very differently from the chance acquaintances I make in society. It would be strange if I did not, having known you so long and been your mother's guest so often. But you talk almost as if I had been making love to you."

"No," said Douglas, forgetting his ceremonious manner and speaking angrily and naturally; "but you talk as though I had not been making love to *you*."

"If you have, I never knew it. I never dreamt it."

"Then, since you are not the stupidest lady of my acquaintance, you must be the most innocent."

"Tell me of one single occasion on which anything has passed between us that justifies your speaking to me as you are doing now."

"Innumerable occasions. But since I cannot compel you to acknowledge them, it would be useless to cite them."

"All I can say is that we have utterly misunderstood one another," she said, after a pause.

He said nothing, but took up his hat, and looked down at it with angry determination. Marian, too uneasy to endure silence, added:

"But I shall know better in future."

"True," said Douglas, hastily putting down his hat and advancing a step. "You cannot plead misunderstanding now. Can you give me the assurance I seek?"

"What assurance?"

Douglas shook his shoulders impatiently.

"You expect me to know everything by intuition," she said.

"Well, my declaration shall be definite enough, even for you. Do you love me?"

"No, I dont think I do. In fact, I am quite sure I do not—in the way you mean. I wish you would not talk like this, Sholto. We have all got on so pleasantly together: you, and I, and Nelly, and Marmaduke, and my father. And now you begin making love, and stuff of that kind. Pray let us agree to forget all about it, and remain friends as before."

"You need not be anxious about our future relations: I shall not embarrass you with my society again. I hoped to find you a woman capable of appreciating a man's passion, even if you should be unable to respond to it. But I perceive that you are only a girl, not yet aware of the deeper life that underlies the ice of conventionality."

"That is a very good metaphor for your own case," said Marian, interrupting him. "Your ordinary manner is all ice, hard and chilling. One may suspect that there are depths beneath, but that is only an additional inducement to keep on the surface."

"Then even your amiability is a delusion! Or is it that you are amiable to the rest of the world, and reserve taunts of coldness and treachery for me?"

"No, no," she said, angelic again. "You have taken me up wrongly. I did not mean to taunt you."

"You conceal your meaning as skilfully as—according to you—I have concealed mine. Good-morning."

"Are you going already?"

"Do you care one bit for me, Marian?"

"I do indeed. Believe me, you are one of my special friends."

"I do not want to be *one* of your friends. Will you be my wife?"

"Sholto!"

"Will you be my wife?"

"No. I—"

"Pardon me. That is quite sufficient. Good-morning."

The moment he interrupted her, a change in her face shewed she had a temper. She did not move a muscle until she heard the house door close behind him. Then she ran upstairs to the drawing-room, where Miss McQuinch was still practising.

"Oh, Nelly," she cried, throwing herself into an easy chair, and covering her face with her hands. "Oh! Oh! Oh! Oh! Oh!" She opened her fingers and looked whimsically at her cousin, who, despising this stage business, said, impatiently:

"Well?"

"Do you know what Sholto came for?"

"To propose to you."

"Stop, Nelly. You do not know what horrible things one may say in jest. He *has* proposed."

"When will the wedding be?"

"Dont joke about it, please. I scarcely know how I have behaved, or what the meaning of the whole scene is, yet. Listen. Did you ever suspect that he was—what shall I say?— *courting* me?"

"I saw that he was trying to be tender in his own conceited way. I fully expected he would propose some day, if he could once reconcile himself to a wife who was not afraid of him."

"And you never told me."

"I thought you saw it for yourself; particularly as you encouraged him."

"There! The very thing he has been accusing me of! He said I had given him unequivocal tokens—yes, unequivocal tokens—that I was madly in love with him."

"What did you say?—if I may ask."

"I tried to explain things to him; but he persisted in asking me would I be his wife; and when I refused he would not listen to anything else, and went off in a rage."

"Yes, I can imagine Sholto's feelings on discovering that he had humbled himself in vain. Why did you refuse him?"

"Why! Fancy being Sholto's wife! I would as soon think of marrying Marmaduke. But I cannot forget what he said about my flirting with him. Nelly: will you promise to tell me whenever you think I am behaving in a way that might lead anybody on to—like Sholto, you know?"

"Nonsense! If men choose to make fools of themselves, you cannot prevent them. Hush! I hear someone coming upstairs. It is Marmaduke, I think."

"Marmaduke would never come up so slowly. He generally comes up three steps at a time."

"Sulky after last night, no doubt. I suppose he wont speak to me."

Marmaduke entered listlessly. "Good morning, Marian," he

said, sitting down on an uncomfortable chair. "Good morrow, Nell."

Elinor, surprised at the courtesy, looked up and saluted him snappishly.

"Is there anything the matter, Duke?" said Marian. "Are you ill?"

"No, I'm all right. Rather busy: thats all."

"Busy!" said Elinor. "There must be something even more unusual than that, when you are too low spirited to keep up a quarrel with me. Why dont you sit on the easy chair, or sprawl on the ottoman, after your manner?"

"Anything for a quiet life," he replied, moving to the ottoman.

"You must be hungry," said Marian, puzzled by his obedience. "Let me get you something."

"No, thank you," said Marmaduke. "I couldnt eat. Just had lunch. Ive come to pack up a few things of mine that you have here."

"We have your banjo."

"Oh, I dont want that. You may keep it, or put it in the fire, for all I care. I want some clothes I left behind me when we had the theatricals."

"Are you leaving London?"

"Yes. I am getting tired of loafing about here. I think I ought to go home for a while. My mother wants me to."

Miss McQuinch, by a subdued but expressive snort, conveyed the most entire scepticism as to his solicitude about his mother. She then turned to the piano calmly, observing, "You have probably eaten something that disagrees with you."

"What a shame!" said Marian. "Come, Duke: I have plenty of good news for you. Nelly and I are invited to Carbury Park for the autumn; and there will be no visitors but us three. We shall have the whole place to ourselves."

"Time enough to think of the autumn yet awhile," said Marmaduke, gloomily.

"Well," said Miss McQuinch, "here is some better news for you. Constance—*Lady* Constance—will be in town next week."

Marmaduke muttered something.

"I beg your pardon?" said Elinor, quickly.

"I didnt say anything."

"I may be wrong; but I thought I heard you say 'Hang Lady Constance!'."

"Oh, Marmaduke!" cried Marian, affectedly. "How dare you speak so of your betrothed, sir?"

"Who says she is my betrothed?" he said, turning on her angrily.

"Why, everybody. Even Constance admits it."

"She ought to have the manners to wait until I ask her," he said, subsiding. "I'm not betrothed to her; and I dont intend to become so in a hurry, if I can help it. But you neednt tell your father I said so. It might get round to my governor; and then there would be a row."

"You *must* marry her some day, you know," said Elinor, maliciously.

"*Must* I? I shant marry at all. I've had enough of women."

"Indeed? Perhaps they have had enough of you." Marmaduke reddened. "You seem to have exhausted the joys of this world since the concert last night. Are you jealous of Mr. Conolly's success?"

"Your by-play when you found how early it was at the end of the concert was not lost on us," said Marian demurely. "You were going somewhere, were you not?"

"Since you are so jolly curious," said Marmaduke, unreasonably annoyed, "I went to the theatre with Connolly; and my by-play, as you call it, simply meant my delight at finding that we could get rid of you in time to enjoy the evening."

"With Conolly!" said Marian, interested. What kind of man is he?"

"He is nothing particular. You saw him yourself."

"Yes. But is he well educated, and—and so forth?"

"Dont know, I'm sure. We didnt talk about mathematics and classics."

"Well; but—do you like him?"

"I tell you I dont care a damn about him one way or the other," said Marmaduke, rising and walking away to the window. His cousins, astonished, exchanged looks.

"Very well, Marmaduke," said Marian softly, after a pause: "I wont tease you any more. Dont be angry."

"You havnt teased me," said he, coming back somewhat shamefacedly from the window. "I feel savage to-day, though there is no reason why I should not be as jolly as a shrimp. Perhaps Nelly will play some Chopin, just to soothe me. I should like to hear that polonaise again."

"I should enjoy nothing better than taking you at your word," said Elinor. "But I heard Mr. Lind come in, a moment ago; and he is not so fond of Chopin as you and I."

Mr. Lind entered whilst she was speaking. He was a dignified gentleman, with delicately chiselled features and portly figure. His silky light brown hair curled naturally about his brow and set it off imposingly. His hands were white and small, with tapering fingers, and small thumbs.

"How do you do, sir?" said Marmaduke, blushing.

"Thank you: I am better than I have been."

Marmaduke murmured congratulations, and looked at his watch as if pressed for time. "I must be off now," he said, rising. "I was just going when you came in."

"So soon! Well, I must not detain you, Marmaduke. I heard from your father this morning. He is very anxious to see you settled in life."

"I suppose I shall shake down some day, sir."

"You have very good opportunities—very exceptional opportunities. Has Marian told you that Constance is expected to arrive in town next week?"

"Yes: we told him," said Marian.

"He thought it too good to be true, and would hardly believe us," added Elinor.

Mr. Lind smiled at his nephew, happily forgetful, worldly wise as he was, of the inevitable conspiracy of youth against age. They smiled too, except Marmaduke, who, being under observation, kept his countenance like the Man in the Iron

George Bernard Shaw

Mask. "It is quite true, my boy," said the uncle, kindly. "But before she arrives, I should like to have a talk with you. When can you come to breakfast with me?"

"Any day you choose to name, sir. I shall be very glad."

"Let us say to-morrow morning. Will that be too soon?"

"Not at all. It will suit me quite well. Good evening, sir."

"Good evening to you."

When Marmaduke was in the street, he stood for a while considering which way to go. Before the arrival of his uncle, he had intended to spend the afternoon with his cousins. He was now at a loss for a means of killing time. On one point he was determined. There was a rehearsal that day at the Bijou Theatre; and thither, at least, he would not go. He drove to Charing Cross, and drifted back to Leicester Square. He turned away from the theatre, and wandered down Piccadilly. Then he thought he would return as far as the Criterion, and drink. Finally he arrived at the stage door of the Bijou Theatre, and inquired whether the rehearsal was over.

"Theyve bin at it since eleven this mornin, and will be pretty nigh til the stage is wanted for to-night," said the janitor. "I'd as lief youd wait here as go up, if you dont mind, sir. The guvnor is above; and he aint in the best o' tempers. I'll send word up."

Marmaduke looked round irresolutely. A great noise of tramping and singing began.

"Thats the new procession," continued the doorkeeper. "Sixteen hextras took on for it. It's Miss Virtue's chance for lunch, sir: you wont have long to wait now."

Here there was a rapid pattering of feet down the staircase. Marmaduke started, and stood biting his lips as Mademoiselle

Lalage, busy, hungry, and in haste, hurried towards the door.

"Come! Come on," she said impatiently to him, as she went out. "Go and get a cab, will you. I must have something to eat; and I have to get back sharp. Do be qu—there goes a hansom. Hi!" She whistled shrilly, and waved her umbrella. The cab came, and was directed by Marmaduke to a restaurant in Regent Street.

"I am absolutely starving," she said as they drove off. "I have been in since eleven this morning; and of course they only called the band for half-past. They are such damned fools: they drive me mad."

"Why dont you walk out of the theatre, and make them arrange it properly for next day?"

"Oh yes! And throw the whole day after the half, and lose my rehearsal. It is bad enough to lose my temper. I swore, I can tell you."

"I have no doubt you did."

"This horse thinks he's at a funeral. What o'clock is it?"

"It's only eight minutes past four. There is plenty of time."

When they alighted, Lalage hurried into the restaurant; scrutinized the tables; and selected the best lighted one. The waiter, a decorous elderly man, approached with some severity of manner, and handed a bill of fare to Marmaduke. She snatched it from him, and addressed the waiter sharply.

"Bring me some thin soup; and get me a steak to follow. Let it be a thick juicy one. If its purple and raw I wont have it; and if its done to a cinder, I wont have it: it must be red. And get me some spring cabbage and potatoes, and a pint of dry champagne—the decentest you have. And be quick."

"And what for you, sir?" said the waiter, turning to Marmaduke.

"Never mind him," interrupted Susanna. "Go and attend to me."

The waiter bowed and retired.

"Old stick-in-the-mud!" muttered Miss Lalage. "Is it half-past four yet?"

"No. It's only quarter past. There's lots of time."

Mademoiselle Lalage ate until the soup, a good deal of bread, the steak, the vegetables, and the pint of champagne—less a glassful taken by her companion—had disappeared. Marmaduke watched her meanwhile, and consumed two ices.

"Have an ice to finish up with?" he said.

"No. I cant work on sweets," she replied. "But I am beginning to feel alive again and comfortable. Whats the time?"

"Confound the time!" said Marmaduke. "It's twenty minutes to five."

"Well, I'll drive back to the theatre. I neednt start for quarter of an hour yet."

"Thank heaven!" said Marmaduke. "I was afraid I should not be able to get a word with you."

"That reminds me of a crow I have to pluck with you, Mr. Marmaduke Lind. What did you mean by telling me your name was Sharp?"

"It's the name of a cousin of mine," said Marmaduke, attempting to dismiss the subject with a laugh.

"It may be your cousin's name; but it's not yours. By the bye, is that the cousin youre engaged to?"

"What cousin? I'm not engaged to anybody."

"That's a lie, like your denial of your name. Come, come, Master Marmaduke: you cant humbug me. Youre too young. Hallo! What do *you* want?"

It was the waiter, removing some plates, and placing a bill on the table. Marmaduke put his hand into his pocket.

"Just wait a minute, please," said Susanna. The waiter retired.

"Now then," she resumed, placing her elbows on the table, "let us have no more nonsense. What is your little game? Are you going to pay that bill or am I?"

"I am, of course."

"There is no of course in it—not yet, anyhow. What are you hanging about the theatre after me for? Tell me that. Dont stop to think."

Marmaduke looked foolish, and then sulky. Finally he brightened, and said, "Look here. Youre angry with me for bringing your brother last night. But upon my soul I had no idea—"

"That's not what I mean at all. You are dodging a plain question. When you came to the theatre, I thought you were a nice fellow; and I made friends with you. Now I find you have been telling me lies about yourself, and trying to play fast and loose. You must either give that up or give me up. I wont have you pass that stage door again if you only want to amuse yourself like other lounging cads about town."

"What do you mean by playing fast and loose, and being a cad about town?" said Marmaduke angrily.

"I hope youre not going to make a row here in public."

"No; but I have you where *you* cant make a row; and I intend to have it out with you once and for all. If you quarrel now, so help me Heaven I'll never speak to you again!"

"It is you who are quarrelling."

"Very well," said Susanna, opening her purse as though the matter were decided. "Waiter."

"I am going to pay."

"So you can—for what you had yourself. I dont take dinners from strange men, nor pay for their ices."

Marmaduke did not reply. He took out his purse determinedly; glanced angrily at her; and muttered, "I never thought you were that sort of woman."

"What sort of woman?" demanded Susanna, in a tone that made the other occupants of the room turn and stare.

"Never mind," said Marmaduke. She was about to retort, when she saw him looking into his purse with an expression of dismay. The waiter came. Susanna, instead of attempting to be beforehand in proffering the money, changed her mind, and waited. Marmaduke searched his pockets. Finding nothing, he muttered an imprecation, and, fingering his watch chain, glanced doubtfully at the waiter, who looked stolidly at the tablecloth.

"There," said Susanna, putting down a sovereign.

Marmaduke looked on helplessly whilst the waiter changed the coin and thanked Susanna for her gratuity. Then he said, "You must let me settle with you for this to-night. Ive left nearly all my cash in the pocket of another waistcoat."

"You will not have the chance of settling with me, either to-night or any other night. I am done with you." And she rose and left the restaurant. Marmaduke sat doggedly for quarter of a minute. Then he went out, and ran along Regent Street, anxiously looking from face to face in search of her. At last he saw her walking at a great pace a little distance ahead of him. He made a dash and overtook her.

"Look here, Lalage," he said, keeping up with her as she walked: "this is all rot. I didnt mean to offend you. I dont know what you mean, or what you want me to do. Dont be so unreasonable."

No answer.

"I can stand a good deal from you; but it's too much to be kept at your heels as if I were a beggar or a troublesome dog. *Lalage.*" She took no notice of him; and he stopped, trying to compose his features, which were distorted by rage. She walked on, turning into Glasshouse Street. When she had gone twenty yards, she heard him striding behind her.

"If you wont stop and talk to me," he said, "I'll make you. If anybody interferes with me I'll smash him into jelly. It would serve you right if I did the same to you."

He put his hand on her arm; and she instantly turned and struck him across the face, knocking off his hat. He, who a moment before had been excited, red, and almost in tears, was appalled. There was a crowd in a moment; and a cabman drew up close to the kerb with a calm conviction that his hansom would be wanted presently.

"How dare you put your hand on me, you coward?" she exclaimed, with remarkable crispness of utterance and energy of style. "Who are you? I dont know you. Where are the police?" She paused for a reply; and a bracelet, broken by the blow she had given him, dropped on the pavement, and was officiously picked up and handed to her by a battered old

George Bernard Shaw

woman who shewed in every wrinkle her burning sympathy with Woman turning at bay against Man. Susanna looked at the broken bracelet, and tears of vexation sprang to her eyes. "Look at what youve done!" she cried, holding out the bracelet in her left hand and shewing a scrape which had drawn blood on her right wrist. "For two pins I'd knock your head off!"

Marmaduke, quite out of countenance, and yet sullenly very angry, vacillated for a moment between his conflicting impulses to knock her down and to fly to the utmost ends of the earth. If he had been ten years older he would probably have knocked her down: as it was, he signed to the cabman, who gathered up the reins and held them clear of his fare's damaged hat with the gratification of a man whose judgment in a delicate matter had just been signally confirmed by events.

As they started, Susanna made a dash at the cab, which was pulled up, amid a shout from the crowd, just in time to prevent an accident. Then, holding on to the rail and standing on the step, she addressed herself to the cabman, and, sacrificing all propriety of language to intensity of vituperation, demanded whether he wanted to run his cab over her body and kill her. He, with undisturbed foresight, answered not a word, but again shifted the reins so as to make way for her bonnet. Acknowledging the attention with one more epithet, she seated herself in the cab, from which Marmaduke at once indignantly rose to escape. But the hardiest Grasmere wrestler, stooping under the hood of a hansom, could not resist a vigorous pull at his coat tails; and Marmaduke was presently back in his seat again, with Susanna clinging to him and half sobbing:

"Oh, Bob, youve killed me. How could you?" Then, with a suspiciously sudden recovery of energy, she screamed "Bijou Theatre. Drive on, will you" up at the cabman, who was looking down through the trapdoor. The horse plunged forward, and, with the jolt, she was fawning on Marmaduke's arm again, saying, "Dont be brutal to me any more, Bob. I cant bear it. I have enough trouble without your turning on me."

He was young and green, and too much confused by this time to feel sure that he had not been the aggressor. But he did, on the whole, the wisest thing—folded his arms and sat silent, with his cheeks burning.

"Say something to me," she said, shaking his arm. "I have nothing to say," he replied. "I shall leave town for home to-night. I cant shew my face again after this."

"Home," she said, in her former contemptuous tone, flinging his arm away. "That means your cousin Constance."

"Who told you about her?"

"Never mind. You are engaged to her."

"You lie!"

Susanna was shaken. She looked hard at him, wondering whether he was deceiving her or not. "Look me in the face, Bob," she said. If he had complied, she would not have believed him. But he treated the challenge with supreme disdain and stared straight ahead, obeying his male instinct, which taught him that the woman, with all the advantages on her side, would nevertheless let him win if he held on. At last she came caressingly to his shoulder again, and said:

"Why didnt you tell me about her yourself?"

"Damn it all," he exclaimed, violently, "there is nothing to tell! I am not engaged to her: on my oath I am not. My people at home talk about a match between us as if it were a settled thing, though they know I don't care for her. But if you want to have the truth, I cant afford to say that I wont marry her, because I am too hard up to quarrel with the governor, who has set his heart on it. You see, the way I am circumstanced—"

"Oh, bother your circumstances! Look here, Bob, I dont want you to introduce me to your swell relations; it is not worth *my* while to waste time on people who cant earn their own living. And never mind your governor: we can get on without him. If you are hard up for money, and he is stingy, you had better get it from me than from the Jews."

"I couldnt do that," said Marmaduke, touched. "In fact, I am well enough off. By the bye, I must not forget to pay you for that lunch. But if I ever am hard up, I will come to you. Will that do?"

"Of course: that is what I meant. Confound it, here we are already. You mustnt come in, you would only be in the way. Come to-night after the burlesque, if you like. Youre not angry with me, are you?"

Her breast touched his arm just then; and as if she had released some spring, all his love for her suddenly surged up within him and got the better of him. "Wait—listen," he said, in a voice half choked with tenderness. "Look here, Lalage: the honest truth is that I shall be ruined if I marry you openly. Let us be married quietly, and keep it dark until I am more independent."

"Married! Catch me at it—if you can. No, dear boy, I am very fond of you, and you are one of the right sort to make me the offer; but I wont let you put a collar round *my* neck. Matrimony is all very fine for women who have no better way of supporting themselves, but it wouldn't suit me. Dont look so dazed. What difference does it make to *you*?"

"But—" He stopped, bewildered, gazing at her.

"Get out, you great goose!" she said, and suddenly sprang out of the hansom and darted into the theatre.

He sat gaping after her, horrified—genuinely horrified.

CHAPTER III

The Earl of Carbury was a youngish man with no sort of turn for being a nobleman. He could not bring himself to behave as if he was anybody in particular; and though this passed for perfect breeding whenever he by chance appeared in his place in society, on the magisterial bench, or in the House of Lords, it prevented him from making the most of the earldom, and was a standing grievance with his relatives, many of whom were the most impudent and uppish people on the face of the earth. He was, if he had only known it, a born republican, with no natural belief in earls at all; but as he was rather too modest to indulge his consciousness with broad generalizations of this kind, all he knew about the matter was that he was sensible of being a bad hand at his hereditary trade of territorial aristocrat. At a very early age he had disgraced himself by asking his mother whether he might be a watchmaker when he grew up, and his feeble sense on that occasion of the impropriety of an earl being anything whatsoever except an earl had given his mother an imperious contempt for him which afterward got curiously mixed with a salutary dread of his moral superiority to her, which considerable. His aspiration to become a watchmaker was an early symptom of his extraordinary turn for mechanics. An apprenticeship of six years at the bench would have made an educated workman of him: as it was, he pottered at every mechanical pursuit as a gentleman amateur in a laboratory and workshop which he had got built for himself in his park. In this magazine of toys—for such it virtually was at first—he satisfied his itchings to play with tools and machines. He was no sportsman; but if

　　　　George Bernard Shaw

he saw in a shop window the most trumpery patent improvement in a breechloader, he would go in and buy it; and as to a new repeating rifle or liquefied gas gun, he would travel to St. Petersburg to see it. He wrote very little; but he had sixteen different typewriters, each guaranteed perfect by an American agent, who had also pledged himself that the other fifteen were miserable impostures. A really ingenious bicycle or tricycle always found in him a ready purchaser; and he had patented a roller skate and a railway brake. When the electric chair for dental operations was invented, he sacrificed a tooth to satisfy his curiosity as to its operation. He could not play brass instruments to any musical purpose; but his collection of double slide trombones, bombardons with patent compensating pistons, comma trumpets, and the like, would have equipped a small military band; whilst his newly tempered harmonium with fifty-three notes to each octave, and his pianos with simplified keyboards that nobody could play on, were the despair of all musical amateurs who came to stay at Towers Cottage, as his place was called. He would buy the most expensive and elaborate lathe, and spend a month trying to make a true billiard ball at it. At the end of that time he would have to send for a professional hand, who would cornet the ball with apparently miraculous skill in a few seconds. He got on better with chemistry and photography; but at last he settled down to electrical engineering, and, giving up the idea of doing everything with his own half-trained hand, kept a skilled man always in his laboratory to help him out.

All along there had been a certain love of the marvelous at the bottom of his fancy for inventions. Therefore, though he did not in the least believe in ghosts, he would "investigate" spiritualism, and part with innumerable guineas to mediums, slatewriters, clairvoyants, and even of turbaned rascals from the East, who would boldly offer at midnight to bring him out into the back yard and there and then raise the devil for him. And just as his tendency was to magnify the success and utility of his patent purchases, so he would lend himself more or less to gross impostures simply because they interested him. This confirmed his reputation for being a bit of a crank; and as he had in addition all the restlessness and eccentricity of the active spirits of his class, arising from the fact that no matter what he busied himself with, it never really mattered whether he accomplished it or not, he remained an unsatisfied and (considering the money he cost) unsatisfactory specimen of a true man in a false position.

Towers Cottage was supposed to be a mere appendage to Carbury Towers, which had been burnt down, to the great relief of its noble owners, in the reign of William IV. The Cottage, a handsome one-storied Tudor mansion, with tall chimneys, gabled roofs, and transom windows, had since served the family as a very sufficient residence, needing a much smaller staff of servants than the Towers, and accommodating fewer visitors. At first it had been assumed on all hands that the stay at the Cottage was but a temporary one, pending the re-erection of the Towers on a scale of baronial magnificence; but this tradition, having passed through its primal stage of being a standing excuse with the elders into that of being a standing joke with the children, had naturally lapsed as the children grew up. Indeed, the Cottage was now too large for the family; for the Earl was still unmarried, and all his sisters had contracted splendid alliances except the youngest, Lady Constance Carbury, a maiden of twenty-two, with a thin face and slight angular figure, who was still on her mother's hands. The illustrious matches made by her sisters had, in fact, been secured by extravagant dowering, which had left nothing for poor Lady Constance except a miserable three hundred pounds a year, at which paltry figure no man had as yet offered to take her. The Countess (Dowager) habitually assumed that Marmaduke Lind ardently desired the hand of his cousin; and Constance herself supported tacitly this view; but the Earl was apt to become restive when it was put forward, though he altogether declined to improve his sister's pecuniary position, having already speculated quite heavily enough in brothers-in-law.

In the August following the Wandsworth concert Lord Carbury began to take his electrical laboratory with such

George Bernard Shaw

intensified seriousness that he flatly refused to entertain any visitors until the 12th, and held fast to his determination in spite of his mother's threat to leave the house, alleging, with a laugh, that he had got hold of a discovery with money in it at last. But he felt at such a disadvantage after this incredible statement that he hastened to explain that his objection to visitors did not apply to relatives who would be sufficiently at home at Towers Cottage to require no attention from him. Under the terms of this capitulation Marian, as universal favorite, was invited; and since there was no getting Marian down without Elinor, she was invited too, in spite of the Countess's strong dislike for her, a sentiment which she requited with a pungent mixture of detestation and contempt. Marian's brother, the Reverend George Lind, promised to come down in a day or two; and Marmaduke, who was also invited, did not reply.

The morning after her arrival, Marian was awakened at six o'clock by a wagon rumbling past the window of her room with a sound quite different from that made by the dust-cart in Westbourne Terrace. She peeped out at it, and saw that is was laden with packages of irregular shape, which, judging by some strange-looking metal rods that projected through the covering, she took to be apparatus for Lord Jasper's laboratory. From the wagon, with its patiently trudging horse and dull driver, she lifted her eyes to the lawn, where the patches of wet shadow beneath the cedars refreshed the sunlit grass around them. It looked too fine a morning to spend in bed. Had Marian been able to taste and smell the fragrant country air she would not have hesitated a moment. But she had been accustomed to believe that fresh air was unhealthy at night, and though nothing would have induced her to wash in dirty water, she thought nothing of breathing dirty air; and so the window was shut and the room close. Still, the window did not exclude the loud singing of the birds or the sunlight. She ventured to open it a little, not without a sense of imprudence. Twenty minutes later she was dressed.

She first looked into the drawing-room, but it was stale and dreary. The dining-room, which she tried next, made her hungry. The arrival of a servant with a broom suggested to her that she had better get out of the way of the household work. She felt half sorry for getting up, and went out on the lawn to recover her spirits. There she heard a man's voice trolling a stave somewhere in the direction of the laboratory. Thinking that it might be Lord Carbury, and that, if so, he would probably not wait until half past nine to break his fast, she ran gaily off round the southwest corner of the Cottage to a terrace, from which there was access through a great double window, now wide open, to a lofty apartment roofed with glass.

At a large table in the middle of the room sat a man with his back to the window. He had taken off his coat, and was bending over a small round block with little holes sunk into it. Each hole was furnished with a neat brass peg, topped with ebony; and the man was lifting and replacing one of these pegs whilst he gravely watched the dial of an instrument that resembled a small clock. A large straw hat concealed his head, and protected it from the rays that were streaming through the glass roof and open window. The apparent triviality of his occupation, and his intentness upon it, amused Marian. She stole into the laboratory, came close behind him, and said:

"Since you have nothing better to do than play cribbage with yourself, I—"

She had gently lifted up his straw hat, and found beneath a head that was not Lord Carbury's. The man, who had cowered with surprise at her touch and voice, but had waited even then to finish an observation of his galvanometer before turning, now turned and stared at her.

"I *beg* your pardon," said Marian, blushing vigorously. "I thought it was Lord Carbury. I have disturbed you very rudely. I—"

"Not at all," said the man. "I quite understand. I was not

playing cribbage, but I was doing nothing very important. However, as you certainly did take me by surprise, perhaps you will excuse my coat."

"Oh, pray dont mind me. I must not interrupt your work." She looked at his face again, but only for an instant, as he was watching her. Then, with another blush, she put out her hand and said, "How do you do, Mr. Conolly. I did not recognize you at first."

He shook hands, but did not offer any further conversation. "What a wonderful place!" she said, looking round, with a view to making herself agreeable by taking an interest in everything. "Wont you explain it all to me? To begin with, what is electricity?"

Conolly stared rather at this question, and then shook his head. "I don't know anything about that," he said; "I am only a workman. Perhaps Lord Carbury can tell you: he has read a good deal about it."

Marian looked incredulously at him. "I am sure you are joking," she said. "Lord Carbury says you know ever so much more than he does. I suppose I asked a stupid question. What are those reels of green silk for?"

"Ah," said Conolly, relaxing. "Come now, I can tell you that easily enough. I dont know what it *is*, but I know what it does, and I can lay traps to catch it. Here now, for instance—"

And he went on to deliver a sort of chatty Royal Institution Children's Lecture on Electricity which produced a great impression on Marian, who was accustomed to nothing better than small talk. She longed to interest him by her comments and questions, but she found that they had a most discouraging effect on him. Redoubling her efforts, she at last reduced him to silence, of which she availed herself to remark, with great earnestness, that science was a very wonderful thing.

"How do you know?" he said, a little bluntly.

"I am sure it must be," she replied, brightening; for she thought he had now made a rather foolish remark. "Is Lord Carbury a very clever scientist?"

Conolly looked just grave enough to suggest that the question was not altogether a discreet one. Then, brushing off that consideration, he replied:

"He has seen a great deal and read a great deal. You see, he has great means at his disposal. His property is as good as a joint-stock company at his back. Practically, he is very good, considering his method of working: not so good, considering the means at his disposal."

"What would you do if you had his means?"

Conolly made a gesture which plainly signified that he thought he could do a great many things.

"And is science, then, so expensive? I thought it was beyond the reach of money."

"Oh, yes: science may be. But I am not a scientific man: I'm an inventor. The two things are quite different. Invention is the most expensive thing in the world. It takes no end of time, and no end of money. Time is money; so it costs both ways."

"Then why dont you discover something and make your fortune?"

"I have already discovered something."

"Oh! What is it?"

"That it costs a fortune to make experiments enough to lead to an invention."

"You are exaggerating, are you not? What do you mean by a fortune?"

"In my case, at least four or five hundred pounds."

"Is that all? Surely you would have no difficulty in getting five hundred pounds."

Conolly laughed. "To be sure," said he. "What is five hundred pounds?"

"A mere nothing—considering the importance of the object. You really ought not to allow such a consideration as that to delay your career. I have known people spend as much in one day on the most worthless things."

"There is something in that, Miss Lind. How would you recommend me to begin?"

"First," said Marian, with determination, "make up your mind to spend the money. Banish all scruples about the largeness of the sum. Resolve not to grudge even twice as much to science."

"That is done already. I have quite made up my mind to spend the money. What next?"

"Well, I suppose the next thing is to spend it."

"Excuse me. The next thing is to get it. It is a mere detail, I know; but I should like to settle it before we go any further."

"But how can I tell you that? You forget that I am quite unacquainted with your affairs. You are a man, and understand business, which of course I dont."

"If you wanted five hundred pounds, Miss Lind, how would you set about getting it?—if I may ask."

"What? I! But, as I say, I am only a woman. I should ask my

father for it, or sign a receipt for my trustees, or something of that sort."

"That is a very simple plan. But unfortunately I have no father and no trustees. Worse than that, I have no money. You must suggest some other way."

"Do what everybody else does in your circumstances. Borrow it. I am sure Lord Carbury would lend it to you."

Conolly shook his head. "It doesnt do for a man in my position to start borrowing the moment he makes the acquaintance of a man in Lord Carbury's," he said. "We are working a little together already on one of my ideas, and that is as far as I care to ask him to go. I am afraid I must ask you for another suggestion."

"Save up all your money until you have enough."

"That would take some time. Let me see. As I am an exceptionally fortunate and specially skilled workman, I can now calculate on making from seventy shillings to six pounds a week. Say four pounds on the average."

"Ah," said Marian, despondingly, "you would have to wait more than two years to save five hundred pounds."

"And to dispense with food, clothes, and lodging in the meantime."

"True," said Marian. "Of course, I see that it is impossible for you to save anything. And yet it seems absurd to be stopped by the want of such a sum. I have a cousin who has no money at all, and no experiments to make, and he paid a thousand pounds for a race-horse last spring."

Conolly nodded, to intimate that he knew that such things happened.

Marian could think of no further expedient. She stood still, thinking, whilst Conolly took up a bit of waste and polished a brass cylinder.

"Mr. Conolly," she said at last, "I cannot absolutely promise you; but I think I can get you five hundred pounds." Conolly stopped polishing the cylinder, and stared at her. "If I have not enough, I am sure we could make the rest by a bazaar or something. I should like to begin to invest my money; and if you make some great invention, like the telegraph or steam engine, you will be able to pay it back to me, and to lend me money when *I* want it."

Conolly blushed. "Thank you, Miss Lind," said he, "thank you very much indeed. I—It would be ungrateful of me to refuse; but I am not so ready to begin my experiments as my talking might lead you to suppose. My estimate of their cost was a mere guess. I am not satisfied that it is not want of time and perseverance more than of money that is the real obstacle. However, I will—I will—a—Have you any idea of the value of money, Miss Lind? Have you ever had the handling of it?"

"Of course," said Marian, secretly thinking that the satisfaction of shaking his self-possession was cheap at five hundred pounds. "I keep house at home, and do all sorts of business things."

Conolly glanced about him vaguely; picked up the piece of waste again as if he had been looking for that; recollected himself; and looked unintelligibly at her. Her uncertainty as to what he would do next was a delightful sensation: why, she did not know nor care. To her intense disappointment, Lord Carbury entered just then, and roused her from what was unaccountably like a happy dream.

Nothing more of any importance happened that day except the arrival of a letter from Paris, addressed to Lady Constance in Marmaduke's handwriting. Miss McQuinch first heard of it in the fruit garden, where she found Constance sitting with her arm around Marian's waist in a summer-house. She sat down opposite them, at a rough oak table.

"A letter, Nelly!" said Marian. "A letter! A letter from Marmaduke! I have extorted leave for you to read it. Here it is. Handle it carefully, pray."

"Has he proposed?" said Elinor, taking it.

Constance changed color. Elinor opened the letter in silence, and read:

> My dear Constance:
>
> I hope you are quite well. I am having an awfully jolly time of it here. What a pity it is you dont come over! I was wishing for you yesterday in the Louvre, where we spent a pleasant day looking at the pictures. I send you the silk you wanted, and had great trouble hunting through half-a-dozen shops for it. Not that I mind the trouble, but just to let you see my devotion to you. I have no more to say at present, as it is nearly post hour. Remember me to the clan.
>
> Yours ever,
> DUKE.
>
> P.S.—How do Nelly and your mother get along together?

Whilst Elinor was reading, the gardener passed the summer-house, and Constance went out and spoke to him. Elinor looked significantly at Marian.

"Nelly," returned Marian, in hushed tones of reproach, "you have stabbed poor Constance to the heart by telling her that Marmaduke never proposed to her. That is why she has gone out."

"Yes," said Elinor, "it was brutal. But I thought, as you made such a fuss about the letter, that it must have been a proposal at least. It cant be helped now. It is one more enemy for me, that is all."

"What do you think of the letter? Was it not kind of him to write—considering how careless he is usually?"

"Hm! Did he match the silk properly?".

"To perfection. He must really have taken some trouble. You know how he botched getting the ribbon for his fancy dress at the ball last year."

"That is just what I was thinking about. Do you remember also how he ridiculed the Louvre after his first trip to Paris, and swore that nothing would ever induce him to enter it again?"

"He has got more sense now. He says in the letter that he spent yesterday there."

"Not exactly. He says 'we spent a pleasant day looking at the pictures.' Who is 'we'?"

"Some companion of his, I suppose. Why?"

"I was just thinking could it be the person who has matched the silk so well. The same woman, I mean."

"Oh, Nelly!"

"Oh, Marian! Do you suppose Marmaduke would spend an afternoon at the Louvre with a man, who could just as well go by himself? Do men match silks?"

"Of course they do. Any fly-fisher can do it better than a woman. Really, Nell, you have an odious imagination."

"Yes—when my imagination is started on an odious track. Nothing will persuade me that Marmaduke cares a straw for

Constance. He does not want to marry her, though he is too great a coward to own it."

"Why do you say so? I grant you he is unceremonious and careless. But he is the same to everybody."

"Yes: to everybody *we* know. What is the use of straining after an amiable view of things, Marian, when a cynical view is most likely to be the true one."

"There is no harm in giving people credit for being good."

"Yes, there is, when people are not good, which is most often the case. It sets us wrong practically, and holds virtue cheap. If Marmaduke is a noble and warmhearted man, and Constance a lovable, innocent girl, all I can say is that it is not worth while to be noble or lovable. If amiability consists in maintaining that black is white, it is a quality anyone may acquire by telling a lie and sticking to it."

"But I dont maintain that black is white. Only it seems to me that as regards white, you are color blind. Where I see white, you see black; and—hush! Here is Constance."

"Yes," whispered Elinor: "she comes back quickly enough when it occurs to her that we are talking about her."

Instead of simply asking why Constance should not behave in this very natural manner if she chose to, Marian was about to defend Constance warmly by denying all motive to her return, when that event took place and stopped the discussion. Marian and Nelly spent a considerable part of their lives in bandying their likes and dislikes under the impression that they were arguing important points of character and conduct.

They knew that Constance wanted to answer Marmaduke's letter; so they alleged correspondence of their own, and left her to herself.

Lady Constance went to her brother's study, where there was a comfortable writing-table. She began to write without hesitation, and her pen gabbled rapidly until she had covered two sheets of paper, when, instead of taking a fresh sheet, she wrote across the lines already written. After signing the letter, she read it through, and added two postscripts. Then she remembered something she had forgotten to say; but there was no more room on her two sheets, and she was reluctant to use a third, which might, in a letter to France, involve extra postage. Whilst she was hesitating her brother entered.

"Am I in your way?" she said. "I shall have done in a moment."

"No, I am not going to write. By-the-bye, they tell me you had a letter from Marmaduke this morning. Has he anything particular to say?"

"Nothing very particular. He is in Paris."

"Indeed? Are you writing to him?"

"Yes," said Constance, irritated by his disparaging tone. "Why not?"

"Do as you please, of course. I am afraid he is a scamp."

"Are you? You know a great deal about him, I dare say."

"I am not much reassured by those who do know about him."

"And who may they be? The only person you know who has seen much of him is Marian, and she doesnt speak ill of people behind their backs."

"Marian takes rather a rose-colored view of everybody, Marmaduke included. You should talk to Nelly about him."

"I knew it. I knew, the minute you began to talk, who had set you on."

"I am afraid Nelly's opinion is worth more than Marians."

"*Her* opinion! Everybody knows what her opinion is. She is bursting with jealousy of me."

"Jealousy!"

"What else? Marmaduke has never taken the least notice of her, and she is madly in love with him."

"This is quite a new light upon the affair. Constance, are you sure you are not romancing?"

"Romancing! Why, she cannot conceal her venom. She taunted me this morning in the summer-house because Marmaduke has never made me a formal proposal. It was the letter that made her do it. Ask Marian."

"I can hardly believe it: I should not have supposed, from what I have observed, that she cared about him."

You should not have supposed it from what she *said*: is that what you mean? I dont care whether you believe it or not."

"Well, if you are so confident, there is no occasion to be acrimonious about Elinor. She is more to be pitied than blamed."

"Yes, everybody is to pity Elinor because she cant have her wish and make me wretched," said Constance, beginning to cry. Whereupon Lord Carbury immediately left the room.

CHAPTER IV

Long before the harvest was home, preparations were made at Towers Cottage to receive another visitor. The Rev. George Lind was coming. Lord Carbury drove in the wagonet to the railway station, and met him on the platform.

"How are you, my dear fellow?" cried the clergyman, shaking the earl's hand. "Why did you trouble to meet me? I could have taken a fly. Most kind of you, I am sure. How is your dear mother? And Constance: how is *she*?"

"All quite well, thank you. Just show my fellow your traps; he will see to them."

"Oh, there is no need to trouble him. I myself or a porter—oh, thank you, I am sure; the brown one with G.L. on it—and that small green metal box too, if you will be so good. Thank you very much. And how are you, Jasper, if I may call you so? Studious still, eh? I hope he will be careful of the box. No, not a word to him, I beg: it does not matter at all. What a charming little trap! What air! Happy man, Jasper! These fields are better than the close alleys and garrets to which my profession leads me."

"Jump in."

"Thank you. And how is Marian?"

"Quite well, thank you. *Everybody* is quite well. The girls are at a tennis party, or they would have come to meet you. Constance desired me particularly to apologize."

"Oh, needless, most needless. Why should they not enjoy themselves? What a landscape! The smiling beauty of nature in the country is like a—like a message to us. This is indeed a delightful drive."

"Yes, she is a capital trotter, this mare of mine. What do you think of her?"

"A noble animal, Jasper. Although I never studied horseflesh much, even in my university days, I can admire a spirited nag on occasion. But I have to content myself with humbler means of locomotion in my own calling. A poor parson cannot entertain his friends as a magnate like you can. Have you any one at the hall now, besides the girls?"

"No. The place will be rather dull for you, I am afraid."

"Not at all, my dear fellow, not at all. I shall be satisfied and thankful under all circumstances."

"We have led a humdrum life for the past month. Marian and Elinor have begun to potter about in my laboratory. They come there every day for an hour to work and study, as they call it."

"Indeed! I have no doubt Marian will find the study of nature most improving. It is very generous of you to allow her to trespass on you."

"I occupy myself chiefly with Nelly McQuinch. Marian is my assistant's pupil, and he has made a very expert workwoman of her already. With a little direction, she can put a machine together as well as I can."

"I am delighted to hear it. And dear Nelly?"

"Oh, dear Nelly treats the subject in her usual way. But she is very amusing."

"Ah, Jasper! Ah! An unstable nature there, an unstable nature! Elinor has not been firmly trained. She needs to be tried by adversity."

"No doubt she will be. Most of us are."

"And dear Constance? Does she study?"

"No."

"Ahem! A—have you—? That is St. Mildred's yonder, is it not?"

"It is. They have put a new clock in the tower, worth about sixty pounds. I believe they collected a hundred and fifty for the purpose. But you were going to say something else."

"No. At least, I intended to ask you about Marmaduke. He is coming down, I understand."

"I dont know what he is doing. Last week he wrote to us that he had just returned from Paris; but I happened to know that he had then been back for some time. He has arranged to come twice, but on each occasion, at the last moment, he has made excuses. He can do as he likes now. I wish he would say definitely that he doesnt intend to come, instead of shilly-shallying from week to week. Hallo, Prentice, have the ladies returned yet?" This was addressed to the keeper of the gate-lodge, at which they had now arrived. He replied that the ladies were still absent.

"Then," said Lord Carbury, "we had better get down and stroll across the lawn. Perhaps you are tired, though?"

"Not at all. I should prefer it. What a lovely avenue! What greenery! How—"

"We were talking about Marmaduke. Do you know what he is doing at present? He talks of being busy, and of not having a moment to spare. I can understand a fellow not having a moment to spare in June or July, but what Marmaduke has to do in London in September is more than I can imagine."

"I do not care to enquire into these things too closely. I had intended to speak to you on the subject. Marmaduke, as I suppose you know, has taken a house at West Kensington."

"A house at West Kensington! No, I did not know it. What has he done that for?"

"I fear he has been somewhat disingenuous with me on the subject. I think he tried to prevent the matter coming to my ears; and when I asked him about it, he certainly implied—in fact, I grieve to say he left me under the impression that he had taken the house with a view to marrying dear Constance, and settling down. I expressed some surprise at his going so far out of town; but he did not volunteer any further explanation, and so the matter dropped." The Rev. George paused, and then continued in a lower tone, "Not long afterward I met him at a very late hour. He had perhaps exceeded a little in his cups; for he spoke to me with the most shocking cynicism, inviting me to supper at this house of his, and actually accusing me of knowing perfectly well the terrible truth about his occupation of it. He assured me that she—meaning, I presume, the unhappy person with whom he lives there—was exceptionally attractive; and I have since discovered that she is connected with the theatre, and of great notoriety. I need not tell you how dreadful all this is to me, Jasper; but to the best of my judgment, which I have fortified by earnest prayers for guidance, it is my imperative duty to tell you of it."

"The vagabond! It is exactly as I have always said: Constance is too tame for him. He does not care a d—"

"Jasper, my dear fellow, gently," said the clergyman, pressing his arm.

George Bernard Shaw

"Pshaw!" said the Earl, "I dont care. I think Constance is well out of it. Let us drop the subject for the present. I hear the carriage."

"Yes, here it is. Dear Lady Carbury has recognized me, and is waving her hand." The Rev. George stood on tiptoe as he spoke, and flourished his low-crowned soft felt hat.

During the ensuing greetings Carbury stood silent, looking at the horses with an expression that made the coachman uneasy. At dinner he ate sedulously, and left the task of entertaining the visitor to his mother and the girls. The clergyman was at no loss for conversation. He was delighted with the dinner, delighted with the house, delighted to see the Countess looking so well, and delighted to hear that the tennis party that day had been a pleasant one. The Earl listened with impatience, and was glad when his mother rose. Before she quitted the dining-room he made a sign to her, and she soon returned, leaving Marian, Constance, and Elinor in the drawing-room.

"You will not mind my staying, I hope, George," she said, as she resumed her seat.

"A delightful precedent, and from a distinguished source," said the Rev. George. "Allow me to pass the bottle. Ha! ha!"

"Thank you, no," said the Countess. "I never take wine." Her tone was inconclusive, as if she intended to take something else.

"Will you take brandy-and-soda?" said her son, rather brusquely.

Lady Carbury lowered her eyelids in protest. Then she said: "A very little, if you please, Jasper. I dare not touch wine," she continued to the clergyman. "I am the slave of my medical man in all matters relating to my unfortunate digestion."

"Mother," said Jasper, "George has brought us a nice piece of news concerning your pet Marmaduke."

The clergyman became solemn and looked steadily at his glass.

"I do not know that it is fair to describe him as my pet exactly," said the Countess, a little troubled. "I trust there is nothing unpleasant the matter."

"Oh, nothing! He has settled down domestically in a mansion at West Kensington, that is all."

"What! Married!"

"Unhappily," said the Rev. George, "no, not married."

"Oh!" said the Countess slowly, as an expression of relief. "It is very shocking, of course; very wrong indeed. Young men *will* do these things. It is especially foolish in Marmaduke's case, for he really cannot afford to make any settlement such as this kind of complication usually involves when the time comes for getting rid of it. Pray do not let it come to Constance's ears. It is not a proper subject for a girl."

"Quite as proper a subject as marriage with a fellow like Marmaduke," said Jasper, rising coolly and lighting a cigaret. "However, it will be time enough to trouble about that when there is any sign of his having the slightest serious intentions toward Constance. For my part I don't believe, and I never did believe, that there was anything real in the business. This last move of his proves it—to my satisfaction, at any rate."

Lady Carbury, with a slight but impressive bridling, and yet with an evident sense of discomfiture, proceeded to assert herself before the clergyman. "I beg you will control yourself, Jasper," she said. "I do not like to be spoken to in that tone. In discharging the very great responsibility which rests with a mother, I am compelled to take the world as I find it, and to acknowledge that certain very deplorable tendencies must be allowed for in society. You, in the solitude of your laboratory,

George Bernard Shaw

contemplate an ideal state of things that we all, I am sure, long for, but which unhappily does not exist. I have never enquired into Marmaduke's private life, and I think you ought not to have done so. I could not disguise from myself the possibility of his having entered into some such relations as those you have alluded to."

Jasper, without the slightest appearance of having heard this speech, strolled casually out of the room. The Countess, baffled, turned to her sympathetic guest.

"I am sure that you, George, must feel that it is absolutely necessary for us to keep this matter to ourselves."

The Rev. George said, gravely, "I do not indeed see what blessing can rest on our interference in such an inexpressibly shocking business. It is for Marmaduke to wrestle with his own conscience."

"Quite so," said the Countess, shrugging her shoulders as if to invite her absent son's attention to this confirmation of her judgment. "Is it not absurd of Jasper to snatch at such an excuse for breaking off the match?"

"I can sympathize with Jasper's feeling, I trust. It is natural for a candid nature to recoil from duplicity. But all our actions need charitable construction; and, remembering that, we should take heed to prevent our forebearance toward others from wavering. Who knows that the alliance with your pure and lovely daughter may not be the means specially ordained to rescue him from his present condition."

"I think it very possible," drawled the Countess, looking at him, nevertheless, with a certain contempt for what she privately considered his priggish, underbred cant. "Besides, such things are recognized, though of course they are not spoken of. No lady could with common decency pretend to know that such connexions are possible, much less assign one of them as a reason for breaking off an engagement."

"Pardon me," said the Rev. George; "but can these worldly considerations add anything to the approval of our consciences? I think not. We will keep our own counsel in this matter in the sight of Heaven. Then, whatever the world may think, all will surely come right in the end."

"Oh, it is sure to come right in the end: these wretched businesses always do. I cannot imagine men having such low tastes—as if there were anything in these women more than in anybody else! Come into the drawing-room, George."

They went into the drawing-room and found it deserted. The ladies were in the veranda. The Countess took up the paper and composed herself for a nap. George went into the porch, where the girls, having seen the sun go down, were now watching the deepening gloom among the trees that skirted the lawn. Marian proposed that they should walk through the plantation whilst there was still a little light left, and the clergyman readily assented. He rather repented of this when they got into the deep gloom under the trees, and Elinor began to tell stories about adders, wild cats, poachers, and anything else that could possibly make a nervous man uncomfortable under such circumstances. He was quite relieved when they saw the spark of a cigaret ahead of them and heard the voices of Jasper and Conolly coming toward them through the darkness.

"Oh, I believe I have had the pleasure of meeting Mr. Conolly," said the Rev. George, formally, when they met. "I am glad to see you."

"Thank you," said Conolly. "If you ladies have thin shoes on as usual, we had better come out of this."

"As we ladies happen to have our boots on," said Marian, "we shall stay as long as we like."

Nevertheless, they soon turned homeward, and as the path was narrow, they walked in pairs. The clergyman, with Constance, led the way. Lord Jasper followed with Elinor. Conolly and Marian came last.

"Does that young man—Mr. Conolly—live at the Hall?" was the Rev. George's first remark to Constance.

"No. He has rooms in Rose Cottage, that little place on Quilter's farm."

"Ha! Then he is very well off here."

"A great deal too well off. Jasper allows him to speak to him as though he were an equal. However, I suppose Jasper knows his own business best."

"I have observed that he is rather disposed to presume upon any encouragement he receives. It is a bad sign in a young man, and one, I fear, that will greatly interfere with his prospects."

"He is an American, and I suppose thinks it a fine thing to be republican. But it is Jasper's fault. He spoils him. He once wanted to have him in the drawing-room in the evenings to play accompaniments; but mamma positively refused to allow it. Jasper is excessively obstinate, and though he did not make a fuss, he got quite a habit of going over to Rose Cottage and spending his evenings there singing and playing. Everybody about the place used to notice it. Mamma was greatly disgusted."

"Do you find him unpleasant—personally, I mean?"

"I! Oh dear, no! I should never dream of speaking to him. His presence is unpleasant, because he exercises a bad influence on Jasper; so I wish, on that account alone, that he would go."

"I trust Marian is careful to limit her intercourse with him as much as possible."

"Well, Marian learns electricity from him; and of course that makes a difference. I do not care about such things; and I never go into the laboratory when he is there; so I do not know whether Marian lets him be familiar with her or not. She is rather easygoing; and he is insufferably conceited. However, if she wants to learn electricity, I suppose she must put up with him. He is no worse, after all, than the rest of the people one has to learn things from. They are all impossible."

"It is a strange fancy of the girls, to study science."

"I am sure I dont know why they do it. It is great nonsense for Jasper to do it, either. He will never keep up his position properly until he shuts up that stupid workshop. He ought to hunt and shoot and entertain a great deal more than he does. It is very hard on us, for we are altogether in Jasper's hands for such matters. I think he is very foolish."

"Not foolish. Dont say that. Excuse my giving you a little lecture; but it is not right to speak, even without thought, of your brother as a fool. No doubt he is a little injudicious; but all men are not called to the same pursuits."

"If people have a certain position, they ought to make up their minds to the duties of their position, whether they are called to them or not."

The Rev. George, missing the deference with which ladies not related to him usually received his admonitions, changed the subject.

Meanwhile, Conolly and Marian, walking more slowly than the rest, had fallen far behind. They had been silent at first. She seemed to be in trouble. At last, after some wistful glances at him, she said:

"Have you resolved to go to London to-morrow; or will you wait until Friday?"

George Bernard Shaw

"To-morrow, Miss Lind. Can I do anything for you in town?"

Marian hesitated painfully.

"Do not mind giving me plenty of bother," he said. "I am so accustomed to superintend the transit of machines as cumbersome as trunks and as fragile as bonnet boxes, that the care of a houseful of ordinary luggage would be a mere amusement for me."

"Thank you; but it is not that. I was only thinking—Are you likely to see my cousin, Mr. Marmaduke Lind, whilst you are in London?"

"N—no. Unless I call upon him, which I have no excuse for doing."

"Oh! I thought you knew him."

"I met him at that concert."

"But I thought you were in the habit of going about with him. At least, I understood him one day to say that you had been to the theatre together."

"So we were; but only once. We went there after the concert, and I have never seen him since."

"Oh, indeed! I quite mistook."

"If you have any particular reason for wishing me to see him, I will. It will be all right if I have a message from you. Shall I call on him? It will be no trouble to me."

"No, oh no. I wanted—it was something that could only be told to him indirectly by an intimate friend—by some one with influence over him. More a hint than anything else. But it does not matter. At least, it cannot be helped."

Conolly did not speak until they had gone some thirty yards or so in silence. Then he said: "If the matter is of serious importance to you, Miss Lind, I think I can manage to have a message conveyed to him by a person who has influence over him. I am not absolutely certain that I can; but probably I shall succeed without any great difficulty."

Marian looked at him in some surprise. "I hardly know what I ought to do," she said, doubtfully.

"Then do nothing," said Conolly bluntly. "Or, if you want anything said to this gentleman, write to him yourself."

"But I dont know his address, and my brother says I ought not to write to him. I dont think I ought, either; but I want him to be told something that may prevent a great deal of unhappyness. It seems so unfeeling to sit down quietly and say, 'It is not my business to interfere,' when the mischief might so easily be prevented."

"I advise you to be very cautious, Miss Lind. Taking care of other people's happiness is thankless and dangerous. You dont know your cousin's address, you say?"

"No. I thought you did."

Conolly shook his head. "Who does know it?" he said.

"My brother George does; but he refused to tell me. I shall not ask him again."

"Of course not. I can find it out for you. But of what use will that be, since you think you ought not to write to him?"

"I assure you, Mr. Conolly, that if it only concerned myself, I would not hesitate to tell you the whole story, and ask your advice. I feel sure you would shew me what was right. But this is a matter which concerns other people only."

"Then you have my advice without telling me. Dont meddle in it."

"But—"

"But what?"

"After all, what I wish to do could not possibly bring about mischief. If Marmaduke could be given a hint to come down here at once—he has been invited, and is putting off his visit from week to week—it would be sufficient. He will get into trouble if he makes any more excuses. And he can set everything right by coming down now."

"Are you sure you dont mean only that he can smooth matters over for the present?"

"No, you mistake. It is not so much to smooth matters over as to rescue him from a bad influence that is ruining him. There is a person in London from whom he must he got away at all hazards. If you only knew—I *wish* you knew."

"Perhaps I know more than you suppose. Come, Miss Lind, let us understand one another. Your family want your cousin to marry Lady Constance. I know that. She does not object. I know that too. He does."

"Oh!" exclaimed Marian, "you are wrong. He does not."

"Anyhow," continued Conolly, "he acts with a certain degree of indifference toward her—keeps away at present, for instance. I infer that the bad influence you have mentioned is the cause of his remissness."

"Yes, you are right; only, looking at it all from without as you do, you are mistaken as to Marmaduke's character. He is easily led away, and very careless about the little attentions that weigh so much with women; but he is thoroughly honorable, and incapable of trifling with Lady Constance. Unfortunately, he is easily imposed on, and impatient of company in which he cannot be a little uproarious. I fear that somebody has taken advantage of this part of his character to establish a great ascendency over him. I"—here Marian became nervous, and controlled her voice with difficulty—"I saw this person once in a theatre; and I can imagine how she would fascinate Marmaduke. She was so clever, so handsome, and—and so utterly abominable. I was angry with Duke for bringing us to the place; and I remember now that he was angry with me because I said she made me shudder."

"Utterly abominable is a strong thing for one woman to say of another," said Conolly, with a certain sternness. "However, I can understand your having that feeling about her. I know her; and it is through her that I hope to find out his address for you."

"But her address is his address now, Mr. Conolly. I think it is somewhere in West Kensington."

Conolly stopped, and turned upon her so suddenly that she recoiled a step, frightened.

"Since when, pray?"

"Very lately, I think. I do not know."

They neither moved nor spoke for some moments: she earnestly regretting that she had lingered so far behind her companions in the terrible darkness. He walked on at last faster than before. No more words passed between them until they came out into the moonlight close to the veranda. Then he stopped again, and took off his hat.

"Permit me to leave you now," he said, with an artificial politeness worthy of Douglas himself. "Good-night."

"Good-night," faltered Marian.

He walked gravely away. Marian hurried into the veranda, where she found Jasper and Elinor. The other couple had gone into the drawing-room.

"Hallo!" said Jasper, "where is Conolly? I want to say a word to him before he goes."

"He has just gone," said Marian, pointing across the lawn. Jasper immediately ran out in the direction indicated, and left the two cousins alone together.

"Well, Marian," said Elinor, "do you know that you have taken more than quarter of an hour longer to come from the plantation than we did, and that you look quite scared? Our sweet Constance, as the parson calls her, has been making some kind remarks about it."

"Do I look disturbed? I hope Auntie wont notice it. I wish I could go straight to bed without seeing anybody."

"Why? What is the matter?"

"I will tell you to-night when you come in to me. I am disgusted with myself; and I think Conolly is mad."

"Mad!"

"On my word, I think Conolly has gone mad," said Lord Jasper, returning at this moment out of breath and laughing.

Elinor, startled, glanced at Marian.

"He was walking quite soberly toward the fence of the yellow field when I caught sight of him. Just as I was about to hail him, he started off and cleared the fence at a running jump. He walked away at a furious rate, swinging his arms about, and laughing as if he was enjoying some uncommonly good joke. I am not sure that I did not see him dance a hornpipe; but as it is so dark I wont swear to that."

"You had better not," said Elinor, sceptically. "Let us go in; and pray do not encourage George to talk. I have a headache, and want to go to bed."

"You have been in very good spirits, considering your headache," he replied, in the same incredulous tone. "It has come on rather suddenly, has it not?"

When they went into the drawing-room they found that Constance had awakened her mother, and had already given her an account of their walk. Jasper added a description of what he had just witnessed. "I have not laughed so much for a long time," he said, in conclusion. "He is usually such a steady sort of fellow."

"I see nothing very amusing in the antics of a drunken workman," said the Countess. "How you could have left Marian in his care even for a moment I am at a loss to conceive."

"He was not drunk, indeed," said Marian.

"Certainly not," said Jasper, rather indignantly. "I was walking with him for some time before we met the girls. You are very pale, Marian. Have you also a headache?"

"I have been playing tennis all day; and I am quite tired out."

Soon afterward, when Marian was in bed, and Miss McQuinch, according to a nightly custom of theirs, was seated on the coverlet with her knees doubled up to her chin inside her bedgown, they discussed the adventure very earnestly.

"Dont understand him at all, I confess," said Elinor, when Marian had related what had passed in the plantation. "Wasnt it rather rash to make a confidant of him in such a delicate matter?"

"That is what makes me feel so utterly ashamed. He might have known that I only wanted to do good. I thought he was

George Bernard Shaw

so entirely above false delicacy."

"I dont mean that. How do you know that the story is true? You only have it from Mrs. Leith Fairfax's letter; and she is perhaps the greatest liar in the world."

"Oh, Nelly, you ought not to talk so strongly about people. She would never venture to tell me a made-up tale about Marmaduke."

"In my opinion, she would tell anybody anything for the sake of using her tongue or pen."

"It is so hard to know what to do. There was nobody whom I could trust, was there? Jasper has always been against Marmaduke; and Constance, of course, was out of the question. There was Auntie, but I did not like to tell her."

"Because she is an evil-minded old Jezebel, whom no nice woman would talk to on such a subject," said Elinor, giving the bed a kick with her heel.

"Hush, Nelly. I am always in terror lest you should say something like that before other people, out of sheer habit."

"Never fear. Well, you have done the best you could. No use regretting what cannot be recalled. You cannot have the security of conventionality along with the self-respect of sincerity. By the bye, do you remember that Jasper and his fond mamma and George had a family council after dinner? You may be sure that George has told them everything."

"What! Then my wretched attempt to have Marmaduke warned was useless. Oh, Nelly, this is too bad. Do you really think so? When I told him before dinner what Mrs. Leith Fairfax wrote, he only said he feared it was true, and refused to give me the address."

"And so threw you back on Conolly. I am glad the

responsibility rests with George. He knew very well that it was true; for he had only just been telling Jasper. Jasper told me as much in the plantation. Master Georgy has no right to be your brother. He is worse than a dissenter. Dissenters try to be gentlemen; but George has no misgivings about himself on that score; so he gives his undivided energy to his efforts to be parsonic. He is an arrant hypocrite."

"I dont think he is a hypocrite. I think he sincerely believes that his duty to the Church requires him to behave as he does."

"Then he is a donkey, which is worse."

"I wish he were more natural in his manner."

"He is natural enough. It is always the same with parsons: 'it is their nature to.' Good-night. Men are all the same, my dear, all the same."

"How do you mean?"

"Never mind. Good-night."

CHAPTER V

A little removed from a pretty road in West Kensington, and communicating with it by a shrubbery and an iron gate, there stood at this time a detached villa called Laurel Grove. On the opposite side were pairs of recently built houses, many of them still unlet. These, without depriving the neighbourhood of its suburban quietude, forbade any feeling of rustic seclusion, and so made it agreeable to Susanna Conolly, who lived at Laurel Grove with Marmaduke Lind.

One morning in September they were at breakfast together. Beside each was a pile of letters. Marmaduke deferred opening his until his hunger was satisfied; but Susanna, after pouring out tea for him, seized the uppermost envelope, thrust her little finger under the flap, and burst it open.

"Hm," she said. "First rehearsal next Monday. Here he is at me again to make the engagement renewable after Christmas. What an old fool he must be not to guess why I dont want to be engaged next spring! Just look at the *Times*, Bob, and see if the piece is advertized yet."

"I should think so, by Jupiter," said Marmaduke, patiently interrupting his meal to open the newspaper.

"Here is a separate advertisement for everybody. 'The latest Parisian success. *La petite Maison du Roi*. Music by M. de Jongleur. Mr. Faulkner has the honor to announce that an adaptation by Mr. Cribbs of M. de Jongleur's opera bouffe *La petite Maison du Roi*, entitled King Lewis on the lewis'—what the deuce does that mean?"

"On the loose, of course."

"But it is spelt l-e-w—oh! its a pun. What an infernal piece of idiocy! Then it goes on as usual, except that each name in the cast has a separate line of large print. Here you are: 'Lalage Virtue as Madame Dubarry'—"

"Is that at the top?"

"Yes."

"Before Rose Stella?"

"Yes. Why!—I didnt notice it before—you are down fifteen times! Every alternate space has your name over again. 'Lalage Virtue as Madame Dubarry. Fred Smith as Louis XV. Lalage Virtue as the Dubarry. Felix Sumner as the Due de Richelieu. Lalage Virtue as *la belle Jeanneton*.' By the way, that is all rot. Cardinal Richelieu died four or five hundred years before Madame Dubarry was born."

"Let me see the paper. I see they have given Rose Stella the last line with a big AND before it. No matter. She is down only once; and I am down fifteen times."

"I wonder what all these letters of mine are about! This is a bill, of course. The West Kensington Wine Company. Whew! We are getting through the champagne at the rate of about thirty pounds a month, not counting what we pay for when we dine in town."

"Well, what matter! Champagne does nobody any harm; and I get awfully low without it."

"All right, my dear. So long as you please yourself, and dont injure your health, I dont care. Here's a letter of yours put

George Bernard Shaw

among mine by mistake. It has been forwarded from your old diggings at Lambeth."

"It's from Ned," said Susanna, turning pale. "He must be coming home, or he would not write. Yes, he is. What shall I do?"

"What does he say?" said Marmaduke, taking the letter from her. "'*Back at 6 on Wednesday evening. Have high tea. N.C.*' Short and sweet! Well, he will not turn up til to-morrow, at all events, even if he knows the address, which of course he doesnt."

"He knows nothing. His note shews that. What *will* he do when he finds me gone? He may get the address at the post-office, where I told them to send on my letters. The landlady has most likely found out for her own information. There is no mistake about it," said Susanna, rising and walking to the window: "I am in a regular funk about him. I have half a mind to go back to Lambeth and meet him. I could let the murder out gradually, or, perhaps, get him off to the country again before he discovers anything."

"Go back! oh no, nonsense! The worst he can do is to cut you—and a good job too."

"I wish he would. It would be a relief to me at present to know for certain that he would."

"He cant be so very thin-skinned as you fancy, considering the time you have been on the stage."

"There's nothing wrong in being on the stage. There's nothing wrong in being here either, in spite of Society. After all, what do I care about Ned, or anybody else? He always went his own way when it suited him; and he has no right to complain if I go mine. Let him come if he likes: he will not get much satisfaction from me." Susanna sat down again, and drank some tea, partly defiant, partly disconsolate.

"Dont think any more about it," said Marmaduke. "He wont come."

"Oh, let him, if he likes," said Susanna, impatiently. Marmaduke did not quite sympathize with her sudden recklessness. He hoped that Conolly would have the good sense to keep away.

"Look here, Bob," said she, when they had finished breakfast. "Let us go somewhere to-day. I feel awfully low. Let us have a turn up the river."

"All right," said Marmaduke, with alacrity. "Whatever you please. How shall we go?"

"Anyhow. Let us go to Hampton by train. When we get there we can settle what to do afterward. Can you come now?"

"Yes, whenever you are ready."

"Then I will run upstairs and dress. Go out and amuse yourself with that blessed old lawn-mower until I come."

"Yes, I think I will," said Marmaduke, seriously. "That plot near the gate wants a trimming badly."

"What a silly old chap you are, Bob!" she said, stopping to kiss him on each cheek as she left the room.

Marmaduke had become attached to the pursuit of gardening since his domestication. He put on his hat; went out; and set to work on the plot near the gate. The sun was shining brightly; and when he had taken a few turns with the machine he stopped, raising his face to the breeze, and saw Conolly standing so close to him that he started backward, and made a vague movement as if to ward off a blow. Conolly, who seemed amused by the mowing, said quietly: "That machine wants oiling: the clatter prevented you from hearing me come. I have just returned from Carbury Towers. Miss Lind is staying there; and she has asked me to give you a message."

This speech perplexed Marmaduke. He inferred from it that Conolly was ignorant of Susanna's proceedings, but he had not sufficient effrontery to welcome him unconcernedly at once. So he stood still and stared at him.

"I am afraid I have startled you," Conolly went on, politely. "I found the gate unlocked, and thought it would be an unnecessary waste of time to ring the bell. You have a charming little place here."

"Yes, it's a pretty little place, isnt it?" said Marmaduke. "A—wont you come in and have a—excuse my bringing you round this way, will you? My snuggery is at the back of the house."

"Thank you; but I had rather not go in. I have a great deal of business to do in town to-day; so I shall just discharge my commission and go."

"At any rate, come into the shade," said Marmaduke, glancing uneasily toward the windows of the house. "This open place is enough to give us sunstroke."

Conolly followed him to a secluded part of the shrubbery, where they sat down on a bench.

"Is there anything up?" said Marmaduke, much oppressed.

"Will you excuse my speaking without ceremony?"

"Oh, certainly. Fire away!"

"Thank you. I must then tell you that the relations between you and Lady Constance are a source of anxiety to her brother. You know the way men feel bound to look after their sisters. You have, I believe, sisters of your own?"

Marmaduke nodded, and stole a doubtful glance at Conolly's face.

"It appears that Lord Carbury has all along considered your courtship too cool to be genuine. In this view he was quite unsupported, the Countess being strongly in your favor, and the young lady devoted to you."

"Well, I knew all that. At least, I suspected it. What is up now?"

"This. The fact of your having taken a villa here has reached the ears of the family at Carbury. They are, not unnaturally, curious to know what use a bachelor can have for such an establishment."

"But I have my rooms in Clarges Street still. This is not my house. It was taken for another person."

"Precisely what they seem to think. But, to be brief with you, Miss Lind thinks that unless you wish to break with the Earl, and quarrel with your family, you should go down to Towers Cottage at once."

"But I cant go away just now. There are reasons."

"Miss Lind is fully acquainted with your reasons. They are her reasons for wishing you to leave London immediately. And now, having executed my commission, I must ask you to excuse me. My time is much occupied."

"Well, I am greatly obliged to you for coming all this way out of town to give me the straight tip," said Marmaduke, relieved at the prospect of getting rid of his visitor without alluding to Susanna. "It is very good of you; and I am very glad to see you. Jolly place, Carbury Park is, isnt it? How will the shooting be?"

"First rate, I am told. I do not know much about it myself." They had risen, and were strolling along the path leading to the gate.

"Shall I see you down there—if I go?"

"Possibly. I shall have to go down for a day at least, to get my luggage, in case I decide not to renew my engagement with Lord Jasper."

"I hope so," said Marmaduke. Then, as they reached the gate, he proffered his hand, in spite of an inward shrinking, and said heartily, "Good-bye, old fellow. Youre looking as well as possible."

Conolly took his hand, and retained it whilst he said: "Good-bye, Mr. Lind. I am quite well, thank you. If I may ask—how is Susanna?"

Marmaduke was prevented by a spasm of the throat from replying. Before he recovered, Susanna herself, attired for her proposed trip to Hampton, emerged from the shrubbery and stood before them, confounded. Conolly, still wearing the cordial expression with which he had shaken Marmaduke's hand, looked at her, then at her protector, and then at her again.

"I have been admiring the villa, Susanna," said he, after an emphatic silence. "It is better than our place at Lambeth. You wont mind my hurrying away: I have a great deal to do in town. Good-bye. Good-bye, Mr. Lind."

Susanna murmured something. Marmaduke, after making an effort to bid his guest good-bye genially, opened the gate, and stood for a minute watching him as he strode away.

"What does *he* care what becomes of me, the selfish brute!" cried Susanna, passionately.

"He didnt complain: he has nothing to complain of," said Marmaduke. "Anyhow, why didnt he stay at home and look after you? By George, Susanna, he is the coolest card I ever came across."

"What brought him here?" she demanded, vehemently.

"That reminds me. I am afraid I must go down to Carbury for a few days."

"And what am I to do here alone? Are *you* going to leave me too?"

"Well, I cannot be in two places at the same time. I suppose you can manage to get on without me for a few days."

"I will go home. I can get on without you altogether. I will go home."

"Come, Susanna! what is the use of kicking up a row? I cant afford to quarrel with all my people because you choose to be unreasonable."

"What do I care about your people, or about you either?"

"Very well, then," said Marmaduke, offended, "you can go home if you like. Perhaps your brother appreciates this sort of thing. I dont."

"Ah, you coward! You taunt me because you think I have no home. Do you flatter yourself that I am dependent on you?"

"Hold your tongue," said Marmaduke, fiercely. "Dont you turn on me in that fashion. Keep your temper if you want me to keep mine."

"You have ruined me," said Susanna, sitting down on the grass, and beginning to cry.

"Oh, upon my soul, this is too much," said Marmaduke, with disgust. "Get up out of that and dont make a fool of yourself.

Ruined indeed! Will you get up?"

"No!" screamed Susanna.

"Then stay where you are and be damned," retorted Marmaduke, turning on his heel and walking toward the house. In the hall he met a maid carrying an empty champagne bottle and goblet.

"Missis is looking for you, sir," said the maid.

"All right," said Marmaduke, "I have seen her. Listen to me. I am going to the country. My man Mason will come here today to pack up my traps, and bring them after me. You had better take a note of my address from the card in the strap of my valise."

"Yes, sir," said the maid. "Any message for missis?"

"No," said Marmaduke. He then changed his coat and hat, and went out again. As he approached the gate he met Susanna, who had risen and was walking toward the house.

"I am going to Carbury," he said. "I dont know when I shall be back."

She passed on disdainfully, as if she had not heard him.

CHAPTER VI

Three days later Lord Carbury came to luncheon with a letter in his hand. Marian had not yet come in; and the Rev. George was absent, his place being filled by Marmaduke.

"Good news for you and Constance, mother."

"Indeed?" said the Countess, smiling.

"Yes. Conolly is coming down this afternoon to collect his traps and leave you forever."

"Really, Jasper, you exaggerate Mr. Conolly's importance. Intelligence of his movements can hardly be news—good or bad—either to me or to Constance."

"I am glad he is going," said Constance, "for Jasper's sake."

"Thank you," replied Jasper. "I thought you would be. He will be a great loss to me."

"Nonsense!" said the Countess. "If another workman is needed, another can easily be had."

"If I can be of any assistance to you, old man," said Marmaduke, "make what use of me you like. I picked up something about the business yesterday."

"Yes," said Elinor. "While you were away, Jasper, he went to

George Bernard Shaw

the laboratory with Constance, and fired off a brass cannon with your new pile until he had used up all the gunpowder and spoiled the panels of the door. That is what he calls picking up something about the business."

"Nothing like experiment for convincing you of the power of electricity," said Marmaduke. "Is there, Conny?"

"It's very wonderful; but I hate shots."

"Where is Marian?" said Lady Carbury.

"I left her in the summer-house in the fruit garden," said Elinor. "She was reading."

"She must have forgotten the hour," said the Countess. "She has been moping, I think, for the last few days. I hope she is not unwell. But she would never stay away from luncheon intentionally. I shall send for her."

"I'll go," said Marmaduke, eagerly.

"No, no, Duke. You must not leave the table. I will send a servant."

"I will fetch her here in half the time that any servant will. Poor Marian, why shouldnt she have her lunch? I shall be back in a jiffy."

"What a restless, extraordinary creature he is!" said Lady Carbury, displeased, as Marmaduke hastily left the room. "The idea of a man leaving the table in that way!"

"I suspect he has his reasons," said Elinor.

"I think it is a perfectly natural thing for him to do," said Constance, pettishly. "I see nothing extraordinary in it."

Marmaduke found Marian reading in the summer-house in

the fruit garden. She looked at him in lazy surprise as he seated himself opposite to her at the table.

"This is the first chance I've had of talking to you privately since I came down," he said. "I believe you have been keeping out of my way on purpose."

"Well, I concluded that you wanted as many chances as possible of talking to some one else in private; so I gave you as many as I could."

"Yes, you and the rest have been uncommonly considerate in that respect: thank you all awfully. But I mean to have it out with you, Miss Marian, now that I have caught you alone."

"With me! Oh, dear! What have I done?"

"What have you done? I'll tell you what youve done. Why did you send Conolly, of all men in the world, to tell me that I was in disgrace here?"

"There was no one else, Marmaduke."

"Well, suppose there wasn't! Suppose there had been no one else alive on the earth except you, and I, and he, and Constance, and Su—and Constance! how could you have offered him such a job?"

"Why not? Was there any special reason—"

"Any special reason! Didnt your common sense tell you that a meeting between him and me must be particularly awkward for both of us?"

"No. At least I—. Marmaduke: I think you must fancy that I told him more than I did. I did not know where you were; and as he was going to London, and I thought you knew him well, and I had no other means of warning you, I had to make use of him. Jasper will tell you how thoroughly trustworthy he is.

George Bernard Shaw

But all I said—and I really could not say less—was that I was afraid you were in bad company, or under bad influence, or something like that; and that I only wanted you to come down here at once."

"Oh! Indeed! That was *all*, was it? Merely that I was in bad company."

"I think I said under bad influence. I was told so; and I believed it at the time. I hope it's not true, Marmaduke. If it is not, I beg your pardon with all my heart."

Marmaduke stared very hard at her for a while, and then said, with the emphasis of a man baffled by utter unreason: "Well, I *am* damned!" at which breach of good manners she winced. "Hang me if I understand you, Marian," he continued, more mildly. "Of course it's not true. Bad influence is all bosh. But it was a queer thing to say to his face. He knew very well you meant his sister. Hallo! what's the matter? Are you going to faint?"

"No, I—Never mind me."

"Never mind you!" said Marmaduke. "What are you looking like that for?"

"Because—it is nothing: I only blushed. Dont be stupid, Duke."

"Blushed! Why dont you blush red, like other people, and not green? Shall I get you something?"

"No, no. Oh, Duke, why did you not tell me? How could you be so heartless as to leave us all in the dark when we were talking about you before him every day! Oh, are you in earnest, Duke? Pray dont jest about it. What do you mean by his sister? I never knew he had one. Who is she? What happened? I mean when you saw him?"

"Nothing happened. I was mowing in the garden. He just walked in; bade me good morning; admired the place; and told me he came with a message from you that things were getting hot here. Then he went off, as cool as you please. He didnt seem to mind."

"And he warned you, in spite of all."

"More for your sake than for mine, I suspect. He's rather sweet on you, isnt he?"

"Oh, Duke, Duke, are you not ashamed of yourself?"

"Deuce a bit. But I'm in trouble; and I want you to stand by me. Look here, Marian, you have no nonsense about you, I know. I may tell you frankly how I am situated, maynt I?"

Marian looked at him apprehensively, and said nothing.

"You see you will only mix up matters worse than before unless you know the truth. Besides, I offered to marry her: upon my soul I did; but she refused. Her real name is Susanna Conolly: his sister, worse luck."

"Dont tell me any more of this, Duke. It is not right."

"I suppose it's not right, as you say. But what am I to do? I must tell you; or you will go on making mischief with Constance."

"As if I would tell her! I promise that she shall never know from me. Is that enough?"

"No: its too much. The plain truth is that I dont care whether she finds me out or not. I want her to understand thoroughly, once and for ever, that I wont marry her."

"Marmaduke!"

"Not if I were fifty Marmadukes!"

"Then you will break her heart."

"Never fear! Her heart is pretty tough, if she has one. Whether or no, I am not going to have her forced on me by the Countess or any one else. The truth is, Marian, they have all tried to bully me into this match. Constance can't complain."

"No, not aloud."

"Neither aloud or alow. I never proposed to her."

"Very well, Marmaduke: there is no use now in blaming Auntie or excusing yourself. If you have made up your mind, there is an end."

"But you cant make out that I am acting meanly, Marian. Why, I have everything to lose by giving her up. There is her money, and I suppose I must prepare for a row with the family; unless the match could be dropped quietly. Eh?"

"And is that what you want me to manage for you?"

"Well—. Come, Marian! dont be savage. I have been badly used in this affair. They forced it on me. I did all I could to keep out of it. She was thrown at my head. Besides, I once really used to think I could settle down with her comfortably some day. I only found out what an insipid little fool she was when I had a woman of sense to compare her with."

"Dont say hard things about her. I think you might have a little forbearance towards her under the circumstances."

"Hm! I dont feel very forbearing. She has been sticking to me for the last few days like a barnacle. Our respectable young ladies think a lot of themselves, but—except you and Nelly—I dont know a woman in society who has as much brains in her whole body as Susanna Conolly has in her little finger nail. I cant imagine how the deuce you all have the cheek to expect men to talk to you, much less marry you."

"Perhaps there is something that honest men value more than brains."

"I should like to know what it is. If it is something that ladies have and Susanna hasnt, it is not either good looks or good sense. If it's respectability, that depends on what you consider respectable. If Conny's respectable and Susanna isnt, then I prefer disrepu—"

"Hush, Duke, you know you have no right to speak to me like this. Let us think of poor Constance. How is she to be told the truth?"

"Let her find it out. I shall go back to London as soon as I can; and the affair will drop somehow or another. She will forget all about me."

"Happy-go-lucky Marmaduke. I think if neglect and absence could make her forget you, you would have been forgotten before this."

"Yes. You see you must admit that I gave her no reason to suppose I meant anything."

"I am afraid you have consulted your own humor both in your neglect and your attentions, Duke. The more you try to excuse yourself, the more inexcusable your conduct appears. I do not know how to advise you. If Constance is told, you may some day forget all about your present infatuation; and then a mass of mischief and misery will have been made for nothing. If she is not told, you will be keeping up a cruel deception and wasting her chances of—but she will never care for anybody else."

"Better do as I say. Leave matters alone for the present. But mind! No speculating on my changing my intentions. I wont marry her."

"I wish you hadnt told me about it."

"Well, Marian, I couldnt help it. I know, of course, that you only wanted to make us all happy; but you nursed this match and kept it in Constance's mind as much as you could. Besides—though it was not your fault—that mistake about Conolly was too serious not to explain. Don't be downcast: I am not blaming you a bit."

"It seems to me that the worst view of things is always the true one in this world. Nelly and Jasper were right about you."

"Aha! So *they* saw what I felt. You cant say I did not make my intentions plain enough to every unbiassed person. The Countess was determined to get Constance off her hands; Constance was determined to have me; and you were determined to stick up for your own notions of love and honeysuckles."

"I was determined to stick up for *you*, Marmaduke."

"Dont be indignant: I knew you would stick up for me in your own way. But what I want to shew is, that only three people believed that I was in earnest; and those three were prejudiced."

"I wish you had enlightened Constance, and deceived all the rest of the world, instead. No doubt I was wrong, very wrong. I am very sorry."

"Pshaw! It doesnt matter. It will all blow over some day. Hush, I hear the garden gate opening. It is Constance, come to spy what I am doing here with you. She is as jealous as a crocodile—very nearly made a scene yesterday because I played with Nelly against her at tennis. I have to drive her to Bushy Copse this afternoon, confound it!"

"And *will* you, after what you have just confessed?"

"I must. Besides, Jasper says that Conolly is coming this evening to pack up his traps and go; and I want to be out of the way when he is about."

"This evening!"

"Yes. Between ourselves, Marian, Susanna and I were so put out by the cool way he carried on when he called, that we had a regular quarrel after he went; and we haven't made it up yet."

"Pray dont talk about it to me, Duke. Here is Constance."

"So you are here," said Constance, gaily, but with a quick glance at them. "That is a pretty way to bring your cousin in to luncheon, sir."

"We got chatting about you, my ownest," said Marmaduke; "and the subject was so sweet, and the moments were so fleet, that we talked for quite an hour on the strict q.t. Eh, Marian?"

"As a punishment, you shall have no lunch. Mamma is very angry with you both."

"Always ready to make allowances for her, provided she sends you to lecture me, Conny. Why dont you wear your hat properly?" He arranged her hat as he spoke. Constance laughed and blushed. Marian shuddered. "Now youre all that fancy painted you: youre lovely, youre divine. Are you ready for Bushy Copse?"

Constance replied by singing:

"Oh yes, if you please, kind sir, she said; sir, she said; sir, she said; Oh! yes if you ple—ease, kind sir, she said."

"Then come along. After your ladyship," he said, taking her elbows as if they were the handles of a wheelbarrow, and pushing her out before him through the narrow entrance to the summer-house. On the threshold he turned for a moment;

met Marian's reproachful eyes with a wink; grinned; and disappeared.

For half an hour afterward Marian sat alone in the summer-house, thinking of the mistake she had made. Then she returned to the Cottage, where she found Miss McQuinch writing in the library, and related to her all that had passed in the summer-house. Elinor listened, seated in a rocking-chair, restlessly clapping her protended ankles together. When she heard of Conolly's relationship to Susanna, she kept still for a few moments, looking with widely opened eyes at Marian. Then, with a sharp laugh, she said:

"Well, I beg his pardon. I thought he was another of that woman's retainers. I never dreamt of his being her brother."

Marian was horror stricken. "You thought—! Oh, Nelly, what puts such things into your head?"

"So would you have thought it if you had the least gumption about people. However, I was wrong; and I'm glad of it. However, I was right about Marmaduke. I told you so, over and over and over again."

"I know you did; but I didnt think you were in earnest."

"No, you never can conceive my being in earnest when I differ from you, until the event proves me to be right."

"I am afraid it will kill Constance."

"*Dont*, Marian!" cried Elinor, giving her chair a violent swing.

"I am quite serious. You know how delicate she is."

"Well, if she dies of any sentiment, it will be wounded vanity. Serve her right for allowing a man to be forced into marrying her. I believe she knows in her soul that he does not care about her. Why else should she be jealous of me, of you, and of everybody?"

"It seems to me that instead of sympathizing with the unfortunate girl, both you and Marmaduke exult in her disappointment."

"I pity her, poor little wretch. But I dont sympathize with her. I don't pity Marmaduke one bit: if the whole family cuts him he will deserve it richly, but I do sympathize with him. Can you wonder at his preference? When we went to see that woman last June I envied her. There she was, clever, independent, successful, holding her own in the world, earning her living, fascinating a crowd of people, whilst we poor respectable nonentities sat pretending to despise her—as if we were not waiting until some man in want of a female slave should offer us our board and lodging and the privilege of his lordly name with 'Missis' before it for our lifelong services. You may make up as many little bread-and-butter romances as you please, Marian; but I defy you to give me any sensible reason why Marmaduke should chain himself for ever to a little inane thing like Constance, when he can enjoy the society of a capable woman like that without binding himself at all."

"Nonsense, Nelly! Really, you oughtnt to say such things."

"No. I ought to keep both eyes tight shut so that I may be contented in that station to which it has pleased God to call me."

"Imagine his proposing to marry her, Nell! I am just as wicked as you; for I am very glad she refused; though I cant conceive why she did it."

"Perhaps," said Miss McQuinch, becoming excited, "she refused because she had too much good sense: aye, and too much common decency to accept. It is all very well for us fortunate good-for-nothings to resort to prostitution—"

"Oh, Nelly!"

"—I say, to prostitution, to secure ourselves a home and an income. Somebody said openly in Parliament the other day that marriage was the true profession of women. So it is a profession; and except that it is a harder bargain for both parties, and that society countenances it, I dont see how it differs from what we—bless our virtuous indignation!—stigmatize as prostitution. *I* dont mean ever to be married, I can tell you, Marian. I would rather die than sell myself forever to a man, and stand in a church before a lot of people whilst George or somebody read out that cynically plain-spoken marriage service over me."

"Stop Nelly! Pray stop! If you thought for a moment you would never say such awful things."

"I thought we had agreed long ago that marriage is a mistake."

"Yes; but that is very different to what you are saying now."

"I cannot see—"

"Pray stop, Nelly. Dont go on in that strain. It does no good; and it makes me very uncomfortable."

"I'll take it out in work," said Nelly calmly, returning to her manuscript. "I can see that, as you say, talking does no good. All the more reason why I should have another try at earning my own living. When I become a great novelist I shall say what I like and do what I please. For the present I am your obedient, humble servant."

At any other time Marian would have protested, and explained, and soothed. Now she was too heavily preoccupied by her guilty conscience. She strolled disconsolately to the window, and presently, seeing that Miss McQuinch was at work in earnest and had better not be disturbed, went off for a lonely walk. It was a glorious afternoon; and nature heaped its peculiar consolations on her; so that she never thought of returning until the sun was close to the horizon. As she came, tired, through the plantation, with the evening glow and the light wind, in which the branches were rustling and the leaves dropping, lulling her luxuriously, she heard some one striding swiftly along the path behind. She looked back; but there was a curve in the way; and she could not see who was coming. Then it occurred to her that it might be Conolly. Dreading to face him after what had happened, she stole aside among the trees a little way, and sat down on a stone, hoping that he might pass by without seeing her. The next moment he came round the curve, looking so resolute and vigorous that her heart became fainter as she watched him. Just opposite where she sat, he stopped, having a clear view of the path ahead for some distance, and appeared puzzled. Marian held her breath. He looked to the left through the trees, then to the right, where she was.

"Good-evening, Miss Lind," he said respectfully, raising his hat.

"Good-evening," said she, trembling.

"You are not looking quite well."

"I have walked too much; and I feel a little tired. That is why I had to sit down. I shall be rested presently."

Conolly sat down on a felled trunk opposite Marian. "This is my last visit to Carbury Towers," he said. "No doubt you know that I am going for good."

"Yes," said Marian. "I—I am greatly obliged to you for all the pains you have taken with me in the laboratory. You have been very patient. I suppose I have often wasted your time unreasonably."

"No," said Conolly, unceremoniously, "you have not wasted my time: I never let anybody do that. My time belonged to Lord Carbury, not to myself. However, that is neither here nor there. I enjoyed giving you lessons. Unless you enjoyed taking

George Bernard Shaw

them, the whole obligation rests on me."

"They were very pleasant."

He shifted himself into an easier position, looking well pleased. Then he said, carelessly, "Has Mr. Marmaduke Lind come down?"

Marian reddened and felt giddy.

"I want to avoid meeting him," continued Conolly; "and I thought perhaps you might know enough of his movements this evening to help me to do so. It does not matter much; but I have a reason."

Marian felt the hysteric globe at her throat as she tried to speak; but she repressed it, and said:

"Mr. Conolly: I know the reason. I did not know before: I am sure you did not think I did. I made a dreadful mistake."

"Why!" said Conolly, with some indignation, "who has told you since?"

"Marmaduke," said Marian, roused to reply quickly by the energy of the questioner. "He did not mean to be indiscreet: he thought I knew."

"Thought! He never thought in his life, Miss Lind. However, he was right enough to tell you; and I am glad you know the truth, because it explains my behavior the last time we met. It took me aback a bit for the moment."

"You were very forbearing. I hope you will not think me intrusive if I tell you how sincerely sorry I am for the misfortune which has come to you."

"What misfortune?"

Marian lost confidence again, and looked at him in silent distress.

"To be sure," he interposed, quickly. "I know; but you had put it all out of my head. I am much obliged to you. Not that I am much concerned about it. You will perhaps think it an instance of the depravity of my order, Miss Lind; but I am not one of those people who think it pious to consider their near relatives as if they were outside the natural course of things. I never was a good son or a good brother or a good patriot in the sense of thinking that my mother and my sister and my native country were better than other people's because I happened to belong to them. I knew what would happen some day, though, as usual, my foreknowledge did not save me from a little emotion when the event came to pass. Besides, to tell you the truth, I dont feel it as a misfortune. You know what my sister's profession is. You told me how you felt when you saw her act. Now, tell me fairly, and without stopping to think of whether your answer will hurt me, would you consent to know her in private even if you had heard nothing to her disadvantage? Would you invite her to your house, or go to a party at which all the other women were like her? Would you introduce young ladies to her, as you would introduce them to Miss McQuinch? Dont stop to imagine exceptional circumstances which might justify you in doing these things; but tell me yes or no, *would* you?"

"You see, Mr. Conolly, I should really never have an opportunity of doing them."

"By your leave, Miss Lind, that means No. Honestly, then, what has Susanna to lose by disregarding your rules of behavior? Even if, by marrying, she conciliated the notions of your class, she would only give some man the right to ill-treat her and spend her earnings, without getting anything in return—and remember there is a special danger of that on the stage, for several reasons. She would not really conciliate you by marrying, for you wouldnt associate with her a bit the more because of her marriage certificate. Of course I am putting her

George Bernard Shaw

self-respect out of the question, that being a matter between herself and her conscience, with which we have no concern. Believe me, neither actresses nor any other class will trouble themselves about the opinion of a society in which they are allowed to have neither part nor lot. Perhaps I am wrong to talk about such matters to you; but you are trained to feel all the worst that can be felt for my sister; and I feel bound to let you know that there is something to be said in her defence. I have no right to blame her, as she has done me no harm. The only way in which her conduct can influence my prospects will be through her being an undesirable sister-in-law in case I should want to marry."

"If the person you choose hesitate on that account, you can let her go without regret," said Marian. "She will not be worthy of your regard."

"I am not so sure of that," said Conolly, laughing. "You see, Miss Lind, if that invention of mine succeeds, I may become a noted man; and it is fashionable nowadays for society to patronize geniuses who hit on a new illustration of what people call the marvels of science. I am ambitious. As a celebrity, I might win the affections of a duchess. Who knows?"

"I should not advise you to marry a duchess. I do not know many of them, as I am a comparatively humble person; but I am sure you would not like them."

"Aye. And possibly a lady of gentle nurture would not like me."

"On the contrary, clever people are so rare in society that I think you would have a better chance than most men."

"Do you think my manners would pass? I learnt to dance and bow before I was twelve years old from the most experienced master in Europe; and I used to mix with all the counts, dukes, and queens in my father's opera company, not to mention the fashionable people I have read about in novels."

"You are jesting, Mr. Conolly. I do not believe that your manners give you the least real concern."

"And you think that I may aspire in time—if I am successful in public—to the hand of a lady?"

"Surely you know as much of the world as I. Why should you not marry a lady, if you wish to?"

"I am afraid class prejudice would be too strong for me, after all."

"I dont think so. What hour is it now, Mr. Conolly?"

"It wants ten minutes of seven."

"Oh!" cried Marian, rising. "Miss McQuinch is probably wondering whether I am drowned or lost. I must get back to the Hall as fast as I can. They have returned from Bushy Copse before this; and I am sure they are asking about me."

Conolly rose silently and walked with her as far as the path from the cottage to the laboratory.

"This is my way, Miss Lind," said he. "I am going to the laboratory. Will you be so kind as to give my respects to Miss McQuinch. I shall not see her again, as I must return to town by the last train to-night."

"And are you not coming back—not at all, I mean?"

"Not at all."

"Oh!" said Marian slowly.

"Good bye, Miss Lind."

He was about to raise his hat as usual; but Marian, with a smile, put out her hand. He took it for the first time; looked at her for a moment gravely; and left her.

Lest they should surprise one another in the act, neither of them looked back at the other as they went their several ways.

BOOK II

CHAPTER VII

In the spring, eighteen months after his daughter's visit to Carbury Towers, Mr. Reginald Harrington Lind called at a house in Manchester Square and found Mrs. Douglas at home. Sholto's mother was a widow lady older than Mr. Lind, with a rather glassy eye and shaky hand, who would have looked weak and shiftless in an almshouse, but who, with plenty of money, unlimited domestic service, and unhesitating deference from attendants who were all trained artists in their occupation, made a fair shew of being a dignified and interesting old lady. When he was seated, her first action was to take a new photograph from a little table at her side, and hand it to him without a word, awaiting his recognition of it with a shew of natural pride and affection which was amateurish in comparison to the more polished and skilful comedy with which her visitor took it and pretended to admire it.

"Capital. Capital," said Mr. Lind. "He must give us one."

"You dont think that the beard has spoiled him, do you?" said Mrs. Douglas.

"Certainly not: it is an improvement," said Mr. Lind, decisively. "You are glad to have him back again with you, I dare say. Ah yes, yes" (Mrs. Douglas's eyes had answered for her). "Did he tell you that he met me? I saw him on Wednesday last for the first time since his return to London. How

George Bernard Shaw

long was he away?"

"Two years," she replied, with slow emphasis, as if such an absence were hardly credible. "Two long years. He has been staying in Paris, in Venice, in Florence: a month here, a week there, dissatisfied everywhere. He would have been almost as happy with me at home. And how is Marian?"

"Well," said Mr. Lind, smiling, "I believe she is still disengaged; and she professes to be fancy free. She is fond of saying, generally, that she will never marry, and so forth. That is the new fashion with young women—if saying what they dont mean can be called a new fashion."

"Marian is sure to get married," said Mrs. Douglas. "She must have had offers already. There are few parents who have not cause to envy you."

"We have both been happy in that respect, Mrs. Douglas. Sholto is a highly distinguished young man. I wish I had started in life with half his advantages. I thought at one time he was perhaps becoming attached to Marian."

"You are quite sure, Mr. Lind, that you could forgive his being a plain gentleman? A little bird whispered to me that you desired a title for Marian."

"My dear Mrs. Douglas, we, who are familiar with titles, understand their true value. I should be very sorry to see Marian lose, by an unsuitable alliance, the social position I have been able to give her. I should set my face resolutely against such an alliance. But few English titles can boast a pedigree comparable with Sholto's. The name of Douglas is historic—far more so than that of Lind, which is not even English except by naturalization. Besides, Sholto's talents are very remarkable. He will certainly adopt a political career; and, with his opportunities and abilities, a peerage is anything but a remote contingency."

"Sholto, you know, is perfectly unembarrassed. There is not a charge on his property. I think that even Marian, good as she is, and lovely as she is, will not easily find a better match. But I am well known to be a little crazy about my dear boy. That is because I know him so much better than anyone else does. Now let us talk about other matters. Let me see. Oh yes, I got a prospectus of some company from the city the other day; and whose name should there be upon the list of directors but Reginald Harrington Lind's! And Lord Carbury's, too! Pray, is the entire family going into business?"

"Well, I believe the undertaking to be a commercially sound one; and—"

"Fancy *you* talking about commercial soundness!"

"True. It must sound strange to you. But it is no longer unusual for men in my position to take an active part in the direction of commerce. We have duties as well as privileges. I gave my name and took a few shares chiefly on the recommendation of Jasper and of my own stockbroker. I think there can be no doubt that Jasper and Mr. Conolly have made a very remarkable discovery, and one which must prove highly remunerative and beneficial."

"What is the discovery? I did not quite understand the prospectus."

"Well, it is called the Conolly Electro-motor."

"Yes, I know that."

"And it—it turns all sorts of machinery. I cannot explain it scientifically to you: you would not understand me. But it is, in short, a method of driving machinery by electricity at a less cost than by steam. It is connected in principle with the conservation of energy and other technical matters. You must come and see the machinery at work some day."

"I must, indeed. And is it true that Mr. Conolly was a common working man?"

"Yes, a practical man, undoubtedly, but highly educated. He speaks French and Italian fluently, and is a remarkable musician. Altogether a man of very superior attainments, and by no means deficient in culture."

"Dear me! Jasper told me something of that sort about him; but Lady Carbury gave him a very different character. She assured me that he was sprung from the dregs of the people, and that she had a great deal of trouble to teach him his proper place. Still, we know that she is not very particular as to what she says when she dislikes people. Yet she ought to know; for he was Jasper's laboratory servant—at least so she said."

"Oh, surely not a servant. Jasper never regarded him in that light. The Countess disapproves of Jasper's scientific pursuits, and sets her face against all who encourage him in them. However, I really know nothing about Mr. Conolly's antecedents. His manner when he appears at our board meetings is quiet and not unpleasant. Marian, it appears, met him at Towers Cottage the year before last, and had some scientific lessons from him. He was quite unknown then. It was rather a curious coincidence. I did not know of it until about a month ago, when he read a paper at the Society of Arts on his invention. I attended the meeting with Marian; and when it was over, I introduced him to her, and was surprised to learn that they knew one another already. He told me afterward that Marian had shewn an unusual degree of cleverness in studying electricity, and that she greatly interested him at the time."

"No doubt. Marian interests everybody; and even great discoverers, when they are young, are only human."

"Ah! Perhaps so. But she must have shewn some ability or she would never have elicited a remark from him. He is full of his business."

"And what is the latest news of the family scamp?"

"Do you mean my Reginald?"

"Dear me, no! What a shame to call poor Reggy a scamp! I mean young Marmaduke, of course. Is it true that he has a daughter now?"

"Oh yes. Perfectly true."

"The reprobate! And he was always such a pleasant fellow."

"Yes; but he is annoyingly inconsiderate. About a fortnight ago, Marian and Elinor went to Putney to a private view at Mr. Scott's studio. On their way back they saw Marmaduke on the river, and, rather unnecessarily, I think, entered into conversation with him. He begged them to come to Hammersmith in his boat, saying that he had something there to shew them. Elinor, it appears, had the sense to ask whether it was anything they ought not to see; but he replied on his honor that it was something perfectly innocent, and promised that they should be delighted with it. So they foolishly consented, and went with him to Hammersmith, where they left the river and walked some distance with him. He left them in a road somewhere in West Kensington, and came back after about fifteen minutes with a little girl. He actually presented her to Marian and Elinor as a member of the family whom they, as a matter of course, would like to know."

"Well, *such* a thing to do! And what happened?"

"Marian seems to have thought of nothing but the prettiness of the unhappy child. She gravely informed me that she forgave Marmaduke everything when she saw how he doted on it. Elinor has always shewn a disposition to defend him—"

"She is full of perversity, and always was."

"—and this incident did not damage his credit with *her.*

However, after the little waif had been sufficiently petted and praised to gratify Master Marmaduke's paternal feelings, they came home, and, instead of holding their tongues, began to tell all our people what a dear little child Marmaduke had, and how they considered that it ought not to be made to suffer for his follies. In fact, I think they would have adopted it, if I had allowed them."

"That is Marian all over. Some of her ideas will serve her very well when she goes to heaven; but they will get her into scrapes in this wicked world if you do not take care of her."

"I fear so. For that reason I tolerate a degree of cynicism in Elinor's character which would otherwise be most disagreeable to me. It is often useful in correcting Marian's extravagances. Unfortunately, the incident at Hammersmith did not pass off without making mischief. It happens that my sister Julia is interested in a Home for foundling girls—a semi-private place, where a dozen children are trained as domestic servants."

"Yes. I have been through it. It is very neat and pretty; but they really treat the poor girls as if they ought to be thankful for permission to exist. Their dresses are so ugly!"

"Possibly. I assure you that presentations are much sought after, and are very difficult to get. Julia is a patroness. Marian told her about this child of Marmaduke's; and it happened that a vacancy had just occurred at the Home in consequence of one of the girls dying of melancholia and spinal affection. Julia, who has perhaps more piety than tact, wrote to Marmaduke offering to present his daughter, and expatiating on the advantages of the Home to the poor little lost one. In her desire to reclaim Marmaduke also, she entrusted the letter to George, who undertook to deliver it, and further Julia's project by personal persuasion. George described the interview to me, and shewed me, I am sorry to say, how much down-right ferocity may exist beneath an apparently frank, jovial, reckless exterior like Marmaduke's."

"Well, I hardly wonder at his refusing. Of course, he might have known that the motive of the offer was a kind one."

"Refused! A gentleman can always refuse an offer with dignity. Marmaduke was outrageous. George—a clergyman—owed his escape from actual violence to the interference of the woman, and to a timely representation that he had undertaken to bear the message in order to soften any angry feelings that it might give rise to. Marmaduke repeatedly applied foul language to his aunt and to her offer; and George with great difficulty dissuaded him from writing a most offensive letter to her. Julia was so hurt by this that she complained to Dora— Marmaduke's mother—who had up to that time been kept in ignorance of his doings; and now it is hard to say where the mischief will end. Dora is overwhelmed by the revelation of the life her son is leading. Marmaduke has consequently forfeited his father's countenance, which had to be extended to him so far as to allow of his occasional appearance at home, in order to keep Dora in the dark. Now that she is enlightened, of course there is an end of all that, and he is forbidden the house."

"What a lot of mischief! Dear me!"

"So I said to Marian. Had she refused to go up the river with Marmaduke, as she should have done, all this would not have occurred. She will not see it in that light, but lays all the blame on her aunt Julia, whose offer fell somewhat short of her own notions of providing for the child's future."

"How does Marmaduke stand with respect to money? I suppose his father has stopped his allowance."

"No. He threatened to do it, and went so far as to make his solicitor write to that effect to Marmaduke, who had the consummate impudence to reply that he should in that case be compelled to provide for himself by contracting a marriage of which he could not expect his family to approve. Still, he added, if the family chose to sever their connexion with him, they could not expect him to consult their feelings in his future disposal of himself. In plain English, he threatened to marry this woman if his income was cut off. He carried his point, too; for no alteration has been made in his allowance. Indeed, as he has money of his own, and as part of the property is entailed, it would be easier to irritate him uselessly than to subject him to any material deprivation."

"The young scamp! I wonder he was clever enough to take advantage like that."

"He has shewn no lack of acuteness of late. I suspect he is under shrewd guidance."

"Have you ever seen the—the guidance?"

"Not in person. I seldom enter a theatre now. But I am of course familiar with her appearance from the photographic portraits of her. They are in all the shop windows."

"Yes. I think I have noticed them."

"And now, Mrs. Douglas, I fear I have paid you a very long visit."

"Why dont you come oftener?"

"I wish I could find time. I have not so much leisure for enjoyment as I used."

"I am not so sure of that. But we are always glad to have a chat with one another, I know. We are agreed about the dear children, I think?"

"Cordially. Cordially. Good-bye."

"Good-bye."

CHAPTER VIII

On the morning of the first Friday in May Marian received this letter:

"Uxbridge Road, Holland Park, W.

"DEAR MISS LIND: I must begin by explaining why I make this communication to you by letter instead of orally. It is because I am about to ask you to do me a favor. If you asked me to do anything for you, then, no matter how much my judgment might protest against my compliance, I could not without pain to myself refuse you face to face. I have no right to assume that your heart would plead on my behalf against your head in this fashion; but, on the other hand—the wish is father to the thought here—I have no right to assume that it would not. Therefore, to spare you all influences except the fair ones of your own interest and inclination, I make my proposal in writing. You will please put the usual construction on the word 'proposal.' What I desire is your consent to marry me. If your first impulse now is to refuse, I beg you to do so in plain terms at once, and destroy this letter without reading further. If you think, on the contrary, that we could achieve a future as pleasant as our past association has been—to me at least, here is what, as I think, you have to consider.

"You are a lady, rich, well-born, beautiful, loved by many persons besides myself, too happily circumstanced to have any pressing inducement to change your condition, and too

George Bernard Shaw

fortunately endowed in every way to have reason to anticipate the least difficulty in changing it to the greatest worldly advantage when you please.

"What I am and have been, you know. I may estrange from you some of the society which you enjoy, and I can introduce you to none that would compensate you for the loss. I am what you call poor: my income at present does not amount to much more than fifteen hundred pounds; and I should not ask you to marry me if it were not that your own inheritance is sufficient, as I have ascertained, to provide for you in case of my early death. You know how my sister is situated; how your family are likely to feel toward me on her account and my own; and how impatient I am of devoting much time to what is fashionably supposed to be pleasure. On the other hand, as I am bidding for a consent and not for a refusal, I hope you will not take my disadvantages for more, or my advantages for less, than they are honestly worth. At Carbury Park you often said that you would never marry; and I have said the same myself. So, as we neither of us overrate the possi- bilities of happiness in marriage, perhaps we might, if you would be a little forbearing with me, succeed in proving that we have greatly underrated them. As for the prudence of the step, I have seen and practised too much prudence to believe that it is worth much as a rule of conduct in a world of accidents. If there were a science of life as there is one of mechanics, we could plan our lives scientifically and run no risks; but as it is, we must—together or apart—take our chance: cautiousness and recklessness divide the great stock of regrets pretty equally.

"Perhaps you will wonder at my selfishness in wanting you, for my own good, to forfeit your present happy indepen- dence among your friends, and involve your fortunes with those of a man whom you have only seen on occasions when ceremony compelled him to observe his best behavior. I can only excuse myself by reminding you that no matter whom you marry, you must do so at the same disadvantages, except as to the approval of your friends, of which the value is for you to consider. That being so, why should I not profit by your hazard as well as another? Besides, there are many other feelings impelling me. I should like to describe them to you, and would if I understood them well enough to do it accurately.

"However, nothing is further from my intention than to indite a love letter; so I will return to graver questions. One, in particular, must be clearly understood between us. You are too earnest to consider an allusion to religious matters out of place here. I do not know exactly what you believe; but I have gathered from stray remarks of yours that you belong to what is called the Broad Church. If so, we must to some extent agree to differ. I should never interfere in any way with your liberty as far as your actions concerned yourself only. But, frankly, I should not permit my wife to teach my children to know Christianity in any other way than that in which an educated Englishman knows Buddhism. I will not go through any ceremony whatever in a church, or enter one except to play the organ. I am prejudiced against religions of all sorts. The Church has made itself the natural enemy of the theatre; and I was brought up in the theatre until I became a poor workman earning wages, when I found the Church always taking part against me and my comrades with the rich who did no work. If the Church had never set itself against me, perhaps I should never have set myself against the Church; but what is done is done: you will find me irreligious, but not, I hope, unreasonable.

"I will be at the Academy to-morrow at about four o'clock, as I do not care to remain longer in suspense than is absolutely necessary; but if you are not prepared to meet me then, I shall faithfully help you in any effort I may perceive you make to avoid me.

"I am, dear Miss Lind,
    "Yours sincerely,

"EDWARD CONOLLY."

This letter conveyed to Marian hardly one of the considerations set forth in it. She thought it a frank, strong, admirable letter, just what she should have hoped from her highest estimate of him. In the quaint earnestness about religion, and the exaggerated estimate (as she thought) of the advantages which she might forfeit by marrying him, there was just enough of the workman to make them characteristic. She wished that she could make some real sacrifice for his sake. She was afraid to realize her situation at first, and, to keep it off, occupied herself during the forenoon with her household duties, with some pianoforte practice, and such other triflings as she could persuade herself were necessary. At last she quite suddenly became impatient of further delay. She sat down in a nook behind the window curtain, and re-read the letter resolutely. It disappointed her a little, so she read it again. The third time she liked it better than the first; and she would have gone through it yet again but for the arrival of Mrs. Leith Fairfax, with whom they had arranged to go to Burlington House.

"It is really a tax on me, this first day at the Academy," said Mrs. Fairfax, when they were at luncheon. "I have been there at the press view, besides seeing all the pictures long ago in the studios. But, of course, I am expected to be there."

"If I were in your place," said Elinor, "I—"

"Last night," continued Mrs. Fairfax, deliberately ignoring her, "I was not in bed until half-past two o'clock. On the night before, I was up until five. On Tuesday I did not go to bed at all."

"Why do you do such things?" said Marian.

"My dear, I *must*. John Metcalf, the publisher, came to me on Tuesday at three o'clock, and said he must have an article on the mango experiments at Kew ready for the printer before ten next morning. For his paper, the *Fortnightly Naturalist*, you know. 'My dear John Metcalf,' I said, 'I dont know what a mango is.' 'No more do I, Mrs. Leith Fairfax,' said he: 'I think it's something that blooms only once in a hundred years. No matter what it is, you must let me have the article. Nobody else can do it.' I told him it was impossible. My London letter for the *Hari Kari* was not even begun; and the last post to catch the mail to Japan was at a quarter-past six in the morning. I had an article to write for your father, too. And, as the sun had been shining all day, I was almost distracted with hay fever. 'If you were to go down on your knees,' I said, 'I could not find time to read up the *flora* of the West Indies and finish an article before morning.' He went down on his knees. 'Now Mrs. Leith Fairfax,' said he, 'I am going to stay here until you promise.' What could I do but promise and get rid of him? I did it, too: how, I dont know; but I did it. John Metcalf told me yesterday that Sir James Hooker, the president of the Society for Naturalizing the Bread Fruit Tree in Britain, and the greatest living authority on the subject, has got the credit of having written my article."

"How flattered he must feel!" said Elinor.

"What article had you to write for papa?" said Marian.

"On the electro-motor—the Conolly electro-motor. I went down to the City on Wednesday, and saw it working. It is most wonderful, and very interesting. Mr. Conolly explained it to me himself. I was able to follow every step that his mind has made in inventing it. I remember him as a common workman. He fitted the electric bell in my study four years ago with his own hands. You may remember that we met him at a concert once. He is a thorough man of business. The Company is making upward of fifty pounds an hour by the motor at present; and they expect their receipts to be a thousand a day next year. My article will be in the *Dynamic Statistician* next week. Have you seen Sholto Douglas since he came back from the continent?"

"No."

"I want to see him. When you meet him next, tell him to call on me. Why has he not been here? Surely you are not keeping up your old quarrel?"

"What old quarrel?"

"I always understood that he went abroad on your account."

"I never quarreled with him. Perhaps he did with me, as he has not come to see us since his return. It used to be so easy to offend him that his retirement in good temper after a visit was quite exceptional."

"Come, come, my dear child! that is all nonsense. You must be kind to the poor fellow. Perhaps he will be at the Academy."

"I hope not," said Marian, quickly.

"Why?"

"I mean if he cherishes any grudge against me; for he will be very disagreeable."

"A grudge against you! Ah, Marian, how little you understand him! What perverse creatures all you young people are! I must bring about an *eclaircissement*."

"I advise you not to," said Elinor. "If you succeed, no one will admit that you have done anything; and if you fail, everybody will blame you."

"But there is nothing to be *eclairci*," said Marian. We are talking nonsense, which is silly—"

"And French, which is vulgar," interposed Miss McQuinch, delivering the remark like a pistol shot at Mrs. Fairfax, who had been trying to convey by facial expression that she pitied the folly of Elinor's advice, and was scandalized by her presumption in offering it. "It is time to start for the Academy."

When they arrived at Burlington House, Mrs. Fairfax put on her gold rimmed spectacles, and led the way up the stairs like one having important business in a place to which others came for pleasure. When they had passed the turnstiles, Elinor halted, and said:

"There is no sort of reason for our pushing through this crowd in a gang of three. Besides, I want to look at the pictures, and not after you to see which way you go. I shall meet you here at six o'clock, sharp. Good-bye."

"What an extraordinary girl!" said Mrs. Fairfax, as Elinor opened her catalogue at the end, and suddenly disappeared to the right amongst the crowd.

"She always does so," said Marian; "and I think she is quite right. Two people cannot make their way about as easily as one; and they never want to see the same pictures."

"But, my dear, consider the impropriety of a young girl walking about by herself."

"Surely there is no impropriety in it. Lots of people—all sensible women do it. Who can tell, in this crowd, whether you are by yourself or not? And what does it matter if—"

Here Mrs. Fairfax's attention was diverted by the approach of one of her numerous acquaintances. Marian, after a moment's indecision, slipped away and began her tour of the rooms alone, passing quickly through the first in order to escape pursuit. In the second she tried to look at the pictures; but as she now for the first time realized that she might meet Conolly at any moment, doubt as to what answer she should give him seized her; and she felt a strong impulse to fly. The pictures were unintelligible to her: she kept her face turned to the inharmonious shew of paint and gilding only because she

George Bernard Shaw

shrank from looking at the people about. Whenever she stood still, and any man approached and remained near her, she contemplated the wall fixedly, and did not dare to look round or even to stir until he moved away, lest he should be Conolly. When she passed from the second room to the large one, she felt as though she were making a tremendous plunge; and indeed the catastrophe occurred before she had accomplished the movement, for she came suddenly face to face with him in the doorway. He did not flinch: he raised his hat, and prepared to pass on. She involuntarily put out her hand in remonstrance. He took it as a gift at once; and she, confused, said anxiously: "We must not stand in the doorway. The people cannot pass us," as if her action had meant nothing more than an attempt to draw him out of the way. Then, perceiving the absurdity of this pretence, she was quite lost for a moment. When she recovered her self-possession they were standing together in the less thronged space near a bust of the Queen; and Conolly was saying:

"I have been here half an hour; and I have not seen a single picture."

"Nor I," she said timidly, looking down at her catalogue. "Shall we try to see some now?"

He opened his catalogue; and they turned together toward the pictures and were soon discussing them sedulously, as if they wished to shut out the subject of the very recent crisis in their affairs, which was nevertheless constantly present in their minds. Marian was saluted by many acquaintances. At each encounter she made an effort to appear unconcerned, and suffered immediately afterward from a suspicion that the effort had defeated its own object, as such efforts often do. Conolly had something to say about most of the pictures: generally an unanswerable objection to some historical or technical inaccuracy, which sometimes convinced her, and always impressed her with a confiding sense of ignorance in herself and infallible judgment in him.

"I think we have done enough for one day," she said at last. "The watercolors and the sculpture must wait until next time."

"We had better watch for a vacant seat. You must be tired."

"I am, a little. I think I should like to sit in some other room. Mrs. Leith Fairfax is over there with Mr. Douglas—a gentleman whom I know and would rather not meet just now. You saw him at Wandsworth."

"Yes. That tall man? He has let his beard grow since."

"That is he. Let us go to the room where the drawings are: we shall have a better chance of a seat there. I have not seen Sholto for two years; and our last meeting was rather a stormy one."

"What happened?"

Marian was a little hurt by being questioned. She missed the reticence of a gentleman. Then she reproached herself for not understanding that his frank curiosity was a delicate appeal to her confidence in him, and answered: "He proposed to me."

Conolly immediately dropped the subject, and went in search of a vacant seat. They found one in the little room where the architects' drawings languish. They were silent for some time.

Then he began, seriously: "Is it too soon to call you by your own name? 'Miss Lind' is distant; but 'Marian' might shock you if it came too confidently without preparation."

"Whichever you please."

"Whichever I please!"

"That is the worst of being a woman. Little speeches that are sheer coquetry when you analyze them, come to our lips and escape even when we are most anxious to be straightforward."

"In the same way," said Conolly, "the most enlightened men often express themselves in a purely conventional manner on subjects on which they have the deepest convictions." This sententious utterance had the effect of extinguishing the conversation for some moments, Marian being unable to think of a worthy rejoinder. At last she said:

"What is your name?"

"Edward, or, familiarly, Ned. Commonly Ted. In America, Ed. With, of course, the diminutives Neddy, Teddy, and Eddy."

"I think I should prefer Ned."

"I prefer Ned myself."

"Have you any other name?"

"Yes; but it is a secret. Why people should be plagued with two Christian names, I do not know. No one would have believed in the motor if they had known that my name was Sebastian."

"Sebastian!"

"Hush. I was actually christened Edoardo Sebastiano Conolly. My father used to spell his name Conollj whilst he was out of Italy. I have frustrated the bounty of my godfathers by suppressing all but the sensible Edward Conolly."

There was a pause. Then Marian spoke.

"Do you intend to make our—our engagement known at once?"

"I have considered the point; and as you are the person likely to be inconvenienced by its publication, I am bound to let you conceal it for the present, if you wish to. It must transpire sometime: the sooner the better. You will feel uncomfortably deceitful with such a secret; and as for me, every time your father greets me cordially in the City I shall feel mean. However, you can watch for your opportunity. Let me know at once when the cat comes out of the bag."

"I will. I think, as you say, the right course is to tell at once."

"Undoubtedly. But from the moment you do so until we are married you will be worried by remonstrances, entreaties, threats, and what not; so that we cannot possibly make that interval too short."

"We must take Nelly into our confidence. You will not object to that?"

"Certainly not. I like Miss McQuinch."

"You really do! Oh, I am so glad. Well, we are accustomed to go about together, especially to picture galleries. We can come to the Academy as often as we like; and you can come as often as you like, can you not?"

"Opening day, for instance."

"Yes, if you wish."

"Let us say between half-past four and five, then. I would willingly be here when the doors open in the morning; but my business will not do itself while I am philandering and making you tired of me before your time. The consciousness of having done a day's work is necessary to my complete happiness."

"I, too, have my day's work to do, silly as it is. I have to housekeep, to receive visitors, to write notes about nothing, and to think of the future. We can say half-past four or any later hour that may suit you."

"Agreed. And now, Marian—"

"Dont let me disturb you," said Miss McQuinch, at his elbow, to Marian; "but Mrs. Leith Fairfax will be here with Sholto Douglas presently; and I thought you might like to have an opportunity of avoiding him. How do you do, Mr. Conolly?"

"I must see him sooner or later," said Marian, rising. "Better face him at once and get it over. I will go back by myself and meet them." Then, with a smile at Conolly, she went out through the door leading to the water-color gallery.

"Marian does not stand on much ceremony with you, Mr. Conolly," said Miss McQuinch, glancing at him.

"No," said Conolly. "Do you think you could face the Academy again on Monday at half-past four?"

"Why?"

"Miss Lind is coming to meet me here at that hour."

"Marian!"

"Precisely. Marian. She has promised to marry me. At present it is a secret. But it was to be mentioned to you."

"It will not be a secret very long if you allow people to overhear you calling her by her Christian name in the middle of the Academy, as you did me just now," said Elinor, privately much taken aback, but resolute not to appear so.

"Did you overhear us? I should have been more careful. You do not seem surprised."

"Just a little, at your audacity. Not in the least at Marian's consenting."

"Thank you."

"I did not mean it in that way at all," said Elinor resentfully. "I think you have been very fortunate, as I suppose you would have married somebody in any case. I believe you are able to appreciate her. That's a compliment."

"Yes. I hope I deserve it. Do you think you will ever forgive me for supplanting the hero Marian deserves?"

"If you had let your chance of her slip, I should have despised you, I think: at least, I should if you had missed it with your eyes open. I am so far prejudiced in your favor that I think Marian would not like you unless you were good. I have known her to pity people who deserved to be strangled; but I never knew her to be attracted by any unworthy person except myself; and even I have my good points. You need not trouble yourself to agree with me: you could not do less, in common politeness. As I am rather tired, I shall go and sit in the vestibule until the others are ready to go home. In the meantime you can tell me all the particulars you care to trust me with. Marian will tell me the rest when we go home."

"That is an undeserved stab," said Conolly.

"Never mind: I am always stabbing people. I suppose I like it," she added, as they went together to the vestibule.

Meanwhile, Mrs. Leith Fairfax had not been wasting her time. She had come upon Douglas in the large room, and had recognized him by his stature and proud bearing, in spite of the handsome Assyrian beard he had allowed to grow during his stay abroad.

"I have been very anxious to see you," said she, forcing a conversation upon him, though he had saluted her formally, and had evidently intended to pass on without speaking. "If your time were not too valuable to be devoted to a poor hard-working woman, I should have asked you to call on me. Dont deprecate my forbearance. You are Somebody in the literary world now."

George Bernard Shaw

"Indeed? I was not aware that I had done anything to raise me from obscurity."

"I assure you you are very much mistaken, or else very modest. Has no one told you about the effect your book produced here?"

"I know nothing of it, Mrs. Leith Fairfax. I never enquire after the effect of my work. I have lived in comparative seclusion; and I scarcely know what collection of fugitive notes of mine you honor by describing as a book."

"I mean your 'Note on three pictures in last year's *Salon*,' with the sonnets, and the fragment from your unfinished drama. Is it finished, may I ask?"

"It is not finished. I shall never finish it now."

"I will tell you—between ourselves—that I heard one of the foremost critics of the age say, in the presence of a great poet (whom we both know), that it was such another fragment as the Venus of Milo, 'whose lost arms,' said he, 'we should fear to see, lest they should be unworthy of her.' 'You are right,' said the poet: 'I, for one, should shudder to see the fragment completed.' That is a positive fact. But look at some of the sonnets! Burgraves says that his collection of English sonnets is incomplete because it does not contain your 'Clytemnestra,' which he had not seen when his book went to press. You stand in the very forefront of literature—far higher than I, who am—dont tell anybody—five years older than you."

"You are very good. I do not value any distinction of the sort. I write sometimes because, I suppose, the things that are in me must come out, whether I will or not. Let us talk of something else. You are quite well I hope?"

"Very far from it. I am never well; but since I never have a moment's rest from work, I must bear with it. People expect me to think, when I have hardly time to eat."

"If you have no time to think, I envy you. But I am truly sorry that your health remains so bad."

"Thank you. But what is the cause of all this gloomy cynicism, Mr. Douglas? Why should you, who are young, distinguished, gifted, and already famous, envy me for having no leisure to think?"

"You exaggerate the sadness of my unfortunate insensibility to the admiration of the crowd," said Douglas, coldly. "I am, nevertheless, flattered by the interest you take in my affairs."

"You need not be, Mr. Douglas," said Mrs. Fairfax, earnestly, fearing that he would presently succeed in rebuffing her. "I think you are much better off than you deserve. You may despise your reputation as much as you like: that only affects yourself. But when a beautiful girl pays you the compliment of almost dying of love for you, I think you ought to buy a wedding-ring and jump for joy, instead of sulking in remote corners of the continent."

"And pray, Mrs. Leith Fairfax, what lady has so honored me?"

"You must know, unless you are blind."

"Pardon me. I do not habitually imply what is not the case. I beg you to believe that I do *not* know."

"Not know! What moles men are! Poor Marian!"

"Oblige me by taking this seat," said Douglas, sternly, pointing to one just vacated. "I shall not detain you many minutes," he added, sitting down beside her. "May I understand that Miss Lind is the lady of whom you spoke just now?"

"Yes. Remember that I am speaking to you as a friend, and that I trust to you not to mention the effort I am making to clear up the misunderstanding which causes her so much unhappiness."

"Are you then in Miss Lind's confidence? Did she ask you to tell me this?"

"What do you mean, Mr. Douglas?"

"I am quite innocent of any desire to shock or offend you, Mrs. Leith Fairfax. Does your question imply a negative?"

"Most certainly. Marian ask me to tell! you must be dreaming. Do you think, even if Marian were capable of making an advance, that *I* would consent to act as a go-between? Really, Mr. Douglas!"

"I confess I do not understand these matters; and you must bear with my ineptitude. If Miss Lind entertains any sentiment for me but one of mistrust and aversion, her behavior is singularly misleading."

"Mistrust! Aversion! I tell you she is in love with you."

"But you have not, you admit, her authority for saying so, whereas I *have* her authority for the contrary."

"You do not understand girls. You are mistaken."

"Possibly; but you must pardon me if I hesitate to set aside my own judgment in deference to your low estimate of it."

"Very well," said Mrs. Fairfax, her patience yielding a little to his persistent stiffness: "be it so. Many men would be glad to beg what you will not be bribed to accept."

"No doubt. I trust that when they so humble themselves they may not encounter a flippant repulse."

"If they do, it will spring from her unmerited regard for you."

He bowed slightly, and turned away, arranging his gloves as if about to rise.

"Pray what is that large picture which is skied over there to the right?" said Mrs. Fairfax, after a pause, during which she had feigned to examine her catalogue. "I cannot see the number at this distance."

"Do you defend her conduct on the ground of that senseless and cruel caprice which your sex seem to consider becoming to them; or has she changed her mind in my absence?"

"Oh! you are talking of Marian. I do not know what you have to complain of in her conduct. Mind, she has never breathed a word to me on the subject. I am quite ignorant of the details of your difference with her. But she has confessed to me that she is very sorry for what passed—I am abusing her confidence by telling you so—and I am a woman, with eyes and brains, and know what the poor girl feels well enough. I will tell you nothing more: I have no right to; and Marian would be indignant if she knew how much I have said already. But I know what I should do were I in your place."

"Expose myself to another refusal, perhaps?"

Mrs. Fairfax, learning now for the first time that he had actually proposed to Marian, looked at him for some moments in silence with a smile which was assumed to cover her surprise. He thought it expressed incredulity at the idea of his being refused again.

"Are you sure?" he began, speaking courteously to her for the first time. "May I rely upon the accuracy of your impressions on this subject? I know you are incapable of trifling in a matter which might expose me to humiliation; but can you give me any guarantee—any—"

"Certainly not, Mr. Douglas. I am really sorry that I cannot give you a written undertaking that your suit shall succeed: perhaps that might encourage you to brave the scorn of a poor child who adores you. But if you need so much encouragement, I fear you do not greatly relish the prospect of success.

Doubtless it has already struck her that since you found absence from her very bearable for two years, and have avoided meeting her on your return, her society cannot be very important to your happiness."

"But it was her own fault. If she accuses me of having gone away to enjoy myself, her thoughts are a bitter sarcasm on the truth."

"Granted that it was her own fault, if you please. But surely you have punished her enough by your long seclusion, and can afford to shew a tardy magnanimity by this time. There she is, I think, just come in at the door on the left. My sight is so wretched. Is it not she?"

"Yes."

"Then let us get up and speak to her. Come."

"You must excuse me, Mrs. Leith Fairfax. I have distinctly given her my word that I will not intrude upon her again."

"Dont be so foolish."

Douglas's face clouded. "You are privileged to say so," he said.

"Not at all," said Mrs. Fairfax, frightened. "But when I think of Marian, I feel like an old woman, and venture to remonstrate with all the presumption of age. I beg your pardon."

He bowed. Then Marian joined them, and Mrs. Fairfax again gave tongue.

"Where have you been?" she cried. "You vanished from my side like a sprite. I have been searching for you ever since."

"I have been looking at the pictures, of course. I am so glad you have come back, Sholto. I think you might have made time to pay us a visit before this. You look so strong and well!

Your beard is a great improvement. Have you met Nelly?"

"I think we saw her at some distance," said Douglas. "I have not been speaking to her."

"How did you enjoy yourself while you were away?"

"As best I could."

"You look as if you had succeeded very fairly. What o'clock is it? Remember that we have to meet Nelly at the turnstiles at six."

"It is five minutes to six now, Miss Lind."

"Thank you, Mr. Douglas. We had better go, I think."

As they left the room, Mrs. Fairfax purposely lingered behind them.

"Am I right in concluding that you are as frivolous as ever, Marian?" he said.

"Quite," she replied. "To-day especially so. I am very happy to-day."

"May I ask why?"

"Something has happened. I will tell you what it is some day perhaps, but not now. Something that realizes a romantic dream of mine. The dream has been hovering vaguely about me for nearly two years; but I never ventured to teach myself exactly what it was until to-day."

"Realized here? in the Academy?"

"It was foreshadowed—promised, at home this morning; but it was realized here."

"Did you know beforehand that I was coming?"

"Not until to-day. Mrs. Leith Fairfax said that you would most likely be here."

"And you are happy?"

"So much so that I cannot help talking about my happiness to you, who are the very last person—as you will admit when everything is explained—to whom I should unlock my lips on the subject."

"And why? Am I not interested in your happiness?"

"I suppose so. I hope so. But when you learn the truth, you will be more astonished than gratified."

"I dare swear that you are mistaken. Is this dream of yours an affair of the heart?"

"Now you are beginning to ask questions."

"Well, I will ask no more at present. But if you fear that my long absence has rendered me indifferent in the least degree to your happiness, you do me a great injustice."

"Well, you were not in a very good humor with me when you went away."

"I will forget that if you wish me to."

"I do wish you to forget it. And you forgive me?"

"Most assuredly."

"Then we are the best friends in the world again. This is a great deal better than meeting and pretending to ignore the very thing of which our minds are full. You will not delay visiting us any longer now, I hope."

"I will call on your father to-morrow morning. May I?"

"He is out of town until Monday. He will be delighted to see you then. He has been talking to me about you a great deal of late. But if you want to see him in the morning you had better go to the club. I will write to him to-night if you like; so that he can write to you and make an appointment."

"Do. Ah, Marian, instinct is better and truer than intellect. I have been for two years trying to believe all kinds of evil of you; and yet I knew all the time that you were an angel."

Marian laughed. "I suppose that under our good understanding I must let you say pretty things to me. You must write me a sonnet before your enthusiasm evaporates. I am sure I deserve it as well as Clytemnestra."

"I will. But I fear I shall tear it up for its unworthiness afterward."

"Dont: I am not a critic. Talking of critics, where has Mrs. Leith Fairfax gone to? Oh, there she is!"

Mrs. Fairfax came up when she saw Marian look round for her. "My dear," she said: "it is past six. We must go. Elinor may be waiting for us."

They found Elinor seated in the vestibule with Conolly, at whom Mrs. Fairfax plunged, full of words. Conolly and Douglas, introduced to one another by Marian, gravely raised their hats. When they had descended the stairs, they stood in a group near one of the doors whilst Conolly went aside to get their umbrellas. Just then Marmaduke Lind entered the building, and halted in surprise at finding himself among so many acquaintances.

"Hallo!" he cried, seizing Douglas's hand, and attracting the attention of the bystanders by his boisterous tone. "Here you are again, old man! Delighted to see you. Didnt spot you at first, in the beard. George told me you were back. I met your mother in Knightsbridge last Thursday; but she pretended not to see me. How have you enjoyed yourself abroad, eh? Very much in the old style, I suppose?"

"Thank you," said Douglas. "I trust your people are quite well."

"Hang me if I know!" said Marmaduke. "I have not troubled them much of late. How d'ye do, Mrs. Leith Fairfax? How are all the celebrities?" Mrs. Fairfax bowed coldly.

"Dont roar so, Marmaduke," said Marian. "Everybody is looking at you."

"Everybody is welcome," said Marmaduke, loudly. "Douglas: you must come and see me. By Jove, now that I think of it, come and see me, all of you. I am by myself on week-nights from six to twelve; and I should enjoy a housewarming. If Mrs. Leith Fairfax comes, it will be all proper and right. Let us have a regular party."

Mrs. Fairfax looked indignantly at him. Elinor looked round anxiously for Conolly. Marian, struck with the same fear, moved toward the door.

"Here, Marmaduke," she said, offering him her hand. "Good-bye. You are in one of your outrageous humors this afternoon."

"What am I doing?" he replied. "I am behaving myself perfectly. Let us settle about the party before we go."

"Good evening, Mr. Lind," said Conolly, coming up to them with the umbrellas. "This is yours, I think, Mrs. Leith Fairfax."

"Good evening," said Marmaduke, subsiding. "I—Well, you are all off, are you?"

"Quite time for us, I think," said Elinor. "Good-bye."

Mrs. Fairfax, with a second and more distant bow, passed out with Conolly and Douglas. Elinor waited a moment to whisper to Marmaduke.

"First rate," said Marmaduke, in reply to the whisper; "and beginning to talk like one o'clock. Oh yes, I tell you!" He shook Elinor's hand at such length in his gratitude for the inquiry that she was much relieved when a servant in livery interrupted him.

"Missus wants to speak to you, sir, afore she goes," said the man.

Elinor shook her head at Marmaduke, and hurried away to rejoin the rest outside. As they went through the courtyard, they passed an open carriage, in which reclined a pretty woman with dark eyes and delicate artificial complexion. Her beauty and the elegance of her dress attracted their attention. Suddenly Marian became aware that Conolly was watching her as she looked at the woman in the carriage. She was about to say something, when, to her bewilderment, Elinor nudged her. Then she understood too, and looked solemnly at Susanna. Susanna, observing her, stared insolently in return, and Marian averted her head like a guilty person and hurried on. Conolly saw it all, and did not speak until they rejoined Mrs. Fairfax and Douglas in Piccadilly.

"How do you propose to go home?" said Douglas.

"Walk to St. James's Street, where the carriage is waiting at the club; take Uncle Reginald with us; and drive home through the park," said Elinor.

"I will come with you as far as the club, if you will allow me," said Douglas.

Conolly then took leave of them, and stood still until they

George Bernard Shaw

disappeared, when he returned to the courtyard, and went up to his sister's carriage.

"Well, Susanna," said he. "How are you?"

"Oh, there's nothing the matter with me," she replied carelessly, her eyes filling with tears, nevertheless.

"I hear that I have been an uncle for some time past."

"Yes, on the wrong side of the blanket."

"What is its name?" he said more gravely.

"Lucy."

"Is it quite well?"

"I suppose not. According to Nurse, it is always ill."

Conolly shrugged his shoulders, and relapsed into the cynical manner in which he had used to talk with his sister. "Tired of it already?" he said. "Poor little wretch!"

"It is very well off," she retorted, angrily: "a precious deal better than I was at its age. It gets petting enough from its father, heaven knows! He has nothing else to do. I have to work."

"You have it all your own way at the theatre now, I suppose. You are quite famous."

"Yes," she said, bitterly. "We are both celebrities. Rather different from old times."

"We certainly used to get more kicks than halfpence. However, let us hope all that is over now."

"Who were those women who were with you a minute ago?"

"Cousins of Lind. Miss Marian Lind and Miss McQuinch."

"I remember. She is pretty. I suppose, as usual, she hasnt an idea to bless herself with. The other looks more of a devil. Now that you are a great man, why dont you marry a swell?"

"I intend to do so."

"The Lord help her then!"

"Amen. Good-bye."

"Oh, good-bye. Go on to Soho," she added, to the coachman, settling herself fretfully on the cushions.

CHAPTER IX

On Monday morning Douglas received a note inviting him to lunch at Mr. Lind's club. He had spent the greater part of the previous night composing a sonnet, which he carried with him in his pocket to St. James's Street. Mr. Lind received him cordially; listened to an account of his recent stay abroad; and described his own continental excursions, both gentlemen expressing great interest at such coincidences as their having put up at the same hotel or travelled by the same line of railway. When luncheon was over, Mr. Lind proposed that they should retire to the smoking-room.

"I should like to have a few words with you first, as we are alone here," said Douglas.

"Certainly," said Mr. Lind, assuming a mild dignity in anticipation of being appealed to as a parent. "Certainly, Sholto."

"What I have to say, coming so soon after my long absence, will probably surprise you. I had it in contemplation before my departure, and was only prevented from broaching it to you then by circumstances which have happily since lost their significance. When I tell you that my communication has reference to Marian, you will perhaps guess its nature."

"Indeed!" said Mr. Lind, affecting surprise. "Well, Sholto, if it be so, you have my heartiest approval. You know what a lonely life her marriage will entail on me; so you will not expect me to consent without a few regrets. But I could not desire a better settlement for her. She must leave me some day. I have no right to complain."

"We shall not be very far asunder, I hope; and it is in Marian's nature to form many ties, but to break none."

"She is an amiable girl, my—my darling child. Does she know anything of this?"

"I am here at her express request; and there remains to me the pleasure of getting her own final consent, which I would not press for until armed with your sanction."

Except for an involuntary hitch of his eyelids, Mr. Lind looked as if he believed perfectly in Douglas's respect for his parental claims. "Quite right," he said, "quite right. You have my best wishes. I have no doubt you will succeed: none. There are, of course, a few affairs to be settled—a few contingencies to be provided for—children—accidents—and so forth. No difficulty is likely to arise between us on that score; but still, these things have to be arranged."

"I propose a very simple method of arranging them. You are a man of honor, and more conversant with business than I. Give me your instructions. My lawyer shall have them within half an hour."

"That is said like a gentleman and a Douglas, Sholto. But I must consider before giving you an answer. You have thrown upon me the duty of studying your position as well as Marian's; and I must neither abuse your generosity nor neglect her interest."

"You will, nevertheless, allow me to consider the conditions as settled, since I leave them entirely in your hands."

"My own means have been seriously crippled by the extravagance of Reginald. Indeed both my boys have cost me much money. I had not, like you, the good fortune to be an only son. I was the fourth son of a younger son: there was very little left for me. I will treat Marian as liberally as I can; but I fear I cannot do anything for her that will bear comparison with your munificence."

"Surely I can give her enough. I should prefer to be solely responsible for her welfare."

"Oh no. That would be too bad. Oh no, Sholto: I will give her something, please God."

"As you wish, Mr. Lind. We can arrange it to your satisfaction afterward. Do you intend returning to Westbourne Terrace soon?"

"I am afraid not. I have to go into the City. If you would care to come with me, I can shew you the Company's place there, and the working of the motor. It is well worth seeing. Then you can return with me to the Terrace and dine with us. After dinner you can talk to Marian."

Douglas consented; and they went to Queen Victoria Street, to a building which had on each doorpost a brass shield inscribed THE CONOLLY ELECTRO-MOTOR COMPANY OF LONDON, LIMITED. At the offices, on the first floor, they were received obsequiously and informed that Mr. Conolly was within. They then went to a door on which appeared the name of the inventor, and entered a handsomely furnished office containing several working models of machinery, and a writing-table, from his seat at which Conolly rose to salute his visitors.

"Good evening, Mr. Lind. How do you do, Mr. Douglas?"

"Oh!" said Mr. Lind. "You two are acquainted. I did not know that."

"Yes," said Conolly, "I had the pleasure of meeting Mr. Douglas at the Academy yesterday evening."

"Indeed? Marian did not mention that you were there. Well, can we see the wonders of the place, Mr. Conolly; or do we disturb you?"

"Not at all," replied Conolly, turning to one of the models, and beginning his showman's lecture with disquieting promptitude. "Hitherto, as you are no doubt aware, Mr. Douglas, steam has kept electricity, as a motive power, out of the field; because it is much less expensive. Even induced magnetic currents, the cheapest known form of electric energy, can be obtained only by the use of steam power. You generate steam by the combustion of coal: electricity, without steam, can only be generated by the combustion of metals. Coal is much cheaper than metal: consider the vast amount of coal consumed in smelting metals. Still, electricity is a much greater force than steam: it's stronger, so to speak. Sixpennorth of electricity would do more work than sixpennorth of steam if only you could catch it and hold it without waste. Up to the present the waste has been so enormous in electric engines as compared with steam engines that steam has held its own in spite of its inferior strength. What I have invented is, to put it shortly, an electric engine in which there is hardly any waste; and we can now pump water, turn mill-stones, draw railway trains, and lift elevators, at a saving, in fuel and labor, of nearly seventy per cent, of the cost of steam. And," added Conolly, glancing at Douglas, "as a motor of six-horsepower can be made to weigh less than thirty pounds, including fuel, flying is now perfectly feasible."

"What!" said Douglas, incredulously. "Does not all trustworthy evidence prove that flying is a dream?"

"So it did; because a combination of great power with little weight, such as an eagle, for instance, possesses, could not formerly be realized in a machine. The lightest known four-horse-power steam engine weighs nearly fifty pounds. With my motor, a machine weighing thirty pounds will give rather more than six-horse-power, or, in other words, will produce a wing power competent to overcome much more than its own

George Bernard Shaw

gravity. If the Aeronautical Society does not, within the next few years, make a machine capable of carrying passengers through the air to New York in less than two days, I will make one myself."

"Very wonderful, indeed," said Douglas, politely, looking askance at him.

"No more wonderful than the flight of a sparrow, I assure you. We shall presently be conveyed to the top of this building by my motor. Here you have a model locomotive, a model steam hammer, and a sewing machine: all of which, as you see, I can set to work. However, this is mere show. You must always bear in mind that the novelty is not in the working of these machines, but the smallness of the cost of working."

Douglas endured the rest of the exhibition in silence, understanding none of the contrivances until they were explained, and not always understanding them even then. It was disagreeable to be instructed by Conolly—to feel that there were matters of which Conolly knew everything and he nothing. If he could have but shaped a pertinent question or two, enough to prove that he was quite capable of the subject if he chose to turn his attention to it, he could have accepted Conolly's information on the machinery as indifferently as that of a policeman on the shortest way to some place that it was no part of a gentleman's routine to frequent. As it was, he took refuge in his habitual reserve, and, lest the exhibition should be prolonged on his account, took care to shew no more interest in it than was barely necessary to satisfy Mr. Lind. At last it was over; and they returned westward together in a hansom.

"He is a Yankee, I suppose,'" said Douglas, as if ingenuity were a low habit that must be tolerated in an American.

"Yes. They are a wonderful people for that sort of thing. Curious turn of mind the mechanical instinct is!"

"It is one with which I have no sympathy. It is generally

subject to the delusion that it has a monopoly of utility. Your mechanic hates art; pelts it with lumps of iron; and strives to extinguish it beneath all the hard and ugly facts of existence. On the other hand, your artist instinctively hates machinery. I fear I am an artist."

"I dont think you are quite right there, Sholto. No. Look at the steam engine, the electric telegraph, the—the other inventions of the century. How could we get on without them?"

"Quite as well as Athens got on without them. Our mechanical contrivances seem to serve us; but they are really mastering us, crowding and crushing the beauty out of our lives, and making commerce the only god."

"I certainly admit that the coarser forms of Radicalism have made alarming strides under the influence of our modern civilization. But the convenience of steam conveyance is so remarkable that I doubt if we could now dispense with it. Nor, as a consistent Liberal, a moderate Liberal, do I care to advocate any retrogression, even in the direction of ancient Greece."

Douglas was seized with a certain impatience of Mr. Lind, as of a well-mannered man who had never learned anything, and had forgotten all that he had been taught. He did not attempt to argue, but merely said, coldly: "I can only say that I wish Fate had made me an Athenian instead of an Englishman of the nineteenth century."

Mr. Lind smiled complacently: he knew Douglas, if not Athens, better, but was in too tolerant a humor to say so. Little more passed between the two until they reached Westbourne Terrace, where Marian and her cousin were dressing for dinner. When Marian came down, her beauty so affected Douglas that his voice was low and his manner troubled as he greeted her. He took her in to dinner, and sat in silence beside her, heedless alike of his host's commonplaces and Miss McQuinch's acridities.

Mr. Lind unceremoniously took a nap after his wine that evening, and allowed his guest to go upstairs alone. Douglas hoped that Elinor would be equally considerate, but, to his disappointment, he found her by herself in the drawing-room. She hastened to explain.

"Marian is looking for some music. She will be back directly."

He sat down and took an album from the table, saying: "Have you many new faces here?"

"Yes. But we never discard old faces for new ones. It is the old ones that are really interesting."

"I have not seen this one of Mr. Lind before. It is capital. Ah! this of you is an old friend."

"Yes. What do you think of the one of Constance on the opposite page?"

"She looks as if she were trying to be as lugubrious as possible. What dress is that? Is it a uniform?"

"Yes. She joined a nursing guild. Didnt Mrs. Douglas tell you?"

"I believe so. I forgot. She went into a cottage hospital or something of that kind, did she not?"

"She left it because one of the doctors offended her. He was rather dreadful. He said that in two months she had contributed more to the mortality among the patients than he had in two years, and told her flatly that she had been trained for the drawing-room and ought to stay there. She was glad enough to have an excuse for leaving; for she was heartily sick of making a fool of herself."

"Indeed! Where is she now?"

"Back at Towers Cottage, moping, I suppose. That's Mr. Conolly the inventor, there under Jasper."

"So I perceive. Clever head, rather! A plain, hard nature, with no depths in it. Is that his wife, with the Swiss bonnet?"

"His wife! Why, that is a Swiss girl, the daughter of a guide at Chamounix, who nursed Marian when she sprained her ankle. Mr. Conolly is not married."

"I thought men of his stamp always married early."

"No. He is engaged, and engaged to a lady of very good position."

"He owes that to the diseased craving of modern women for notoriety of any sort. What an admirable photograph of Marian! I never saw it before. It is really most charming. When was it taken?"

"Last August, at Geneva. She does not like it—thinks it too coquettish."

"Then perhaps she will give it to me."

"She will be only too glad, I daresay. You have caught her at a soft moment to-night."

"I cannot find that duet anywhere," said Marian, entering. "What! Up already, Sholto? Where is papa?"

"I left him asleep in the dining-room. I have just been asking Miss McQuinch whether she thought you would give me a copy of this carte."

"That Geneva one. It is most annoying how people persist in admiring it. It always looks to me as if it belonged to an assortment of popular beauties at one shilling each. I dont think I have another. But you may take that if you wish."

"Thank you," said Douglas, drawing it from the book.

"I think you have a copy of every photograph I have had taken in my life," she said, sitting down near him, and taking the album. "I have several of yours, too. You must get one taken soon for me; I have not got you with your beard yet. I have a little album upstairs which Aunt Dora gave me on my eighth birthday; and the first picture in it is you, dressed in flannels, holding a bat, and looking very stern as captain of your eleven at Eton. I used to stand in great awe of you then. Do you remember telling me once that 'Zanoni' was a splendid book, and that I ought to read it?"

"Pshaw! No. I must have been a young fool. But it seems that I had the grace even then to desire your sympathy."

"I assure you I read it most reverently down in Wiltshire, where Nelly kept a select library of fiction concealed underneath her mattress; and I believed every word of it. Nelly and I agreed that you were exactly like Zanoni; but she was hardly to blame; for she had never seen you."

"Things like that make deep impressions on children," said Elinor, thoughtfully. "You were a Zanoni in my imagination for years before I saw you. When we first met you treated me insufferably. If you had known how my childish fancy had predisposed me to worship you, you might have vouchsafed me some more consideration, and I might have gone on believing you a demigod to the end of the chapter. I have hardly forgiven you yet for disenchanting me."

"I am sorry," said Douglas sarcastically. "I must have been sadly lacking in impressiveness. But on the other hand I recollect that you did not disappoint me in the least. You fully bore out the expectations I had been led to form of you."

"I have no doubt I did," said Elinor. "Yet I protest that my reputation was as unjust as yours. However, I have outlived my sensitiveness to this injustice, and have even contracted a bad habit of pretending to act up to it occasionally before foolish people. Marian: are you sure that duet is not on the sofa in my room?"

"Oh, the sofa! I looked only in the green case."

"I will go and hunt it out myself. Excuse me for a few minutes."

Douglas was glad to see her go. Yet he was confused when he was alone with Marian. He strolled to the window, outside which the roof of the porch had been converted into a summer retreat by a tent of pink-striped canvass. "The tent is up already," he said. "I noticed it as we came in."

"Yes. Would you prefer to sit there? We can carry out this little table, and put the lamp on it. There is just room for three chairs."

"We need not crowd ourselves with the table," he said. "There will be light enough. We only want to talk."

"Very well," said Marian, rising. "Will you give me that woolen thing that is on the sofa? It will do me for a shawl." He placed it on her shoulders, and they went out.

"I will sit in this corner," said Marian. "You are too big for the campstool. You had better bring a chair. I am fond of sitting here. When the crimson shade is on the lamp, and papa asleep in its roseate glow, the view is quite romantic: there is something ecstatically snug in hiding here and watching it." Douglas smiled, and seated himself as she suggested, near her, with his shoulder against the stone balustrade.

"Marian," said he, after a pause: "you remember what passed between us at the Academy yesterday?"

"You mean our solemn league and covenant. Yes."

"Why did we not make that covenant before? Life is not so long, nor happiness so common, that we can afford to trifle away two years of it. I wish you had told me when I last came here of that old photograph of mine in your album."

"But this is not a new covenant. It is only an old one mended. We were always good friends until you quarrelled and ran away."

"That was not my fault, Marian."

"Then it must have been mine. However, it does not matter now."

"You are right. Prometheus is unbound now; and his despair is only a memory sanctifying his present happiness. You know why I called on your father this morning?"

"It was to see the electro-motor in the city, was it not?"

"Good Heavens, Marian!" he said, rising, "what spirit of woman or spirit of mischief tempts you to coquet with me even now?"

"I really thought that was the reason—besides, of course, your desire to make papa amends for not having been to see him sooner after your return."

"Marian!" he said, still remonstrantly.

She looked at him with sudden dread, and instinctively recognized the expression in his face.

"You know as well as I," he continued, "that I went to seek his consent to our solemn league and covenant, as you call it. If that covenant were written on your heart as it is on mine, you would not inflict on me this pretty petty torture. Your father has consented: he is delighted. Now may I make a guess at that happy secret you told me of yesterday, and promised I should know one day?"

"Stop! Wait," said Marian, very pale. "I must tell you that secret myself."

"Hush. Do not be so moved. Remember that your confession is to be whispered to me alone."

"Dont talk like that. It is all a mistake. My secret has nothing to do with you." Douglas drew back a little way.

"I am engaged to be married."

"What do you mean?" he said sternly, advancing a step and looking down menacingly at her with his hand on the back of his chair.

"I have said what I mean," replied Marian with dignity. But she rose quickly as soon as she had spoken, and got past him into the drawing-room. He followed her; and she turned and faced him in the middle of the room, paler than before.

"You are engaged to *me*," he said.

"I am not," she replied.

"That is a lie!" he exclaimed, struggling in his rage to break through the strong habit of self-control. "It is a damnable lie; but it is the most cruel way of getting rid of me, and therefore the one most congenial to your heartlessness."

"Sholto," said Marian, her cheeks beginning to redden: "you should not speak to me like that."

"I say," he cried fiercely, "that it is a lie!"

"Whats the matter?" said Elinor, coming hastily into the room.

"Sholto has lost his temper," said Marian, firmly, her

indignation getting the better of her fear now that she was no longer alone with him.

"It is a lie," repeated Douglas, unable to shape a new sentence. Elinor and Marian looked at one another in perplexity. Then Mr. Lind entered.

"Gently, pray," said he. "You can be heard all through the house. Marian: what is the matter?"

She did not answer; but Douglas succeeded, after a few efforts, in speaking intelligibly. "Your daughter," he said, "with the assistance of her friend Mrs. Leith Fairfax, and a sufficient degree of direct assurance on her own part, has achieved the triumph of bringing me to her feet a second time, after I had unfortunately wounded her vanity by breaking her chains for two years."

"That is utterly false," interrupted Marian, with excitement.

"I say," said Douglas, in a deeper tone and with a more determined manner, "that she set Mrs. Leith Fairfax on me with a tale of love and regret for my absence. She herself with her own lips deliberately invited me to seek your consent to our union. She caused you to write me the invitation I received from you this morning. She told me that my return realized a dream that had been haunting her for two years. She begged me to forgive her the past, and to write her a sonnet, of which she said she was at least more worthy than Clytemnestra, and of which I say she is at best less worthy than Cressida." He took a paper from his pocket as he spoke; and, with a theatrical gesture, tore it into fragments.

"This is very extraordinary," said Mr. Lind irresolutely. "Is it some foolish quarrel, or what is the matter? Pray let us have no more unpleasantness."

"You need fear none from me," said Douglas. "I do not propose to continue my acquaintance with Miss Lind."

"Mr. Douglas has proposed to marry me; and I have refused him," said Marian. "He has lost his temper and insulted me. I think you ought to tell him to go away."

"Gently, Marian, gently. What am I to believe about this?"

"What I have told you," said Douglas, "I confirm *on my honor*, which you can weigh against the pretences of a twice perjured woman."

"Sholto!"

"I have to speak plainly on my own behalf, Mr. Lind. I regret that you were not in a position this morning to warn me of your daughter's notable secret."

"If it is a secret, and you are a gentleman, you will hold your tongue," interposed Elinor, sharply.

"Papa," said Marian: "I became engaged yesterday to Mr. Conolly. I told Mr. Douglas this in order to save him from making me a proposal. That is the reason he has forgotten himself. I had not intended to tell you so suddenly; but this misunderstanding has forced me to."

"Engaged to Mr. Conolly!" cried Mr. Lind. "I begin to fear that—Enga—" He took breath, and continued, to Marian: "I forbid you to entertain any such engagement. Sholto: there is evidently nothing to be gained by discussing this matter in hot blood. It is some girlish absurdity—some—some—some—"

"I apologize for having doubted the truth of the excuse," said Douglas; "but I see that I have failed to gauge Miss Lind's peculiar taste. I beg you to understand, Mr. Lind, that my pretensions are at an end. I do not aspire to the position of Mr. Conolly's rival."

"You are already in the position of Mr. Conolly's unsuccessful rival; and you fill it with a very bad grace," said Elinor.

George Bernard Shaw

"Pray be silent, Elinor," said Mr. Lind. "This matter does not concern you. Marian: go to your room for the present. I shall speak to you afterwards."

Marian flushed, and repressed a sob. "I wish I were under *his* protection now," she said, looking reproachfully at Douglas as she crossed the room.

"What can you expect from a father but hostility?" said Elinor, bitterly. "You are a coward, like all your sex," she added, turning to Douglas. Then she suddenly opened the door, and passed out through it with Marian, whilst the housemaids fled upstairs, the footman shrank into a corner of the landing, and the page hastily dragged the cook down to the kitchen.

The two men, left together in the drawing-room, were for some moments quite at a loss. Then Mr. Lind, after a preliminary cough or two, said: "Sholto: I cannot describe to you how shocked I am by what I have just heard. I am deeply disappointed in Marian. I trusted her implicitly; but of course I now see that I have been wrong in allowing her so much liberty. Evidently a great deal has been going on of which I had not any suspicion."

Douglas said nothing. His resentment was unabated; but his rage, naturally peevish and thin in quality, was subsiding, though it surged back on him at intervals. But now that he no longer desired to speak passionately, he would not trust himself to speak at all. Suddenly Mr. Lind broke out with a fury that astonished him, preoccupied as he was.

"This—this fellow must have had opportunities of thrusting himself into her society of which I knew nothing. I thought she barely knew him. And if I had known, could I have suspected her of intriguing with an ill-bred adventurer! Yes, I might: my experience ought to have warned me that the taint was in her blood. Her mother did the same thing—left the position I had given her to run away with a charlatan, disgracing me without the shadow of an excuse or reason except her own innate love for what was low. I thought Marian had escaped that. I was proud of her—placed un—unbounded confidence in her."

"She has struck me a blow," said Douglas, "the infernal treachery—." He checked himself, and after a moment resumed in his ordinary formal manner. "I must leave you, Mr. Lind. I am quite unable at present to discuss what has passed. Any conventional expressions of regret would be—Goodnight."

He bowed and left the room. Mr. Lind, taken aback, did not attempt to detain him or even return his bow, but stood biting his lips with a frown of discomfiture and menace. When he was alone, he paced the room several times. Then he procured some writing materials and sat down before them. He wrote nothing, but, after sitting for some time, he went upstairs. Passing Marian's room he listened. The sharp voice and restless movements of his niece were the only sounds he heard. They seemed to frighten him; for he stole on quickly to his own room, and went to bed. Even there he could hear a shrill note of conversation occasionally from the opposite room, where Marian was sitting on a sofa, trying to subdue the hysteria which had been gaining on her since her escape from the balcony; whilst Elinor, seated on the corner of a drawer which projected from the dressing-table, talked incessantly in her most acrid tones.

"Henceforth," she said, "Uncle Reginald is welcome to my heartiest detestation. I have been waiting ever since I knew him for an excuse to hate him; and now he has given me one. He has taken part—like a true parent—against you with a self-intoxicated fool whom he ought to have put out of the house. He has told me to mind my own business. I shall be even with him for that some day. I am as vindictive as an elephant: I hate people who are not vindictive: they are never grateful either, only incapable of any enduring sentiment. And Douglas! Sholto Douglas! The hero, the Newdigate poet, the handsome man! What a noble fellow he is when a little disappointment rubs his varnish off! I am glad I called him a coward to his face. I am thoroughly well satisfied with myself altogether: at last I have come out of a scene without having forgotten the right thing to say. You never see people in all their selfishness until they pretend to love you. See what you owe to your loving suitor, Sholto Douglas! See what you owe to your loving father, Reginald Lind!"

"I do not think that my father should have told me to leave the room," said Marian. "It was Sholto's place to have gone, not mine."

"Mr. Lind, who has so suddenly and deservedly descended from 'papa' to 'my father,' judiciously sided with the stronger and richer party."

"Nelly: I shall be as unhappy after this as even Sholto can desire. I feel very angry with papa; and yet I have no right to be. I suppose it is because I am in the wrong. I deceived him about the engagement."

"Bosh! You didnt tell him because you knew you couldnt trust him; and now you see how right you were."

"Even so, Nelly, I must not forget all his past care of me."

"What care has he ever taken of you? He was very little better acquainted with you than he was with me, when you came to keep house for him and make yourself useful. Of course, he had to pay for your board and lodging and education. The police would not have allowed him to leave you to the parish. Besides, he was proud of having a nice, pretty daughter to dispose of. You were quite welcome to be happy so long as you did not do anything except what he approved of. But the moment you claim your independence as a grown woman, the moment you attempt to dispose of yourself instead of letting him dispose of you! Bah! *I* might have been *my* father's pet, if I had been a nonentity. As it was, he spared no pains to make me miserable; and as I was only a helpless little devil of a girl, he succeeded to his heart's content. Uncle Reginald will try to do exactly the same to-morrow, he will come and bully you, instead of apologizing as he ought. See if he doesnt!"

"If I had as much reason to complain of my childhood as you have, perhaps I should not feel so shocked and disappointed by his turning on me to-night. Surely, when he saw me attacked as I was, he ought to have come to my assistance."

"Any stranger would have taken your part. The footman would, if you had asked him. But then, James is not your father."

"It seems a very small thing to be bidden to leave the room. But I will never expose myself to a repetition of it."

"Quite right. But what do you mean to do? for, after all, though parental love is an imposition, parental authority is a fact."

"I will get married."

"Out of the frying pan into the fire! Certainly, if you are resolved to marry, the present is as good as another time, and more convenient. But there must be some legal formalities to go through. You cannot turn into the first church you meet, and be married off-hand."

"Ned must find out all that. I am sadly disappointed and disilluded, Nelly."

"Time will cure you as it does everybody; and you will be the better for being wiser. By the bye, what did Sholto mean about Mrs. Fairfax?"

"I dont know."

"She has evidently been telling him a parcel of lies. Do you remember her hints about him yesterday at lunch? I have not

George Bernard Shaw

the least doubt that she has told him you are frantically in love with him. She as good as told you the same about him."

"Oh! she is not capable of doing such a thing."

"Isnt she? We shall see."

"I dont know what to think," said Marian, despondently. "I used to believe that both you and Ned thought too little of other people; but it seems now that the world is nothing but a morass of wickedness and falsehood. And Sholto, too! Who would have believed that he could break out in that coarse way? Do you remember the day that Fleming, the coachman, lost his temper with Auntie down at the Cottage. Sholto was exactly like that; not a bit more refined or dignified."

"Rather less so, because Fleming was in the right. Let us go to bed. We can do nothing to-night, but fret, and wish for to-morrow. Better get to sleep. Resentment does not keep me awake, I can vouch for that: I got well broken in to it when I was a child. I heard Uncle Reginald going to his room some time ago. I am getting sleepy, too, though I feel the better for the excitement."

"Very well. To bed be it," said Marian. But she did not sleep at all as well as Nelly.

CHAPTER X

Next morning Mr. Lind rose before his daughter was astir, and went to his club, where he breakfasted. He then went to the offices in Queen Victoria Street. Finding the board-room unoccupied, he sat down there, and said to one of the clerks:

"Go and tell Mr. Conolly that I desire to speak to him, if he is disengaged. And if anyone wants to come in, say that I am busy here. I do not wish to be disturbed for half an hour or so."

"Yes, sir," said the clerk, departing. A minute later, he returned, and said: "Mr. Conly is disengaged; and he says will you be so good as to come to his room, sir."

"I told you to ask him to come here," said Mr. Lind.

"Well, thats what he said, sir," said the clerk, speaking in official Board School English. "Shloy gow to him and tell him again?"

"No, no: it does not matter," said Mr. Lind, and walked out through the office. The clerk held the door open for him, and carefully closed it when he had passed through.

"Ow, oy sy!" cried the clerk. "This is fawn, this is."

"Wots the row?" said another clerk.

"Woy, owld Lind sends me in to Conly to cam in to him into the board-room. 'Aw right,' says Conly, 'awsk him to cam in eah to me.' You should 'a seen the owld josser's feaches wnoy towld im. 'Oyd zoyred jou to sy e was to cam in eah to me.' 'Shloy gow and tell him again?' I says, as cool as ennything. 'Now,' says he, 'Oil gow myself.' Thets wot Aw loike in Conly. He tikes tham fellers dahn wen they troy it on owver im."

Meanwhile, Mr. Lind went to Conolly's room; returned his greeting by a dignified inclination of the head; and accepted, with a cold "Thank you," the chair offered him. Conolly, who had received him cordially, checked himself. There was a pause, during which Mr. Lind lost countenance a little. Then Conolly sat down, and waited.

"Ahem!" said Mr. Lind. "I have to speak to you with—with reference to—to a—a matter which has accidentally come to my knowledge. It would be painful and unnecessary—quite unnecessary, to go into particulars."

Conolly remained politely attentive, but said nothing. Mr. Lind began to feel very angry, but this helped him to the point.

"I merely wish—that is, I quite wish you to understand that any intimacy that may have arisen between you and—and a member of my family must—must, in short, be considered to be at an end. My daughter is—I may tell you—engaged to Mr. Sholto Douglas, whom you know; and therefore—you understand."

"Mr. Lind," said Conolly, decisively: "your daughter is engaged to me."

Mr. Lind lost his temper, and rose, exclaiming, "I beg you will not repeat that, either here or elsewhere."

"Pray be seated," said Conolly courteously.

"I have nothing more to say, sir."

Conolly rose, as though the interview were at an end, and seemed to wait for his visitor to go.

"We understand one another, I presume," said Mr. Lind, dubiously.

"Not quite, I think," said Conolly, relenting. "I should suggest our discussing the matter in full, now that we have a favorable opportunity—if you will be so good."

Mr. Lind sat down, and said with condescension, "I am quite willing to listen to you."

"Thank you," said Conolly. "Will you tell me what your objections are to my engagement with your daughter?"

"I had hoped, sir, that your common sense and knowledge of the world would have rendered an explanation superfluous."

"They havnt," said Conolly.

Mr. Lind rose to boiling point again. "Oh, Mr. Conolly, I assure you I have no objection to explain myself: none whatever. I merely wished to spare you as far as possible. Since you insist on my mentioning what I think you must be perfectly well aware of, I can only say that from the point of view of English society our positions are different; and therefore an engagement between you and any member of my family is unsuitable, and—in short—out of the question, however advantageous it might be to you. That is all."

Mr. Lind considered he had had the better of that, and leaned back in his chair more confidently. Conolly smiled and shook his head, appreciative of the clearness with which Mr. Lind had put his case, but utterly unmoved by it. He considered for a moment, and then said, weighing his words carefully:

George Bernard Shaw

"Your daughter, with her natural refinement and delicate habits, is certainly not fit to be married to a foul-mouthed fellow, ignorant, dirty, besotted, and out of place in any company except at the bar in a public house. That is probably your idea of a workman. But the fact of her having consented to marry me is a proof that I do not answer to any such description. As you have hinted, it will be an advantage to me in some ways to have a lady for my wife; but I should have no difficulty in purchasing that advantage, even with my present means, which I expect to increase largely in the course of some years. Do you not underrate your daughter's personal qualities when you assume that it was her position that induced me to seek her hand?"

"I am quite aware of my daughter's personal advantages. They are additional reasons against her contracting an imprudent marriage."

"Precisely. But in what respect would her marriage with me be imprudent? I possess actual competence, and a prospect of wealth. I come of a long lived and healthy family. My name is, beyond comparison, more widely known than yours. [Mr. Lind recoiled]. I now find myself everywhere treated with a certain degree of consideration, which an alliance with your daughter will not diminish."

"In fact, you are conferring a great honor on my family by condescending to marry into it?"

"I dont understand that way of looking at things, Mr. Lind; and so I leave you to settle the question of honor as you please. But you must not condemn me for putting my position in the best possible light in order to reconcile you to an inevitable fact."

"What do you mean by an inevitable fact, sir?"

"My marriage, of course. I assure you that it will take place."

"But I shall not permit it to take place. Do you think to ignore me in the matter?"

"Practically so. If you give your consent, I shall be glad for the sake of Marian, who will be gratified by it. But if you withhold it, we must dispense with it. By opposing us, you will simply— by making Marian's home unbearable to her—precipitate the wedding." Conolly, under the influence of having put the case neatly, here relaxed his manner so far as to rest his elbows on the table and look pleasantly at his visitor.

"Do you know to whom you are speaking?" said Mr. Lind, driven by rage and a growing fear of defeat into desperate self-assertion.

"I am speaking," said Conolly with a smile, "to my future father-in-law."

"I am a director of this company, of which you are the servant, as you shall find to your cost if you persist in holding insulting language to me."

"If I found any director of this company allowing other than strictly business considerations to influence him at the Board, I should insist on his resigning."

Mr. Lind looked at him severely, then indignantly, then unsteadily, without moving him in the least. At last he said, more humbly: "I hope you will not abuse your position, Mr. Conolly. I do not know whether you have sufficient influence over Marian to induce her to defy me; but however that may be, I appeal to your better feelings. Put yourself in my place. If you had an only daughter—"

"Excuse my interrupting you," said Conolly, gently; "but that will not advance the argument unless you put yourself in mine. Besides, I am pledged to Marian. If she asks me to break off the match, I shall release her instantly."

George Bernard Shaw

"You will bind yourself to do that?"

"I cannot help myself. I have no more power to make her marry me than you have to prevent her."

"I have the authority of a parent. And I must tell you, Mr. Conolly, that it will be my duty to enlighten my poor child as to the effect a union with you must have on her social position. You have made the most of your celebrity and your prospects. She may be dazzled for the moment; but her good sense will come to the rescue yet, I am convinced."

"I have certainly spared no pains to persuade her. Unless the habit of her childhood can induce Marian to defer to your prejudice—you must allow me to call it so: it is really nothing more—she will keep her word to me."

Mr. Lind winced, recollecting how little his conduct toward Marian during her childhood was calculated to accustom her to his influence. "It seems to me, sir," he said, suddenly thinking of a new form of reproach, "that, to use your own plain language, you are nothing more or less than a Radical."

"Radicalism is not considered a reproach amongst workmen," said Conolly.

"I shall not fail to let her know the confidence with which you boast of your power over her."

"I have simply tried to be candid with you. You know exactly how I stand. If I have omitted anything, ask me, and I will tell you at once."

Mr. Kind rose. "I know quite as much as I care to know," he said. "I distinctly object to and protest against all your proceedings, Mr. Conolly. If my daughter marries you, she shall have neither my countenance in society nor one solitary farthing of the fortune I had destined for her. I recommend the latter point to your attention."

"I have considered it carefully, Mr. Lind; and I am satisfied with what she possesses in her own right."

"Oh! You have ascertained *that*, have you?"

"I should hardly have proposed to marry her but for her entire pecuniary independence of me."

"Indeed. And have you explained to her that you wish to marry her for the sake of securing her income?"

"I have explained to her everything she ought to know, taking care, of course, to have full credit for my frankness."

Mr. Lind, after regarding him with amazement for a moment, walked to the door.

"I am a gentleman," he said, pausing there for a moment, "and too old-fashioned to discuss the obligations of good breeding with a Radical. If I had believed you capable of the cynical impudence with which you have just met my remonstrances, I should have spared myself this meeting. Good-morning."

"Good-morning," said Conolly, gravely. When the door closed, he sprang up and walked to and fro, chuckling, rubbing his hands, and occasionally uttering a short laugh. When he had sufficiently relieved himself by this exercise, he sat down at his desk, and wrote a note.

"The Conolly Electro-Motor Company of London, Limited. Queen Victoria Street, E.C.

"This is to let your ever-radiant ladyship know that I am fresh from an encounter with your father, who has retired in great wrath, defeated, but of opinion that he deserved no better for arguing with a Radical. I thought it better to put forth my strength at once so as to save future trouble. I send this post haste in order that you may be warned in case he should go straight home and scold you. I hope he will not annoy you much.—E.C."

Having despatched the office boy to Westbourne Terrace with this letter, Conolly went off to lunch. Mr. Lind went back to his club, and then to Westbourne Terrace, where he was informed that the young ladies were together in the drawing-room. Some minutes later, Marian, discussing Conolly's letter with Elinor, was interrupted by a servant, who informed her that her father desired to see her in his study.

"Now for it, Marian!" said Nelly, when the servant was gone. "Remember that you have to meet the most unreasonable of adversaries, a parent asserting his proprietary rights in his child. Dont be sentimental. Leave that to him: he will be full of a father's anguish on discovering that his cherished daughter has feelings and interests of her own. Besides, Conolly has crushed him; and he will try to crush you in revenge."

"I wish I were not so nervous," said Marian. "I am not really afraid, but for all that, my heart is beating very unpleasantly."

"I wish I were in your place," said Elinor. "I feel like a charger at the sound of the trumpet."

"I am glad, for poor papa's sake, that you are not," said Marian, going out.

She knocked at the study door; and her father's voice, as he bade her come in, impressed her more than ever before. He was seated behind the writing-table, in front of which a chair was set for his daughter. She, unaccustomed from her child-hood to submit to any constraint but that which the position of a guest, which she so often occupied, had trained her to impose on herself, was rather roused than awed by this magisterial arrangement. She sat down with less than her usual grace of manner, and looked at him with her brows knitted. It was one of the rare moments in which she reminded him of her mother. An angry impulse to bid her not dare look so at him almost got the better of him. However, he began prudently with a carefully premeditated speech.

"It is my duty, Marian," he said gravely, "to speak of the statement you made last night. We need not allude to the painful scene which took place then: better let that rest and be forgotten as soon as possible. But the discovery of what you have been doing without my knowledge has cost me a sleepless night and a great deal of anxiety. I wish to reason with you now quite calmly and dispassionately; and I trust you will remember that I am older and have far more experience of the world than you, and that I am a better judge of your interests than you yourself can possibly be. Ahem! I have been this morning to the City, where I saw Mr. Conolly, and endeavored to make him understand the true nature of his conduct toward me—and, I may add, toward you—in working his way clandestinely into an intimacy with you. I shall not describe to you what passed; but I may say that I have found him to be a person with whom you could not hope for a day's happiness. Even apart from his habits and tastes, which are those of a mere workman, his social (and, I fear, his religious) views are such as no lady, no properly-minded woman of any class, could sympathize with. You will be better able to judge of his character when I tell you that he informed me of his having taken care, before making any advances to you, to ascertain how much money you had. He boasted in the coarsest terms of his complete influence over you, evidently without a suspicion of the impression of venality and indelicacy which his words were calculated to make on me. Besides, Marian, I am sure you would not like to contract a marriage which would give me the greatest pain; which would offend my family; and which would have the effect of shutting you out from all good society."

"You are mistaken in him, papa."

"I beg you will allow me to finish, Marian. [He had to think for a moment before he could substantiate this pretence of having something more to say.] I have quite made up my mind, from personal observation of Mr. Conolly, that even an

George Bernard Shaw

ordinary acquaintance between you is out of the question. I, in short, refuse to allow anything of the kind to proceed; and I must ask you to respect my wishes in the matter. There is another subject which I will take this opportunity of mentioning; but as I have no desire to force your inclinations, I shall not press you for a declaration of your feelings at present. Sholto Douglas—"

"I do not want to hear *anything* about Sholto Douglas," said Marian, rising.

"I expect you, Marian, to listen to what I have to say."

"On that subject I will not listen. I have felt very sore and angry ever since you told me last night to leave the room when Sholto insulted me, as if I were the aggressor."

"Angry! I am sorry to hear you say so to me."

"It is better to say so than to think so. There is no use in going on with this conversation, papa. It will only lead to more bitterness between us; and I had enough of that when I tasted it for the first time last night. We shall never agree about Mr. Conolly. I have promised to marry him; and therefore I am not free to withdraw, even if I wished to."

"A promise made by you without my sanction is not binding. And—listen to me, if you please—I have obtained Mr. Conolly's express assurance that if you wish to withdraw, he is perfectly willing that you should."

"Of course, he would not marry me if I did not wish it."

"But he is willing that you should withdraw. He leaves you quite free."

"Yes; and, as you told me, he is quite confident that I will keep faith with him; and so I will. I have had a letter from him since you saw him."

"What!" said Mr. Lind, rising also.

"Dont let us quarrel, papa," said Marian, appealingly. "Why may I not marry whom I please?"

"Who wants to prevent you, pray? I have most carefully abstained from influencing you with regard to Sholto Douglas. But this is a totally different question. It is my duty to save you from disgracing yourself."

"Where is the disgrace? Mr. Conolly is an eminent man. I am not poor, and can afford to marry anyone I can respect. I can respect him. What objection have you to him? I am sure he is far superior to Sholto."

"Mr. Douglas is a gentleman, Marian: Mr. Conolly is not; and it is out of the question for you to ally yourself with a—a member of the proletariat, however skilful he may be in his handicraft."

"What *is* a gentleman, papa?"

"A gentleman, Marian, is one who is well born and well bred, and who has that peculiar tone and culture which can only be acquired by intercourse with the best society. I think you should know that as well as I. I hope you do not put these questions from a desire to argue with me."

"I only wish to do what is right. Surely there is no harm in arguing when one is not convinced."

"Humph! Well, I have said all that is necessary. I am sure that you will not take any step calculated to inflict pain on me—at least an act of selfishness on your part would be a new and shocking experience for me.

"That is a very unfair way of putting it, papa. You give me no good reason for breaking my word, and making myself unhappy; and yet you accuse me of selfishness in not being ready to do both."

"I think I have already given you my assurance, weighted as it is by my age, my experience, my regard for your welfare, and, I hope, my authority as a parent, that both your honor and happiness will be secured by your obeying me, and forfeited by following your own headstrong inclinations."

Marian, almost crushed by this, hesitated a moment, twisting her fingers and looking pitiably at him. Then she thought of Conolly; rallied; and said: "I can only say that I am sorry to disagree with you; but I am not convinced."

"Do you mean that you refuse to obey me?"

"I cannot obey you in this matter, papa. I—"

"That is enough," said Mr. Lind, gravely, beginning, to busy himself with the writing materials. Marian for a moment seemed about to protest against this dismissal. Then she checked herself and went out of the room, closing the door quite quietly behind her, thereby unconsciously terrifying her father, who had calculated on a slam.

"Well," said Elinor, when her cousin rejoined her in the drawing-room: "have you been selfish and disobedient? Have you lacerated a father's heart?"

"He is thoroughly unfair," said Marian. "However, it all comes to this: he is annoyed at my wanting to marry Ned: and I believe there will be no more peace for me until I am in a house of my own. What shall we do in the meantime? Where shall we go? I cannot stay here."

"Why not? Uncle Reginald will sulk; sit at dinner without speaking to us; and keep out of our way as much as he can. But you can talk to me: we neednt mind him. It is he who will be out in the cold, biting his nose to vex his face. Such a state of things is new to you; but I have survived weeks of it without a single sympathizer, and been none the worse, except, perhaps, in temper. He will pretend to be inexorable at first: then he will come down to wounded affection; and he will end by giving in."

"No, Nelly, I couldnt endure that sort of existence. If people cannot remain friends they should separate at once. I will not sleep in this house to-night."

"Hurrah!" cried Miss McQuinch. "That will be beginning the war with spirit. If I were in your place, I would stay and fight it out at close quarters. I would make myself so disagreeable that nobody can imagine what life in this house would be. But your plan is the best—if you really mean it."

"Certainly I mean it. Where shall we go, Nelly?"

"Hm! I am afraid none of the family would make us very comfortable under the circumstances, except Marmaduke. It would be a splendid joke to go to West Kensington; only it would tell as much against us and Ned as against the Roman father. I have it! We will go to Mrs. Toplis's in St. Mary's Terrace: my mother always stays there when she is in town. Mrs. Toplis knows us: if she has a room to spare she will give it to us without making any bother."

"Yes, that will do. Are you ready to come now?"

"If you can possibly wait five minutes I should like to put on my hat and change my boots. We will have to come back and pack up when we have settled about the room. We cannot go without clothes. I should like to have a nightdress, at least. Have you any money?"

"I have the housekeeping money; but that, of course, I shall not take. I have thirty pounds of my own."

"And I have my old stocking, which contains nearly seventeen. Say fifty in round numbers. That will keep us going very comfortably for a month."

"Ridiculous! It will last longer than that. Oh!"

"Well?"

"We mustnt go, after all. I forgot *you*."

"What of me?"

"Where will you go when I am married? You cant live by yourself; and papa may not welcome you back if you take my part against him."

"He would not, in any case; so it makes no difference to me. I can go home if the worst comes to the worst. It does not matter: my present luxurious existence must come to an end some time or another, whether we go to Mrs. Toplis's or not."

"I am sure Ned will not object to your continuing with me, if I ask him."

"No, poor fellow! He wont object—at first; but he might not like it. You have no right to inflict me on him. No: I stick to my resolution on that point. Send for the carriage. It is time for us to be off; and Mrs. Toplis will be more impressed if we come in state than if we trudge afoot."

"Hush," said Marian, who was standing near the window. "Here is George, with a face full of importance."

"Uncle Reginald has written to him," said Elinor.

"Then the sooner we go, the better," said Marian.

"I do not care to have the whole argument over again with George."

As they passed through the hall on their way out they met

the clergyman.

"Well, George," said Elinor, "how are the heathen getting on in Belgravia? You look lively."

"Are you going out, Marian," he said, solemnly, disregarding his cousin's banter.

"We are going to engage a couple of rooms for some errant members of the family," said Elinor. "May we give you as a reference?"

"Certainly. I may want to speak to you before I go, Marian. When will you return?"

"I do not know. Probably we shall not be long. You will have plenty of opportunities, in any case."

"Will you walk into the study, please, sir," said the parlormaid.

The Rev. George was closeted with his father for an hour. When he came out, he left the house, and travelled by omnibus to Westbourne Grove, whence he walked to a house in Uxbridge Road. Here he inquired for Mr. Conolly, and, learning that he had just come in, sent up a card. He was presently ushered into a comfortable room, with a pleasant view of the garden. A meal of tea, wheatcakes, and fruit was ready on the table. Conolly greeted his visitor cordially, and rang for another cup. The Rev. George silently noted that his host dined in the middle of the day and had tea in the evening. Afraid though as he was of Conolly, he felt strengthened in his mission by these habits, quite out of the question for Marian. The tea also screwed up his courage a little; but he talked about the electro-motor in spite of himself until the cloth was removed, when Conolly placed two easy chairs opposite one another at the window; put a box of cigarets on a little table close at hand; and invited his visitor to smoke. But as it was now clearly time to come to business, the cigaret was declined solemnly. So Conolly, having settled himself in an easy attitude, waited for the clergyman to begin. The Rev. George seemed at a loss.

"Has your father spoken to you about an interview he had with me this morning?" said Conolly, good-naturedly helping him out.

"Yes. That, in fact, is one of the causes of my visit."

"What does he say?"

"I believe he adheres to the opinion he expressed to you. But I fear he may not have exhibited that self-control in speaking to you which I fully admit you have as much right to expect as anyone else."

"It does not matter. I can quite understand his feeling."

"It does matter—pardon me. We should be sorry to appear wanting in consideration for you."

"That is a trifle. Let us keep the question straight before us. We need make no show of consideration for one another. I have shown none toward your family."

"But I assure you our only desire is to arrange everything in a friendly spirit."

"No doubt. But when I am bent on doing a certain thing which you are equally bent on preventing, no very friendly spirit is possible except one of us surrender unconditionally."

"Hear me a moment, Mr. Conolly. I have no doubt I shall be able to convince you that this romantic project of my sister's is out of the question. Your ambition—if I may say so without offence—very naturally leads you to think otherwise; but the prompting of self-interest is not our safest guide in this life."

"It is the only guide I recognize. If you are going to argue the question, and your arguments are to prevail, they must be addressed to my self-interest."

"I cannot think you quite mean that, Mr. Conolly."

"Well, waive the point for the present: I am open to conviction. You know what my mind is. I have not changed it since I saw your father this morning. You think I am wrong?"

"Not wrong. I do not say for a moment that you are wrong. I—"

"Mistaken. Ill-advised. Any term you like."

"I certainly believe that you are mistaken. Let me urge upon you first the fact that you are causing a daughter to disobey her father. Now that is an awful fact. May I—appealing to that righteousness in which I am sure you are not naturally deficient—ask you whether you have reflected on that fact?"

"It is not half so awful to me as the fact of a father forcing his daughter's inclinations. However, awful is hardly the word for the occasion. Let us come to business, Mr. Lind. I want to marry your sister because I have fallen in love with her. You object. Have you any other motive than aristocratic exclusiveness?"

"Indeed, you quite mistake. I have no such feeling. We are willing to treat you with every possible consideration."

"Then why object?"

"Well, we are bound to look to her happiness. We cannot believe that it would be furthered by an unsuitable match. I am now speaking to you frankly as a man of the world."

"As a man of the world you know that she has a right to choose for herself. You see, our points of view are different. On Sundays, for instance, you preach to a highly privileged

George Bernard Shaw

audience at your church in Belgravia; whilst I lounge here over my breakfast, reading *Reynold's Newspaper*. I have not many social prejudices. Although a workman, I dont look on every gentleman as a bloodsucker who seizes on the fruits of my labor only to pursue a career of vice. I will even admit that there are gentlemen who deserve to be respected more than the workmen who have neglected all their opportunities—slender as they are—of cultivating themselves a little. You, on the other hand, know that an honest man's the noblest work of God; that nature's gentlemen are the only real gentlemen; that kind hearts are more than coronets, and simple faith than Norman blood, and so forth. But when your approval of these benevolent claptraps is brought to such a practical test as the marriage of your sister to a workman, you see clearly enough that they do not establish the suitability of personal intercourse between members of different classes. That being so, let us put our respective philosophies of society out of the question, and argue on the facts of this particular case. What qualifications do you consider essential in a satisfactory brother-in-law?"

"I am not bound to answer that; but, primarily, I should consider it necessary to my sister's happiness that her husband should belong to the same rank as she."

"You see you are changing your ground. I am not in the same rank—after your sense—as she; but a moment ago you objected to the match solely on the ground of unsuitability."

"Where is the difference?" said the clergyman, with some warmth. "I have not changed my ground at all. It is the difference in rank that constitutes the unsuitability.

"Let us see, then, how far you are right—how far suitability is a question of rank. A gentleman may be, and frequently is, a drunkard, a gambler, a libertine, or all three combined."

"Stay, Mr. Conolly! You show how little you understand the only true significance—"

"One moment, Mr. Lind. You are about to explain away the term gentleman into man of honor, honest man, or some other quite different thing. Let me put a case to you. I have a fellow at Queen Victoria Street working for thirty shillings a week, who is the honestest man I know. He is as steady as a rock; supports all his wife's family without complaining; and denies himself beer to buy books for his son, because he himself has experienced what it is to be without education. But he is not a gentleman."

"Pardon me, sir. He is a true gentleman."

"Suppose he calls on you to-morrow, and sends up his name with a request for an interview. You wont know his name; and the first question you will put to your servant is 'What sort of person is he?' Suppose the servant knows him, and, sharing your professed opinion of the meaning of the word, replies 'He is a gentleman!' On the strength of that you will order him to be shewn in; and the moment you see him you will feel angry with your servant for deceiving you completely as to the sort of man you were to expect by using the word gentleman in what you call its true sense. Or reverse the case. Suppose the caller is your cousin, Mr. Marmaduke Lind, and your high-principled servant by mistaking the name or how not, causes you to ask the same question with respect to him. The answer will be that Mr. Marmaduke—being a scamp—is not a gentleman. You would be just as completely deceived as in the other case. No, Mr. Lind, you might as well say that this workman of mine is a true lord or a true prince as a true gentleman. A gentleman may be a rogue; and a knifegrinder may be a philosopher and philanthropist. But they dont change their ranks for all that."

The clergyman hesitated. Then he said timidly, "Even admitting this peculiar view of yours, Mr. Conolly, does it not tell strongly against yourself in the present instance?"

"No; and I will presently shew you why not. When we digressed as to the meaning of the word gentleman, we were considering the matter of suitability. I was saying that a

George Bernard Shaw

gentleman might be a drunkard, or, briefly, a scoundrel. A scoundrel would be a very unsuitable husband for Marian—I perceive I annoy you by calling her by her name."

"N—no. Oh, no. It does not matter."

"Therefore gentility alone is no guarantee of suitability. The only gentlemanliness she needs in a husband is ordinary good address, presentable manners, sense enough to avoid ridiculous solecisms in society, and so forth. Marian is satisfied with me on these points; and her approval settles the question finally. As to rank, I am a skilled workman, the first in my trade; and it is only by courtesy and forbearance that I suffer any man to speak of my class as inferior. Take us all, professions and trades together; and you will find by actual measurement round the head and round the chest, and round our manners and characters, if you like, that we are the only genuine aristocracy at present in existence. Therefore I meet your objection to my rank with a point-blank assertion of its superiority. Now let us have the other objections, if there *are* any others."

The clergyman received this challenge in silence. Then, after clearing his throat uneasily twice, he said:

"I had hoped, Mr. Conolly, to have been able to persuade you on general grounds to relinquish your design. But as you are evidently not within reach of those considerations which I am accustomed to see universally admitted, it becomes my painful duty to assure you that a circumstance, on the secrecy of which you are relying, is known to me, and, through me, to my father."

"What circumstance is that?"

"A circumstance connected with Mr. Marmaduke Lind, whom you mentioned just now. You understand me, I presume?"

"Oh! you have found that out?"

"I have. It only remains for me to warn my sister that she is about to contract a close relationship with one who is—I must say it—living in sin with our cousin."

"What do you suppose will be the result of that?"

"I leave you to imagine," said the clergyman indignantly, rising.

"Stop a bit. You do not understand me yet, I see. You have said that my views are peculiar. What if I have taken the peculiar view that I was bound to tell Marian this before proposing to her, and have actually told her?"

"But surely—That is not very likely."

"The whole affair is not very likely. Our marriage is not likely; but it is going to happen, nevertheless. She knows this circumstance perfectly well. You told her yourself."

"I! When?"

"The year before last, at Carbury Towers. It is worth your consideration, too, that by mistrusting Marian at that time, and refusing to give her my sister's address, you forced her to appeal to me for help, and so advanced me from the position of consulting electrician to that of friend in need. She knew nothing about my relationship to the woman in a state of sin (as you call it), and actually deputed me to warn your cousin of the risk he was running by his intimacy with her. Whilst I was away running this queer errand for her, she found out that the woman was my sister, and of course rushed to the conclusion that she had inflicted the deepest pain on me. Her penitence was the beginning of the sentimental side of our acquaintance. Had you recognized that she was a woman with as good a right as you to know the truth concerning all matters in this world which she has to make her way through, you would have answered her question, and then I suppose I should have gone away without having exchanged a word with her on any more

George Bernard Shaw

personal matters than induction coils and ohms of resistance; and in all probability you would have been spared the necessity of having me for a brother-in-law."

"Well, sir," said the Rev. George dejectedly, "if what you say be true, I cannot understand Marian, I can only grieve for her. I shall not argue with you on the nature of the influence you have obtained over her. I shall speak to her myself; since you will not hear me."

"That is hardly fair. I have heard you, and am willing to hear more, if you have anything new to urge."

"You have certainly listened to my voice, Mr. Conolly. But I fear I have used it to very little purpose."

"You will fail equally with Marian, believe me. Even I, whose ability to exercise influence you admit, never obtained the least over my own sister. She knew me too well on my worst side and not at all on my best. If, as I presume, your father has tried in vain, what hope is there for you?"

"Only my humble trust that a priest may be blessed in his appeal to duty even where a father's appeal to natural affection has been disregarded."

"Well, well," said Conolly, kindly, rising as his visitor disconsolately prepared to go, "you can try. *I* got on by dint of dogged faith in myself."

"And I get on by lowly faith in my Master. I would I could imbue you with the same feeling!"

Conolly shook his head; and they went downstairs in silence. "Hallo!" said he, as he opened the door, "it is raining. Let me lend you a coat."

"Thank you, no. Not at all. Good-night," said the clergyman, quickly, and hastened away through the rain from

Conolly's civilities.

When he arrived at Westbourne Terrace, there was a cab waiting before the house. The door was opened to him by Marian's maid, who was dressed for walking.

"Master is in the drawing-room, sir, with Miss McQuinch," she said, meaning, evidently, "Look out for squalls."

He went upstairs, and found Elinor, with her hat on, standing by the pianoforte, with battle in her nostrils. Mr. Lind, looking perplexed and angry, was opposite to her.

"George," said Mr. Lind, "close the door. Do you know the latest news?"

"No."

"Marian has run away!"

"Run away!"

"Yes," said Miss McQuinch. "She has fled to Mrs. Toplis's, at St. Mary's Terrace, with—as Uncle Reginald was just saying— a most dangerous associate."

"With—?"

"With *me*, in short."

"And you have counselled her to take this fatal step?"

"No. I advised her to stay. But she is not so well used to domestic discomfort as I am; so she insisted on going. We have got very nice rooms: you may come and see us, if you like."

"Is this a time to display your bitter and flippant humor?" said the Rev. George, indignantly. "I think the spectacle of a wrecked home—"

"Stuff!" interrupted Elinor, impatiently. "What else can I say? Uncle Reginald tells me I have corrupted Marian, and refuses to believe what I tell him. And now you attack me, as if it were my fault that you have driven her away. If you want to see her, she is within five minutes walk of you. It is you who have wrecked her home, not she who has wrecked yours."

"There is no use in speaking to Elinor, George," said Mr. Lind, with the air of a man who had tried it. "You had better go to Marian, and tell her what you mentioned this afternoon. What has been the result of your visit?"

"He maintains that she knows everything," said the Rev. George, with a dispirited glance at Elinor. "I fear my visit has been worse than useless."

"It is impossible that she should know. He lies," said Mr. Lind. "Go and tell her the truth, George; and say that I desire her—I order her—to come back at once. Say that I am waiting here for her."

"But, Uncle Reginald," began Elinor, in a softer tone than before, whilst the clergyman stood in doubt—

"I think," continued Mr. Lind, "that I must request you, Elinor, to occupy the rooms you have taken, until you return to your parents. I regret that you have forced me to take this step; but I cannot continue to offer you facilities for exercising your influence over my daughter. I will charge myself with all your expenses until you go to Wiltshire."

Elinor looked at him as if she despaired of his reason. Then, seeing her cousin slowly going to the door, she said:

"You dont really mean to go on such a fool's errand to Marian, George?"

"Elinor!" cried Mr. Lind.

"What else is it?" said Elinor. "You asserted all your authority yourself this morning, and only made matters worse. Yet you expect her to obey you at second hand. Besides, she is bound in honor not to desert *me* now; and I will tell her so, too, if I see any sign of her letting herself be bullied."

"I fear Marian will not pay much heed to what I say to her," said the clergyman.

"If you are coming," said Elinor, "you had better come in my cab. Good-night, Uncle Reginald."

"Stay," said Mr. Lind, irresolutely. "Elinor, I—you—Will you exercise your influence to induce Marian to return? I think you owe me at least so much."

"I will if you will withdraw your opposition to her marriage and let her do as she likes. But if you can give her no better reason for returning than that she can be more conveniently persecuted here than at St. Mary's Terrace, she will probably stay where she is, no matter how I may influence her."

"If she is resolved to quarrel with me, I cannot help it," said Mr. Lind, pettishly.

"You know very well that she is the last person on earth to quarrel with anyone."

"She has been indulged in every way. This is the first time she has been asked to sacrifice her own wishes."

"To sacrifice her whole life, you mean. It is the first time she has ever hesitated to sacrifice her own comfort, and therefore the first time you are conscious that any sacrifice is required. Let me tell her that you will allow her to take her own course, Uncle Reginald. He is well enough off; and they are fond of one another. A man of genius is worth fifty men of rank."

"Tell her, if you please, Elinor, that she must choose between

George Bernard Shaw

Mr. Conolly and me. If she prefers him, well and good: I have done with her. That is my last word."

"So now she has nobody to turn to in the world except him. That is sensible. Come, cousin George! I am off."

"I do not think I should do any good by going," said the clergyman.

"Then stay where you are," said Elinor. "Good-night." And she abruptly left the room.

"It was a dreadful mistake ever to have allowed that young fury to enter the house," said Mr. Lind. "She must be mad. What did *he* say?"

"He said a great deal in attempted self-justification. But I could make no impression on him. We have no feelings in common with a man of his type. No. He is evidently bent on raising himself by a good marriage."

"We cannot prevent it."

"Oh, surely we—"

"I tell you we *cannot* prevent it," repeated Mr. Lind, turning angrily upon his son. "How can we? What can we do? She will marry this—this—this—this beggar. I wish to God I had never seen her mother."

The clergyman stood by, cowed, and said nothing.

"You had better go to that woman of Marmaduke's," continued Mr. Lind, "and try whether she can persuade her brother to commute his interest in the company, and go back to America, or to the devil. I will take care that he gets good terms, even if I have to make them up out of my own pocket. If the worst comes, *she* must be persuaded to leave Marmaduke. Offer her money. Women of that sort drive a hard bargain; but they have their price."

"But, sir, consider my profession. How can I go to drive a bargain with a woman of evil reputation?"

"Well, I must go myself, I suppose."

"Oh, no. I will go. Only I thought I would mention it."

"A clergyman can go anywhere. You are privileged. Come to breakfast in the morning: we can talk over matters then."

George Bernard Shaw

CHAPTER XI

One morning the Rev. George Lind received a letter addressed in a handwriting which he did not remember and never thenceforth forgot. Within the envelope he found a dainty little bag made of blue satin, secured by ribbons of the same material. This contained a note written on scented paper, edged with gold, and decorated with a miniature representation of a *pierrot*, sitting cross-legged, conning a book, on the open pages of which appeared the letters L.V. The clergyman recognized the monogram no more than the writing. But as it was evidently from a lady, he felt a pleasant thrill of expectation as he unfolded the paper.

> "Laurel Grove West Kensington
> "Wednesday
>
> "Dear Mr. George
>
> "I have made poor little Lucy believe that Kew is the most heavenly place on earth to spend a May morning so Bob has had to promise to row her down there to-morrow (Thursday) after breakfast and I shall be at home alone from eleven to one this is very short notice I know but opportunities are scarce and another might not present itself for a month.
>
> "Believe me Dear Mr. George
>
> "Yours sincerely
> Lalage Virtue."

The Rev. George became thoughtful, and absently put the note in a little rack over the mantelpiece. Then, recollecting that a prying servant or landlady might misinterpret it, he transferred it to his pocket. After breakfast, having satisfied himself before the mirror that his dress was faultless, and his expression saintly, he went out and travelled by rail from Sloane Square to West Kensington, whence he walked to Laurel Grove. An elderly maid opened the gate. It was a rule with the Rev. George not to look at strange women; and this morning the asceticism which he thought proper to his office was unusually prominent in his thoughts. He did not look up once while the maid conducted him through the shrubbery to the house; and he fully believed that he had not seen at the first glance that she was remarkably plain, as Susanna took care that all her servants should be. Passing by the drawing-room, where he had been on a previous occasion, they went on to a smaller apartment at the back of the house.

"What room is this?" he asked, uneasily.

"Missus's Purjin bodoor, sir," replied the main.

She opened the door; and the clergyman, entering, found himself in a small room, luxuriously decorated in sham Persian, but containing ornaments of all styles and periods, which had been purchased and introduced just as they had caught Susanna's fancy. She was seated on a ottoman, dressed in wide trousers, Turkish slippers, a voluminous sash, a short Greek jacket, a long silk robe with sleeves, and a turban, all of fine soft materials and rare colors. Her face was skilfully painted, and her dark hair disposed so as not to overweight her small head. The clergyman, foolishly resisting a natural impulse to admire her, felt like St. Anthony struggling with the fascination of a disguised devil. He responded to her smile of welcome by a stiff bow.

"Sit down," she said. "You mustnt mind this absurd dress: it belongs to a new piece I am studying. I always study in character. It is the only way to identify myself with my part, you see."

"It seems a very magnificent dress, certainly," said the clergy-man, nervously.

"Thank you for the compliment—"

"No, no," said he, hastily. "I had no such intention."

"Of course not," said Susanna, with a laugh. "It was merely an unpremeditated remark: all compliments are, of course. I know all about that. But do you think it a proper costume?"

"In what sense, may I ask?"

"Is it a correct Eastern dress? I am supposed to be one of the wives of the Caliph Somebody al Something. You have no idea how difficult it is to get a reliable model for a dress before laying out a heap of money on it. This was designed in Paris; but I should like to hear it criticized—chronologically, or whatever you call it—by a scholar."

"I really do not know, Madam. I am not an Orientalist; and my studies take a widely different direction from yours."

"Yes, of course," said Susanna, with a sigh. "But I assure you I often wish for your advice, particularly as to my elocution, which is very faulty. You are such a master of the art."

The clergyman bowed in acceptance of the compliment, and began to take heart; for to receive flattery from ladies in exchange for severe reproof was part of his daily experience.

"I have come here," he said, "to have a very serious conver-sation with you."

"All right, Doctor. Fire away."

This sudden whim of conferring on him a degree in divinity,

and her change of manner—implying that she had been laughing at him before—irritated him. "I presume," he said, "that you are acquainted with the movements of your brother."

"Of Ned?" said Susanna, frowning a little. "No. What should I know about him?"

"He is, I believe, about to be married."

"No!" screamed Susanna, throwing herself back, and making her bangles and ornaments clatter. "Get out, Doctor. You dont mean it."

"Certainly I mean it. It is not my profession to jest. I must also tell you that his marriage will make it quite impossible for you to continue here with my cousin."

"Why? Who is he going to marry?"

"Ahem! He has succeeded in engaging the affections of my sister."

"What! Your sister? Marian Lind?"

"Yes."

Susanna uttered a long whistle, and then, with a conviction and simplicity which prevented even the Rev. George from being shocked, said: "Well, I *am* damned! I know more than one fool of a girl who will be sick and sorry to hear it." She paused, and added carelessly: "I suppose all your people are delighted?"

"I do not know why you should suppose so. We have had no hand in the matter. My sister has followed her own inclinations."

"Indeed! Let me tell you, young man, that your sister might

have gone farther and fared worse."

"Doubtless. However, you will see now how impossible it is that you should remain in your present—that you should continue here, in fact."

"What do you mean?"

"You cannot," said the clergyman, accustomed to be bold and stern with female sinners, "when you are sister-in-law to Miss Lind, live as you are now doing with her cousin."

"Why not?"

"Because it would be a scandal. I will say nothing at present of the sin of it: you will have to account for that before a greater than I."

"Just so, Doctor. You dont mind the sin; but when it comes to a scandal—!"

"I did not say so. I abhor the sin. I have prayed earnestly for your awakening, and shall do so in spite of the unregenerate hardness of heart—"

"Hallo, Doctor! draw it mild, if you please. I am not one of your parishioners, you know. Perhaps that is the reason your prayers for me have not met with much attention. Let us stick to business: you may talk shop as much as you please afterwards. What do you want me to do?"

"To sever your connexion with Marmaduke at once. Believe me, it will not prove so hard a step as it may seem. You have but to ask for strength to do it, and you will find yourself strong. It will profit you even more than poor Marmaduke."

"Will it? I dont see it, Doctor. You think it will profit *you*: that's plain enough. But it wont profit me; it wont profit Bob; and it wont by any means profit the child."

"Not immediately, perhaps, in a worldly sense—"

"That is the sense I mean. Drop all that other stuff: I dont believe in you parsons: you are about the worst lot going, as far as I can see. Just tell me this, Doctor. Your sister is a very nice girl, I have no doubt: she would hardly have snapped up Ned if she wasn't. But why is she to have everything her own way?"

"I do not understand."

"Well, listen. Here is a young woman who has had every chance in life that hick could give her: silk cradles, gold rattles, rank, wealth, schooling, travelling, swell acquaintances, and anything else she chose to ask for. Even when she is fool enough to want to get married, her luck sticks to her, and she catches Ned, who is a man in a thousand—though Lord forbid we should have many of his sort about! Yet she's not satisfied. She wants *me* to give up my establishment just to keep her family in countenance."

"She knows nothing of my visit, I assure you."

"Even if she doesnt, it makes no odds as to the facts. She can go her own way; and I will go mine. I shant want to visit her; and I don't suppose she will visit me. So she need trouble herself no more than if there was no such person as I in the world."

"But you will find that it will be greatly to your advantage to leave this house. It is not our intention that you shall suffer in a pecuniary point of view by doing so. My father is rich—"

"What is that to me? He doesnt want me to go and live with him, does he?"

"You quite misunderstand me. No such idea ever entered—"

"There! go on. I only said that to get a rise out of you, Doctor. How do you make out that I should gain by leaving

George Bernard Shaw

this house?"

"My father is willing to make you some amends for the withdrawal of such portion of Marmaduke's income as you may forfeit by ceasing your connexion with him."

"You have come to buy me out, in fact: is that it? What a clever old man your father must be! Knows the world thoroughly, eh?"

"I hope I have not offended you?"

"Bless you, Doctor! nobody could be offended with you. Suppose I agree to oblige you (you have a very seductive High Church way about you) who is to make Marmaduke amends for such portion of *my* income as our separation will deprive *him* of? Eh? I see that that staggers you a little. If you will just tot up the rent of this house since we have had it; the price of the furniture; our expenses, including my carriage and Marmaduke's horse and the boat; six hundred pounds of debt that he ran up before he settled down with me; and other little things; and then find out from his father how much money he has drawn within the last two years, I think you will find it rather hard to make the two balance. Your uncle is far too good a man to give Marmaduke money to spend on me; but he was not too good to keep me playing in the provinces all through last autumn just to make both ends meet, when I ought to have been taking my holiday. I wish you would tell his mother, your blessed pious Aunt Dora, to send Bob the set of diamonds his grandmother left him, instead of sermons which he never reads."

"I thought Marmaduke had nearly a thousand a year, independently of his father."

"A thousand a year! What is that? And your uncle would stop even that, if he could, to keep it out of my hands. You may tell him that if it didnt come into my hands it would hardly last a week. Only for the child, and the garden, and the sort of quiet life he leads here, he would spend a thousand a month. And look at *my* expenses! Look at my dresses! I suppose you think that people wear cotton velvet and glazed calico on the stage, as Mrs. Siddons did in the old days when they acted by candlelight. Why, between dress and jewellery, I have about two hundred pounds on my back at the present moment; and you neednt think that any manager alive will find dresses to that tune. At the theatre they think me overpaid at fifty pounds a week, although they might shut up the house to-morrow if my name was taken out of the bills. Tell your father that so far from my living on Bob, it is as much as I can do to keep this place going by my work—not to mention the worry of it, which always falls on the woman."

"I certainly had no idea of the case being as you describe," said the clergyman, losing his former assurance. "But would it not then be better for you to separate?"

"Certainly not. I want my house and home. So does he. If an income is rather tight, halving it is a very good way to make it tighter. No: if I left Bob, he would go to the devil; and very likely I should go to the devil, too, and disgrace you in earnest."

"But, my dear madam, consider the disgrace at present!"

"What disgrace? When your sister becomes Mrs. Ned, what will be the difference between her position and mine? Dont look aghast. What will be the difference?"

"Surely you do not suppose that she will dispense with the sacrament of marriage before casting in her lot with your brother!"

"I bet you my next week's salary that you dont get Ned to enter a church. He will be tied up by a registrar. Of course, your sister will have the law of him somehow: she cant help herself. She is not independent; and so she must be guaranteed against his leaving her without bread and butter. *I* can support myself, and may shew Bob a clean pair of heels to-morrow, if I choose. Even if she has money of her own, she darent stick to her freedom for fear of society. *I* snap my fingers at society, and care as little about it as it cares about me; and I have no doubt she would be glad to do the same if she had the pluck. I confess I shouldnt like to make a regular legal bargain of going to live with a man. I dont care to make love a matter of money; it gives it a taste of the harem, or even worse. Poor Bob, meaning to be honorable, offered to buy me in the regular way at St. George's, Hanover Square, before we came to live here; but, of course, I refused, as any decent woman in my circumstances would. Understand me now, Doctor: I dont want to give myself any virtuous airs, or to boast of behaving better than your sister. I know the world; and I know that she will marry Ned just as much because she thinks it right as because she cant help herself. But dont you try to make me swallow any gammon about my disgracing you and so forth. I intend to stay as I am. I can respect myself; and I dont care whether you or your family respect me or not. If you dont approve of me, why! nobody asks you to associate with me. If you want society, you have your own lot to mix with. If I want it, I can fill this house to-morrow. Not with stupid fine ladies, but with really clever people, who are not at all shy of me. Look at me at the present moment! I am receiving a morning visit from the best born and most popular parson in Belgravia. I wonder, Doctor, what your parishioners would think if they could see you now."

"I must confess that I do not understand you at all. You seem to see everything reversed—upside down. You—I—you bewilder me, Miss Conol—"

"Sh! Mademoiselle Lalage Virtue, if you please. Or you may call me Susanna, if you like, since we are as good as related."

"I fear," said the clergyman, blushing, "that we have no common ground on which to argue. I am sorry I have no power to influence you."

"Oh, dont say that. I really like you, Doctor, and would do more for you than most people. If your father had had the cheek to come himself to offer me money, and so forth, I would have put him out of the house double quick; whereas I have listened to you like a lamb. Never mind your hat yet. Have a bottle of champagne with me?"

"Thank you, no."

"Dont you drink at all?"

"No."

"You should. It would give a fillip to your sermons. Let me send you a case of champagne. Promise to drink a bottle every Sunday in the vestry before you come out to preach, and I will take a pew for the season in your church. Thats good of me, isnt it?"

"I must go," said the Rev. George, rising, after hastily pretending to look at his watch. "Will you excuse me?"

"Nonsense," she said, rising also, and slipping her hand through his arm to detain him. "Wait and have some luncheon. Why, Doctor, I really think youre afraid of me. *Do* stay."

"Impossible. I have much business which I am bound—Pray, let me go," pleaded the clergyman, piteously, ineffectually struggling with Susanna, who had now got his arm against her breast. "You must be mad!" he cried, drops of sweat breaking out on his brow as he felt himself being pulled helplessly toward the ottoman. She got her knee on it at last; and he made a desperate effort to free himself.

"Oh, how rough you are!" she exclaimed in her softest voice, adroitly tumbling into the seat as if he had thrown her down, and clinging to his arms; so that it was as much as he could do to keep his feet as he stooped over her, striving to get upright. At which supreme moment the door was opened by

Marmaduke, who halted on the threshold to survey the two reproachfully for a moment. Then he said:

"George: I'm astonished at you. I have not much opinion of parsons as a rule; but I really did think that *you* were to be depended on."

"Marmaduke," said the clergyman, colouring furiously, and almost beside himself with shame and anger: "you know perfectly well that I am actuated in coming here by no motive unworthy of my profession. You misunderstand what you have seen. I will not hear my calling made a jest of."

"Quite right, Doctor," said Susanna, giving him a gentle pat of encouragement on the shoulder. "Defend the cloth, always. I was only asking him to stay to lunch, Bob. Cant you persuade him?"

"Do, old fellow," said Marmaduke. "Come! you must: I havnt had a chat with you for ever so long. I'm really awfully sorry I interrupted you. What on earth did you make Susanna rig herself out like that for?"

"Hold your tongue, Bob. Mr. George has nothing to do with my being in character. This is what came last night in the box: I could not resist trying it on this morning. I am Zobeida, the light of the harem, if you please. I must have your opinion of the rouge song, Doctor. Observe. This is a powder puff: I suppose you never saw such a thing before. I am making up my face for a visit of the Sultan; and I am apologizing to the audience for using cosmetics. The original French is improper; so I will give you the English version, by the celebrated Robinson, the cleverest adapter of the day:

'Poor odalisques in captive thrall
Must never let their charms pall:
If they get the sack
They ne'er come back;
For the Bosphorus is the boss for all

In this harem, harem, harem, harem, harum scarum place.'

Intellectual, isnt it?"

Susanna, whilst singing, executed a fantastic slow dance, stopping at certain points to clink a pair of little cymbals attached to her ankles, and to look for a moment archly at the clergyman.

"No," he said, hurt and offended into a sincerity of manner which compelled them to respect him for the first time, "I will not stay; and I am very sorry I came." And he left the room, his cheeks tingling. Marmaduke followed him to the gate. "Come and look us up soon again, old fellow," he said.

"Marmaduke," said the clergyman: "you are travelling as fast as you can along the road to Hell."

As he hurried away, Marmaduke leaned against the gate and made the villas opposite echo his laughter.

"On my soul, it's a shame," said he, when he returned to the house. "Poor old George!"

"He found no worse than he had made up his mind to find," said Susanna. "What right has he to come into my house and take it for granted, to my face, that I am a disgrace to his sister? One would think I was a common woman from the streets."

"Pshaw! What does he know? He is only a molly-coddling parson, poor fellow. He will give them a rare account of you when he goes back."

"Let him," said Susanna. "He can tell them how little I care for their opinion, anyhow."

The Rev. George took the next train to the City, and went to the offices of the Electro-Motor Company, where he found his father. They retired together to the board-room, which was

George Bernard Shaw

unoccupied just then.

"I have been to that woman," said the clergyman.

"Well, what does she say?"

"She is an entirely abandoned person. She glories in her shame. I have never before met with such an example of complete and unconscious depravity. Yet she is not unattractive. There is a wonderfully clever refinement even in her coarseness which goes far to account for her influence over Marmaduke."

"No doubt; but apart from her personal charms, about which I am not curious, is she willing to assist us?"

"No. I could make no impression on her at all."

"Well, it cannot be helped. Did you say anything about Conolly's selling his interest here and leaving the country?"

"No," said the clergyman, struck with a sense of remissness. "I forgot that. The fact is, I hardly had the oppor—"

"Never mind. It is just as well that you did not: it might have made mischief."

"I do not think it is of the least use to pursue her with any further overtures. Besides, I really could not undertake to conduct them."

"May I ask," said Mr. Lind, turning on him suddenly, "what objection you have to Marian's wishes being consulted in this matter?"

The Rev. George recoiled, speechless.

"I certainly think," said Mr. Lind, more smoothly, "that Marian might have trusted to my indulgence instead of hurrying away to a lodging and writing the news in all directions. But I must say I have received some very nice letters about it. Jasper is quite congratulatory. The *Court Journal* has a paragraph this week alluding to it with quite good taste. Conolly is a very remarkable man; and, as the *Court Journal* truly enough remarks, he has won a high place in the republic of art and science. As a Liberal, I cannot say that I disapprove of Marian's choice; and I really think that it will be looked on in society as an interesting one."

Mr. Lind's son eyed him dubiously for quite a long time. Then he said, slowly, "Am I to understand that I may now speak of the marriage as a recognized thing?"

"Why not, pray?"

"Of course, since you wish it, and it cannot be helped—" The clergyman again looked at his father, still more dubiously. He saw in his eye that there would be a quarrel if the interview lasted much longer. So he said "I must go home now. I have to write my sermon for next Sunday."

"Very good. Do not let me detain you. Good-bye."

The Rev. George returned to his rooms quite dazed by the novelty of his sensations. He had always respected his father beyond other men; and now he knew that his father did not deserve his respect in the least. That was one conviction uprooted. And Susanna had done something to him—he did not exactly know what; but he felt altogether a different man from the clergyman of the day before. He had come face to face with what he called Vice for the first time, and found it not at all what he had supposed it to be. He had believed that he knew it to be most dangerously attractive to the physical, but utterly repugnant to the moral sense; and such fascination he was prepared to resist to the utmost. But he was attacked in just the opposite way, and thereby so thrown off his guard that he did not know he was attacked at all; so that he told himself vaingloriously that the shafts of the enemy had fallen harmlessly from his breastplate of faith. For he was not in the least

George Bernard Shaw

charmed by Susanna's person. He had detected the paint on her cheeks, and had noted with aversion a certain unhealthy bloat in her face, and an alcoholic taint in her breath. He exulted in the consciousness that he had been genuinely disgusted, not as a matter of duty, but unaffectedly, as a matter of simple nature. What interested him in her was her novel and bold moral attitude, her self-respect in the midst of her sin, her striking arguments in favor of an apparently indefensible course of life. Hers was no common case of loose living, he felt: there was a soul to be saved there, if only Heaven would raise her up a friend in some man absolutely proof against the vulgar fascination of her prettiness. He began to imagine a certain greatness of character about her, a capacity for heroic repentance as well as for heroic sin. Before long he was amusing himself by thinking how it might have gone with her if she had him for her counsellor instead of a gross and thoughtless rake like Marmaduke.

It is not necessary to follow the wild goose chase which the Rev. George's imagination ran from this starting-point to the moment when he was suddenly awakened, by an unmistakable symptom, to the fact that he was being outwitted and beglamoured, like the utter novice he was, by a power which he believed to be the devil. He rushed to the little oratory he had arranged with a screen in the corner of his sitting-room, and prayed aloud, long and earnestly. But the hypnotizing process did not tranquilize him as usual. It excited him, and led him finally to a passionate appeal for pardon and intercession to a statuet of the Virgin Mother, of whom he was a very devout adorer. He had always regarded himself as her especial champion in the Church of England; and now he had been faithless to her, and indelicate into the bargain. And yet, in spite of his contrition, he felt that he was having a tremendous spiritual experience, which he would not for worlds have missed. The climax of it was the composition of his Sunday sermon, the labor of which secured him a sound sleep that night. It was duly delivered on the following Sunday morning in this form:

"Dearly beloved Brethren: In the twenty-third verse of the third chapter of St. Mark's gospel, we find this question: '*How can Satan cast out Satan?*' How can Satan cast out Satan? If you will read what follows, you will perceive that that question was not answered. My brethren, it is unanswerable: it never has been, and it never can be answered.

"In these latter days, when the power of Satan has become so vast, when his empire and throne tower in our midst so that the faithful are cast down by the exceeding great shadow thereof, and when temples innumerable are open for his worship, it is no strange thing that many faint-hearted ones should give half their hearts to Beelzebub, and should hope by the prince of devils to cast out devils. Yes, this is what is taking place daily around us. Oh, you, who seek to excuse this book to infidel philosophers by shewing with how much facility a glib tongue may reconcile it with their so-called science, I tell you that it is science and not the Bible that shall need that apology in the great day of wrath. And, therefore, I would have you, my brethren, earnestly discountenance all endeavors to justify the Word of God by explaining it in conformity with the imaginations of the men of science. How can Satan cast out Satan? He cannot; but he can lead you into the sin of adding to and of taking from the words of this book. He can add plagues unto you, and take away your part out of the holy city.

"In this great London which we inhabit we are come upon evil day's. The rage of the blasphemer, the laugh at the scoffer, the heartless lip-service of the worldling, and the light dalliance of the daughters of music, are offered every hour upon a thousand Baal-altars within this very parish. I would ask some of you who spend your evenings in the playhouses which multiply around us like weeds sown in the rank soil of human frailty, what justification you make to yourselves when you are alone in the watches of the night, and your conscience saith, '*What went ye out for to see?*' You will then complain of the bitterness of life, and prate of the refining influences of music; of the help to spiritual-mindedness given by the exhibition on the public stage of mockeries of God's world, wherein some pitiful temporal triumph of simulated virtue in the last act is the apology for the vicious trifling that has gone before. And in whom do you there see typified that virtue which you should shield in your hearts from the contamination of the theatre? Is it not in some woman whose private life is the scandalous matter of your whispered conversations, and whose shameless face smirks at you from the windows of those picture-shops which are a disgrace to our national morality? Is it from such as she that you will learn to be spiritual-minded? Does she appear before your carnal crowds repentant, her forehead covered with ashes, her limbs covered with sackcloth? No! Her brow is glowing with unquenchable fire to kindle the fuel that the devil has hidden in your hearts. Her raiment is cloth of gold; and she is not covered with it. Naked and unashamed, she smiles and weeps in mockery of the virtue which you would persuade yourselves that she represents to you. Will you learn spiritual-mindedness from the sight of her eyes, from the sound of her mouth, from the measure of her steps, or from the music and the dancing that cease not within the doors of her temple? How can Satan cast out Satan? Whom think ye to deceive by whitening the sepulchre? Is it yourselves? The devil has blinded you already. Is it God? Who shall hide anything from Him? I tell you that he who makes the pursuit of virtue a luxury, and takes refuge from sin, not before the altar, but in the playhouse, is casting out devils by Beelzebub, the prince of the devils.

"As I look about me in this church; I see many things intended to give pleasure to the carnal eye. Were the cost of all these dainty robes, this delicate headgear, these clouds of silk, of satin, of lace, and of sparkling jewels, were the price of these things brought into the Church's treasury, how loudly might the Gospel resound in lands between whose torrid shores and the tropical sun the holy shade of Calvary has not yet fallen! But, you will say, it is a good thing to be comely in the house of the Lord. The sight of what is beautiful elevates the mind. Uncleanness is a vice. This, then, is how you will war with uncleanness. Not by prayer and holy living. Not by pouring of your superfluity into the lap of the poor, and entering by the strait gate upon the narrow path in a garment without seam. No. By the dead and damning gold; by the purple and by the scarlet; by the brightness of the eyes that is born of new wine; by the mincing gait and the gloved fingers; and by the musk and civet instead of the myrrh and frankincense: by these things are you fain to purge your uncleanness. And will they suffice? Can Satan cast out Satan? Beware! *'For though thou wash thee with nitre and take thee much soap, yet thine iniquity is marked before me, saith the Lord God.'* There shall come a day when your lace and feathers shall hang on you as heavy as your chains of gold, to drag you down to him in whose name you have thought to cast out devils. Do not think that these things are harmless vanities. Nothing can fill the human heart and be harmless. If your thoughts be not of God, they will keep your minds distraught from His grace as effectually as the blackest broodings of crime. *'Can a maid forget her ornaments, or a bride her attire? Yet my people have forgotten me days without number, saith the Lord God.'* Yes, your minds are too puny to entertain the full worship of God: do you think they are spacious enough to harbor the worship of Baal side by side with it? Much less dare you pretend that the Baal altar is erected for the honor of God, that you may come into His presence comely and clean. It is but a few days since I stood in the presence of a woman who boasted to me that she bore upon her the value of two hundred pounds of our money. I cared little for the value of money that was upon her. But what shall be said of the weight of sin her attire represented? For, those costly garments were the wages of sin—of hardened, shameless, damnable sin. Yet there is not before me a finer dress or a fairer face. Will you, my sisters, trust to the comeliness of visage and splendor of raiment in which such a woman as this can outshine you? Will you continue to cast out your devils by Beelzebub, the prince of devils? Be advised whilst there is yet time. Ask yourself again and again, how can Satan cast out Satan?

"When sin is committed in a great city for wages, is there no fault on the side of those who pay the wages? There is more than fault: there is crime. I trust there are few among you who have done such crime. But I know full well that it may be said of London to-day '*Thou art full of stirs, a joyous city: thy slain men are not slain with the sword, nor dead in battle.*' No. Our young men are slain by the poison of Beelzebub, the prince of the devils. Nor is the crafty old subterfuge lacking here. There are lost ones in this town who say, 'It is by our means that virtue is preserved to the rich: it is we who appease the wicked rage which would otherwise wreck society.' There are men who boast that they have brought their sins only to the houses of shame, and that they have respected purity in the midst of their foulness. 'Such things must be,' they say: 'let us alone, lest a worse thing ensue.' When they are filled full with sin, they cry 'Lo! our appetite has gone from us and we are clean.' They are willing to slake lust with satiety, but not to combat it with prayer. They tread one woman into the mire, and excuse themselves because the garment of her sister is spotless. How vain is this lying homage to virtue! How can Satan cast out Satan?

"Oh, my brethren, this hypocrisy is the curse and danger of our age. The Atheist, no longer an execration, an astonishment, a curse, and a reproach, poses now as the friend of man and the champion of right. Those who incur the last and most terrible curse in this book, do so in the name of that truth for which they profess to be seeking. Art, profanely veiling its voluptuous nakedness with the attributes of religion, disguises folly so subtly that it seems like virtue in the slothful eyes of those who neglect continually to watch and pray. The vain woman puts on her ornaments to do honor to her Creator's handiwork: the lustful man casts away his soul that society may be kept clean: there is not left in these latter days a sin that does not pretend to work the world's salvation, nor a man who flatters not himself that the sin of one may be the purging of many. To such I say, Look to your own soul: of no other shall any account be demanded of you. A day shall come in which a fire shall be kindled among your gods. The Lord shall array Himself with this land as a shepherd putteth on his garment. Be sure that then if ye shall say 'I am a devil; but I have cast out many devils,' He will reply unto you, How can Satan cast out Satan? Who shall prompt you to an answer to that question? Nay, though in His boundless mercy He give you a thousand years to search, and spread before you all the books of science and sociology in which you were wont to find excuses for sin, what will it avail you? Will a scoff, or a quibble over a doubtful passage, serve your turn? No. You cannot scoff whilst your tongue cleaves to the roof of your mouth for fear, and there will be no passage doubtful in all the Scriptures on that day; for the light of the Lord's countenance will be over all things."

BOOK III

CHAPTER XII

One Sunday afternoon, as the sun was making rainbows in the cloud of spray thrown from the fountain in Kew Gardens, Sholto Douglas appeared there amongst the promenaders on the banks of the pond. He halted on the steps leading down to the basin, gazing idly at the waterfowl paddling at his feet. A lady in a becoming grey dress came to the top of the steps, and looked curiously at him. Somehow aware of this, he turned indifferently, as if to leave, and found that the lady was Marian. Her ripened beauty, her perfect self-possession, a gain in her as of added strength and wisdom, and a loss in her as of gentleness outgrown and timidity overcome, dazzled him for a moment—caused a revulsion in him which he half recognized as the beginning of a dangerous passion. His former love for her suddenly appeared boyish and unreal to him; and this ruin of a once cherished illusion cost him a pang. Meanwhile, there she was, holding out her hand and smiling with a cool confidence in the success of her advance that would have been impossible to Marian Lind.

"How do you do?" she said.

"Thank you: I am fairly well. You are quite well, I hope?"

"I am in rude health. I hardly knew you at first."

"Am I altered?"

"You are growing stout."

"Indeed? Time has not been so bounteous to me as to you."

"You mean that I am stouter than you?" She laughed; and the sound startled him. He got from it an odd impression that her soul was gone. But he hastened to protest.

"No, no. You know I do not. I meant that you have achieved the impossible—altered for the better."

"I am glad you think so. I cling to my good looks desperately now that I am growing matronly. How is Mrs. Douglas?"

"She is quite well, thank you. Mr. Conolly is, I trust—"

"He is suffering from Eucalyptus on the brain at present. Do not trouble yourself to maintain that admirable expression of shocked sadness. Eucalyptus means gum-tree; and Ned is at present studying the species somewhere in the neighborhood. He came here with that object: he never goes anywhere without an object. He wants to plant Eucalyptuses round some new works where the people suffer from ague."

"Oh! You mean that he is here in the gardens."

"Yes. I left him among the trees, as I prefer the flowers. I want to see the lilies. There used to be some in a hot-house, or rather a hot bath, near this."

"That is it on our right. May I go through it with you?"

"Just as you please."

"Thank you. It is a long time since we last met, is it not?"

"More than a year. Fifteen months. I have not seen you since I was married."

Douglas looked rather foolish at this. He was fatter, lazier, altogether less tenacious of his dignity than of old; and his embarrassment brought out the change strikingly. Marian liked him all the better for it; he was less imposing; but he was more a man and less a mere mask. At last, reddening a little, he said, "I remember our last meeting very well. We were very angry then: I was infuriated. In fact, when I recognized you a minute ago, I was not quite sure that you would renew our acquaintance."

"I had exactly the same doubt about you."

"A very unnecessary doubt. Not a sincere one, I am afraid. You know too well that your least beck will bring me to you at any time."

"Dont you think we had better not begin that. I generally repeat my conversations to Ned. Not that he will mind, if you dont."

Douglas now felt at his ease and in his clement. He was clearly welcome to philander. Recovering his poise at once, he began, in his finest voice, "You need not chide me. There can be no mistake on my part now. You can entangle me without fear; and I can love without hope. Ned is an unrepealed statute of Forbiddance. Go on, Mrs. Conolly. Play with me: it will amuse you. And—spiritless wretch that I am!—it will help me to live until you throw me away, crushed again."

"You seem to have been quite comfortable without me: at least you look extremely well. I suspect you are becoming a little lazy and attached to your dinner. Your old haughtiness seems to have faded into a mere habit. It used to be the most active principle in you. Are you quite sure that nobody else has been helping you to live, as you call it?"

"Helping me to forget, you mean. No, not one. Time has taught me the way to vegetate; and so I no longer need to live. As you have remarked, I have habits, not active principles. But one at least of these principles is blossoming again even as I speak. If I could only live as that lily lives now!"

"In a warm bath?"

"No. Floating on the surface of a quiet pool, looking up into your eyes, with no memory for the past, no anticipation of the future."

"Delightful! especially for me. I think we had better go and look for Ned."

"Were I in his place I would not be absent from your side now—or ever."

"That is to say, if you were in his place, you wouldnt be in his place—among the gum trees. Perhaps you would be right."

"He is the only man I have ever stooped to envy."

"You have reason to," said Marian, suddenly grave.

"I envy him sometimes myself. What would you give to be never without a purpose, never with a regret, to regard life as a succession of objects each to be accomplished by so many days' work; to take your pleasure in trifling lazily with the consciousness of possessing a strong brain; to study love, family affection, and friendship as a doctor studies breathing or digestion; to look on disinterestedness as either weakness or hypocrisy, and on death as a mere transfer of your social function to some member of the next generation?"

"I could achieve all that, if I would, at the cost of my soul. I would not for worlds be such a man, save on one condition."

"To wit?"

"That only as such could I win the woman I loved."

"Oh, you would not think so much of an insignificant factor like love if you were Ned."

"May I ask, do you, too, think of love as 'an insignificant factor'?"

"I? Oh, I am not a sociologist. Besides, I have never been in love."

"What! You have never been in love?"

"Not the real, romantic, burning, suicidal love your sonnets used to breathe."

"Then you do not know what love is."

"Do you?"

"You should know whether I do or not."

"Should I? Then I conclude that you do not. You are growing stout. Your dress is not in the least neglected. I am certain you enjoy life thoroughly. No, you have never known love in all its novelistic-poetic outrageousness. That respectable old passion is a myth."

"You look for signs that only children shew. When an oak dies, it does not wither and fall at once as a sapling does. Perhaps you will one day know what it is to love."

"Perhaps so."

"In any case, you will be able to boast of having inspired the passion."

"I hope so—at least, I mean that it is all nonsense. Do look at that vegetable lobster of a thing, that cactus."

"In order to set off its ugliness properly, you should see

yourself against the background of palms, with that great fan-like leaf for a halo, and—"

"Thank you. I see it all in my mind's eye by your eloquent description. You are quite right in supposing that I like compliments; but I am particular about their quality; and I dont need to be told I am pretty in comparison with a hideous cactus. You would not have condescended to make such a speech long ago. You are changed."

"Not toward you, on my honor."

"I did not mean that: I meant toward yourself."

"I am glad you have taken even that slender note of me. I find you somewhat changed, too."

"I did not know that I shewed it; but it is true. I feel as if Marian Lind was a person whom I knew once, but whom I should hardly know again."

"The change in me has not produced that effect. I feel as though Marian Lind were the history of my life."

"You have become quite a master of the art of saying pretty things. You are nearly as glib at it as Ned."

"We have the same incentive to admiration."

"The same! You do not suppose that Ned pays *me* compliments. He never did such a thing in his life. No: I first discovered his talent in that direction at Palermo, where I surprised him in an animated discourse with the dark-eyed daughter of an innkeeper there. That was the first conversation in Italian I succeeded in following. A week later I could understand the language almost as well as he. However, dont let us waste the whole afternoon talking stuff. I want to ask you about your mother. I should greatly like to call upon her; but she has never made me any sign since my marriage; and

Mrs. Leith Fairfax tells me that she never allows my name to be mentioned to her. I thought she was fond of me."

"So she was. But she has never forgiven you for making me suffer as you did. You see she has more spirit than I. She would be angered if she saw me now tamely following the triumphal chariot of my fair tyrant."

"Seriously, do you think, if I made a raid on Manchester Square some morning, I could coax back her old feeling for me?"

"I think you will be quite safe in calling, at all events. Tell me what day you intend to venture. I know my mother will not oppose me if I shew that I wish you to be kindly received."

"Most disinterested of you. Thank you: I will fail or succeed on my own merits, not on your recommendation. You must not say a word to her about me or my project."

"If you command me not to—"

"I do command you."

"I must obey. But I fear that the more submissive I am, the more imperious you will become."

"Very likely. And now look along that avenue to the left. Do you see a man in a brown suit, with straw hat to match, walking towards us at a regular pace, and keeping in a perfectly straight course? He looks at everybody he passes as if he were counting them."

"He is looking back at somebody now, as if he had missed the number."

"Just so; but that somebody is a woman; doubtless a pretty one, probably dark. You recognize him, I see. There is a frost come over you which convinces me that you are preparing to receive him in your old ungracious way. I warn you that I am accustomed to see Ned made much of. He has caught sight of us."

"And has just remarked that there is a man talking to his wife."

"Quite right. See his speculative air! Now he no longer attends to us. He is looking at the passers-by as before. That means that he has recognized you, and has stowed the observation compactly away in his brain, to be referred to when he comes up to us."

"So much method must economize his intellect very profitably. How do you do, Mr. Conolly? It is some time since we have had the pleasure of meeting."

"Glad to see you, Mr. Douglas. We have been away all the winter. Are you staying in London?"

"Yes."

"I hope you will spend an occasional hour with us at Holland Park."

"You are very kind. Thank you: yes, if Mrs. Conolly will permit me."

"I should make you come home with us now," said Marian, "but for this Sunday being a special occasion. Nelly McQuinch is to spend the evening with us; and as I have not seen her since we came back, I must have her all to myself. Come next Sunday, if you care to."

"Do," said Conolly. "Half past three is our Sunday hour. If you cannot face that, we are usually at home afterwards the entire evening. Marian: we have exactly fifteen minutes to catch our train."

"Oh! let us fly. If we miss it, Nelly will be kept waiting half an hour."

Then they parted, Douglas promising to come to them on that day week.

"Dont you think he is growing very fat?" said she, as they walked away.

"Yes. He is beginning to take the world easily. He does not seem to be making much of his life."

"What matter, so long as he enjoys it?"

"Pooh! He doesnt know what enjoyment means."

They said nothing further until they were in the train, where Marian sat looking listlessly through the window, whilst Conolly, opposite, reclining against the cushions, looked thoughtfully at her.

"Ned," said she, suddenly.

"My dear."

"Do you know that Sholto is more infatuated about me than ever?"

"Naturally. You are lovelier than when he last saw you."

"You are nearly as complimentary as he," said Marian, blushing with a gratification which she was very unwilling to betray. "He noticed it sooner than you. I discovered it myself in the glass before either of you."

"No doubt you did. What station is this?"

"I dont know." Then, raising her voice so as to be overheard, she exclaimed "Here is a stupid man coming into our carriage."

A young man entered the compartment, and, after one glance at Marian, who turned her back on him impatiently, spent the remainder of the journey making furtive attempts to catch a second glimpse of her face. Conolly looked a shade graver at his wife's failure in perfect self-control; but he by no means shared her feelings toward the intrusive passenger. Marian and he were in different humors; and he did not wish to be left alone with her.

As they walked from Addison Road railway station to their house, Conolly mused in silence with his eyes on the gardens by the way. Marian, who wished to talk, followed his measured steps with impatience.

"Let me take your arm, Ned: I cannot keep up with you."

"Certainly."

"I hope I am not inconveniencing you," she said, after a further interval of silence.

"Hm—no."

"I am afraid I am. It does not matter. I can get on by myself."

"Arm in arm is such an inconvenient and ridiculous mode of locomotion—you need not struggle in the public street: now that you have got my arm you shall keep it—I say it is such an inconvenient and ridiculous mode of locomotion that if you were any one else I should prefer to wheel you home in a barrow. Our present mode of proceeding would be inexcusable if I were a traction-engine, and you my tender."

"Then let me go. What will the people think if they see a great engineer violating the laws of mechanics by dragging his wife by the arm?"

"They will appreciate my motives; and, in fact, if you watch them, you will detect a thinly-disguised envy in their countenances. I violate the laws of mechanics—to use your own sarcastic phrase—for many reasons. I like to be envied when there are solid reasons for it. It gratifies my vanity to be seen in this artistic quarter with a pretty woman on my arm. Again, the sense of possessing you is no longer an abstraction when I hold you bodily, and feel the impossibility of keeping step with you. Besides, Man, who was a savage only yesterday, has his infirmities, and finds a poetic pleasure in the touch of the woman he loves. And I may add that you have been in such a bad temper all the afternoon that I suspect you of an itching to box my ears, and therefore feel safer with your arm in my custody."

"Oh! *Indeed* I have not been in a bad temper. I have been most anxious to spend a happy day."

"And I have been placidly reflective, and not anxious at all. Is that what has provoked you?"

"I am not provoked. But you might tell me what your reflections are about."

"They would fill volumes, if I could recollect them."

"You must recollect some of them. From the time we left the station until a moment ago, when we began to talk, you were pondering something with the deepest seriousness. What was it?"

"I forget."

"Of course you forget—just because I want to know. What a crowded road this is!" She disengaged herself from his arm; and this time he did not resist her.

"That reminds me of it. The crowd consists partly of people going to the pro-Cathedral. The pro-Cathedral contains an altar. An altar suggests kneeling on hard stone; and that brings me to the disease called 'housemaids' knee,' which was the subject of my reflections."

"A pleasant subject for a fine Sunday! Thank you. I dont want to hear any more."

"But you will hear more of it; for I am going to have the steps of our house taken away and replaced by marble, or slate, or something that can be cleaned with a mop and a pail of water in five minutes."

"Why?"

"My chain of thought began at the door steps we have passed, all whitened beautifully so as to display every footprint, and all representing an expenditure of useless, injurious labor in hearthstoning, that ought to madden an intelligent housemaid. I dont think our Armande is particularly intelligent; but I am resolved to spare her knees and her temper in future by banishing hearthstone from our establishment forever. I shudder to think that I have been walking upon those white steps and flag ways of ours every day without awakening to a sense of their immorality."

"I cannot understand why you are always disparaging Armande. And I hate an ill-kept house front. None of our housemaids ever objected to hearthstoning, or were any the worse for it."

"No. They would not have gained anything by objecting: they would only have lost their situations. You need not fear for your house front. I will order a porch with porphyry steps and alabaster pillars to replace
your beloved hearthstone."

"Yes. That will be clever. Do you know how easy it is to stain marble? Armande will be on her knees all day with a bottle of turpentine and a bit of flannel."

"You are thinking of inkstains, Marian. You forget that it does

George Bernard Shaw

not rain ink, and that Nelly will hardly select the porch to write her novels in."

"Lots of people bring ink on a doorstep. Tax collectors and gasmen carry bottles in their pockets."

"Ask them into the drawing-room when they call, my dear; or, better still, dont pay them, so that they will have no need to write a receipt. Let me remind you that ink shews as much on white hearthstone as it can possibly do on marble. Yet extensive disfigurements of steps from the visits of tax collectors are not common."

"Now, Ned, you know that you are talking utter nonsense."

"Yes, my dear. I think I perceive Nelly looking out of the window for us. Here she is at the door."

Marian hastened forward and embraced her cousin. Miss McQuinch looked older; and her complexion was drier than before. But she had apparently begun to study her appearance; for her hat and shoes were neat and even elegant, which they had never been within Marian's previous experience of her.

"*You* are not changed in the least," she said, as she gave Conolly her hand. "I have just been wondering at the alteration in Marian. She has grown lovely."

"I have been telling her so all day, in the vain hope of getting her into a better temper. Come into the drawing-room. Have you been waiting for us long?"

"About fifteen minutes. I have been admiring your organ. I should have tried the piano; but I did not know whether that was allowable on Sunday."

"Oh! Why did you not pound it to your heart's content? Ned scandalizes the neighbors every Sunday by continually playing. Armande: dinner as soon as possible, please."

"I like this house. It is exactly my idea of a comfortable modern home."

"You must stay long enough to find out its defects," said Conolly. "We read your novel at Verona; but we could not agree as to which characters you meant to be taken as the good ones."

"That was only Ned's nonsense," said Marian. "Most novels are such rubbish! I am sure you will be able to live by writing just as well as Mrs. Fairfax can." Conolly shewed Miss McQuinch his opinion of this unhappy remark by a whimsical glance, which she repudiated by turning sharply away from him, and speaking as affectionately as she could to Marian.

After dinner they returned to the drawing-room, which ran from the front to the back of the house. Marian opened a large window which gave access to the garden, and sat down with Elinor on a little terrace outside. Conolly went to the organ.

"May I play a voluntary while you talk?" he asked. "I shall not scandalize any one: the neighbors think all music sacred when it is played on the organ."

"We have a nice view of the sunset from here," said Marian, in a low voice, turning her forehead to the cool evening breeze.

"Stuff!" said Elinor. "We didnt come here to talk about the sunset, and what a pretty house you have, and so forth. I want to know—good heavens! what a thundering sound that organ makes!"

"Please dont say anything about it to him: he likes it," said Marian. "When he wishes to exalt himself, he goes to it and makes it roar until the whole house shakes. Whenever he feels an emotional impulse, he vents it at the organ or the piano, or by singing. When he stops, he is satisfied; his mind is cleared; and he is in a good-humored, playful frame of mind, such as *I* can gratify."

"But you were always very fond of music. Dont you ever play together, as we used to do; or sing to one another's accompaniments?"

"I cannot. I hardly ever touch the piano when he is in the house."

"Why? Are you afraid of preventing him from having his turn?"

"No: it is not so much that. But—it sounds very silly—if I attempt to play or sing in his presence, I become so frightfully nervous that I hardly know what I am doing. I know he does not like my singing."

"Are you sure that is not merely your fancy? It sounds very like it."

"No. At first I used to play a good deal for him, knowing that he was fond of music, and fancying—poor fool that I was! [here Marian spoke so bitterly that Nelly turned and looked hard at her] that it was part of a married woman's duty in a house to supply music after dinner. At that time he was working hard at his business; and he spent so much time in the city that he had to give up playing himself. Besides, we were flying all about England opening those branch offices, and what not. He always took me with him; and I really enjoyed it, and took quite an interest in the Company. When we were in London, although I was so much alone in the daytime, I was happy in anticipating our deferred honeymoon. Then the time for that paradise came. Ned said that the Company was able to walk by itself at last, and that he was going to have a long holiday after his dry-nursing of it. We went first to Paris, where we heard all the classical concerts that were given while we were there. I found that he never tired of listening to orchestral music; and yet he never ceased grumbling at it. He thought nothing of the great artists in Paris. Then we went for a tour through Brittany; and there, in spite of his classical tastes, he used to listen to the peasants' songs and write them down. He seemed to like folk songs of all kinds, Irish, Scotch, Russian, German, Italian, no matter where from. So one evening, at a lodging where there was a piano, I played for him that old arrangement of Irish melodies—you know—'Irish Diamonds,' it is called."

"Oh Lord! Yes, I remember. 'Believe me if all,' with variations."

"Yes. He thought I meant it in jest: he laughed at it, and played a lot of ridiculous variations to burlesque it. I didnt tell him that I had been in earnest: perhaps you can imagine how I felt about it. Then, after that, in Italy, he got permission—or rather bought it—to try the organ in a church. It was growing dusk; I was tired with walking; and somehow between the sense of repose, and the mysterious twilight in the old church, I was greatly affected by his playing. I thought it must be part of some great mass or symphony; and I felt how little I knew about music, and how trivial my wretched attempts must appear to him when he had such grand harmonies at his fingers' ends. But he soon stopped; and when I was about to tell him how I appreciated his performance, he said, 'What an abominable instrument a bad organ is!' I had thought it beautiful, of course. I asked him what he had been playing. I said was it not by Mozart; and then I saw his eyebrows go up; so I added, as a saving clause, that perhaps it was something of his own. 'My dear girl,' said he, 'it was only an *entr'acte* from an opera of Donizetti's.' He was carrying my shawl at the time; and he wrapped it about my shoulders in the tenderest manner as he said this, and made love to me all the evening to console me. In his opinion, the greatest misfortune that can happen anyone is to make a fool of oneself; and whenever I do it, he pets me in the most delicate manner, as if I were a child who had just got a tumble. When we settled down here and got the organ, he began to play constantly, and I used to practise the piano in the daytime so as to have duets with him. But though he was always ready to play whenever I proposed it, he was quite different then from what he was when he played by himself. He was all eyes and ears, and the moment I played a

George Bernard Shaw

wrong note he would name the right one. Then I generally got worse and stopped. He never lost his patience or complained; but I used to feel that he was urging me on, or pulling me back, or striving to get me to do something which I could not grasp. Then he would give me up in despair, and play on mechanically from the notes before him, thinking of something else all the time. I practised harder, and tried again. I thought at first I had succeeded; because our duets went so smoothly and we were always so perfectly together. But I discovered—by instinct I believe—that instead of having a musical treat, he was only trying to please me. He thought I liked playing duets with him; and accordingly he used to sit down beside me and accompany me faithfully, no matter how I chose to play."

"Dear me! Why doesnt he get Rubinstein to play with him, since he is so remarkably fastidious?"

"It is not so much mechanical skill that I lack; but there is something—I cannot tell what it is. I found it out one night when we were at Mrs. Saunders's. She is an incurable flirt; and she was quite sure that she had captivated Ned, who is always ready to make love to anyone that will listen to him."

"A nice sort of man to be married to!"

"He only does it to amuse himself. He does not really care for them: I almost wish he did, sometimes; but it is often none the less provoking. What is worse, no amount of flirtation on my part would make *him* angry. What happened at Mrs. Saunders's was this. The Scotts, of Putney, were there; and the first remark Ned made to me was, 'Who is the woman that knows how to walk?' It was Mrs. Scott: you know you used to say she moved like a panther. Afterward Mrs. Scott sang 'Caller Herrin' in that vulgar Scotch accent that leaks out occasionally in her speech, with Ned at the piano. Everybody came crowding in to listen; and there was great applause. I cannot understand it: she is as hard and matter-of-fact as a woman can be: I dont believe the expression in her singing comes one bit from true feeling. I heard Ned say to her, 'Thank you, Mrs. Scott: no Englishwoman has the secret of singing a ballad as you have it.' I knew very well what that meant. *I* have not the secret. Well, Mrs. Scott came over to me and said 'Mr. Conolly is a very *pair*tinaceous man. He persuaded me into shewing him the way the little song is sung in Scotland; and I stood up without thinking. And see now, I have been *rag*uilarly singing a song in company for the first time in my life.' Of course, it was a ridiculous piece of affectation. Ned talked about Mrs. Scott all the way home, and played 'Caller Herrin' four times next day. That finished my domestic musical career. I have never sung for him since, except once or twice when he has asked me to try the effect of some passage in one of his music-books."

"And do you never sing when you go out, as you used to?"

"Only when he is not with me, or when people force me to. If he is in the room, I am so nervous that I can hardly get through the easiest song. He never offers to accompany me now, and generally leaves the room when I am asked to sing."

"Perhaps he sees the effect his presence has on you."

"Even so, he ought to stay. He used to like *me* to listen to *him*, at first."

Miss McQuinch looked at the sunset with exceeding glumness. There was an ominous pause. Then she said, abruptly, "You remember how we used to debate whether marriage was a mistake or not. Have you found out?"

"I dont know."

"That sounds rather as if you did know. Are you quite sure you are not in low spirits this evening? He was bantering you about being out of temper when you came in. Perhaps you quarrelled at Kew."

George Bernard Shaw

"Quarrel! He quarrel! I cannot explain to you how we are situated, Nelly. You would not understand me."

"Suppose you try. For instance, is he as fond of you as he was before you married him?"

"I dont know."

Miss McQuinch shrugged herself impatiently.

"Really I do not, Nelly. He has changed in a way—I do not quite know how or why. At first he was not very ceremonious. He used to make remarks about people, and discuss everything that came into his head quite freely before me. He was always kind, and never grumbled about his dinner, or lost his temper, or anything of that kind; but—it was not that he was coarse exactly: he was not that in the least; but he was very open and unreserved and plain in his language; and somehow I did not quite like it. He must have found this out: he sees and feels everything by instinct; for he slipped back into his old manner, and became more considerate and attentive than he had ever been before. I was made very happy at first by the change; but I do not think he quite understood what I wanted. I did not at all object to going down to the country with him on his business trips; but he always goes alone now; and he never mentions his work to me. And he is too careful as to what he says to me. Of course, I know that he is right not to speak ill of anybody; but still a man need not be so particular before his wife as before strangers. He has given up talking to me altogether: that is the plain truth, whatever he may pretend. When we do converse, his manner is something like what it was in the laboratory at the Towers. Of course, he sometimes becomes more familiar; only then he never seems in earnest, but makes love to me in a bantering, half playful, half sarcastic way."

"You are rather hard to please, perhaps. I remember you used to say that a husband should be just as tender and respectful after marriage as before it. You seem to have broken poor Ned into this; and now you are not satisfied."

"Nelly, if there is one subject on which girls are more idiotically ignorant than on any other, it is happiness in marriage. A courtier, a lover, a man who will not let the winds of heaven visit your face too harshly, is very nice, no doubt; but he is not a husband. I want to be a wife and not a fragile ornament kept in a glass case. He would as soon think of submitting any project of his to the judgment of a doll as to mine. If he has to explain or discuss any serious matter of business with me, he does so apologetically, as if he were treating me roughly."

"Well, my dear, you see, when he tried the other plan, you did not like that either. What is the unfortunate man to do?"

"I dont know. I suppose I was wrong in shrinking from his confidence. I am always wrong. It seems to me that the more I try to do right, the more mischief I contrive to make."

"This is all pretty dismal, Marian. What sort of conduct on his part would make you happy?"

"Oh, there are so many little things. He makes me jealous of everything and everybody. I am jealous of the men in the city—I was jealous of the sanitary inspector the other day—because he talks with interest to them. I know he stays in the city later than he need. It is a relief to me to go out in the evening, or to have a few people here once or twice a week; but I am angry because I know it is a relief to him too. I am jealous even of that organ. How I hate those Bach fugues! Listen to the maddening thing twisting and rolling and racing and then mixing itself up into one great boom. He can get on with Bach: he can't get on with me. I have even condescended to be jealous of other women—of such women as Mrs. Saunders. He despises her: he plays with her as dexterously as she thinks she plays with him; but he likes to chat with her; and they rattle away for a whole evening without the least constraint. She has no conscience: she talks absolute nonsense about art and literature: she flirts even more disgustingly than she used to when she was Belle Woodward; but she is quickwitted, like most Irish people; and she enjoys a broad style of jesting which Ned is a great deal too tolerant of, though he would as soon die as indulge in it before me. Then there is Mrs. Scott, who is just as shrewd as Belle, and much cleverer. I have heard him ask her opinion as to whether he had acted well or not in some stroke of business—something that I had never heard of, of course. I wish I were half as hard and strong and self-reliant as she is. *Her* husband would be nothing without her."

"I am afraid I was right all along, Marian. Marriage *is* a mistake. There is something radically wrong in the institution. If you and Ned cannot be happy, no pair in the world can."

"We might be very happy if—" Marian stopped to repress a sob.

"Anybody might be very happy If. There is not much consolation in Ifs. You could not be better off than you are unless you could be Marian Lind again. Think of all the women who would give their souls to have a husband who would neither drink, nor swear at them, nor kick them, nor sulk whenever he was kept waiting half a minute for anything. You have no little pests of children—"

"I wish I had. That would give us some interest in common. We sometimes have Lucy, Marmaduke's little girl, up here; and Ned seems to me to be fond of her. She is a very bold little thing."

"I saw Marmaduke last week. He is not half so jolly as he was."

"He lives in chambers in Westminster now, and only comes out in this direction occasionally to see Lucy. I am afraid *she* has taken to drinking. I believe she is going to America. I hope she is; for she makes me uncomfortable when I think of her."

"Does your—your Ned ever speak of her?"

"No. He used to, before he changed as I described. Now, he never mentions her. Hush! Here he is."

The sound of the organ had ceased; and Conolly came out and stood between them.

"How do you like my consoler, as Marian calls it?" said he.

"Do you mean the organ?"

"Yes."

"I wasn't listening to you."

"You should have: I played the great fugue in A minor expressly for your entertainment: you used to work at Liszt's transcription of it. The organ is only occasionally my consoler. For the most part I am driven to it by habit and a certain itching in my fingers. Marian is my real consoler."

"So she has just been telling me," said Elinor. Conolly's surprise escaped him for just a moment in a quick glance at Marian. She colored, and looked reproachfully at her cousin, who added, "I am sure you must be a nuisance to the neighbors."

"Probably," said Conolly.

"I do not think you should play so much on Sunday," said Marian.

"I know. [Marian winced.] Well, if the neighbors will either melt down the church bells they jangle so horribly within fifteen yards or so of my unfortunate ears, or else hang them up two hundred feet high in a beautiful tower where they would sound angelic, as they do at Utrecht, then perhaps I will stop the organ to listen to them. Until then, I will take the liberty of celebrating the day of rest with such devices as the religious folk cannot forbid me."

"Pray do not begin to talk about religion, Ned."

"My way of thinking is too robust for Marian, Miss McQuinch. I admit that it does not, at first sight, seem pretty or sentimental. But I do not know how even Marian can prefer the church bells to Bach."

"What do you mean by '*even* Marian'?" said Elinor, sharply.

"I should have said, 'Marian, who is tolerant and kind to everybody and everything.' I hope you have forgiven me for carrying her off from you, Miss McQuinch. You are adopting an ominous tone toward me. I fear she has been telling you of our quarrels, and my many domestic shortcomings."

"No," said Elinor. "As far as I can judge from her account, you are a monotonously amiable husband."

"Indeed! Hm! Would you like your coffee out here?"

"Yes."

"Do not stir, Marian: I will ring for it."

When he was gone, Marian said "Nelly: for Heaven's sake say nothing that could make the slightest coldness between Ned and me. I am clinging to him with all my heart and soul; and you must help me. Those sharp things that you say to him stab me cruelly; and he is clever enough to guess everything I have said to you from them."

"If I cannot keep myself from making mischief, I shall go away," said Elinor. "Dont suppose I am in a huff: I am quite serious. I have an unlucky tongue; and my disposition is such that when I see that a jug is cracked, I feel more inclined to smash and have done with it than to mend it and handle it tenderly ever after. However, I hope your marriage is not a cracked jug yet."

CHAPTER XIII

On the following Wednesday Douglas called on his mother at Manchester Square in the afternoon. As if to emphasize the purely filial motive of his visit, he saluted his mother so affectionately that she was emboldened to be more demonstrative with him than she usually ventured to be.

"My darling boy," she said, holding him fondly for a moment, "this is the second visit you have paid your poor old mother this week. I want to speak to you about something, too. Marian has been with me this morning."

"What! Has she gone?" said Douglas.

"Why?" said Mrs. Douglas. "Did you know she was coming?"

"She mentioned to me that she intended to come," he replied, carelessly; "but she bade me not to tell you."

"That accounts for your two visits. Well, Sholto, I do not blame you for spending your time in gayer places than this."

"You must not reproach me for neglecting you, mother. You know my disposition. I am seldom good company for any one; and I do not care to come only to cast a damp on you and your friends when I am morose. I hope you received Marian kindly."

"I did not expect to see her; and I told her so."

George Bernard Shaw

"Mother!"

"But it made no difference. There is no holding her in check now, Sholto; she cares no more for what I say than if I was her father or you. What could I do but kiss and forgive her? She got the better of me."

"Yes," said Douglas, gloomily. "She has a wonderful face."

"The less you see of her face, the better, Sholto. I hope you will not go to her house too often."

"Do you doubt my discretion, mother?"

"No, no, Sholto. But I am afraid of any unpleasantness arising between you and that man. These working men are so savage to their wives, and so jealous of gentlemen. I hardly like your going into his house at all."

"Absurd, mother! You must not think that he is a navvy in fustian and corduroys. He seems a sensible man: his address is really remarkably good, considering what he is. As to his being savage, he is quite the reverse. His head is full of figures and machinery; and I am told that he does nothing at home but play the piano. He must bore Marian terribly. I do not want to go to his house particularly; but Marian and he are, of course, very sensitive to anything that can be construed as a slight; and I shall visit them once or twice to prevent them from thinking that I wish to snub Conolly. He will be glad enough to have me at his dinner-table. I am afraid I must hurry away now: I have an appointment at the club. Can I do anything for you in town?"

"No, thank you, Sholto. I thought you would have stayed with me for a cup of tea."

"Thank you, dear mother, no: not to-day. I promised to be at the club."

"If you promised, of course, you must go. Good-bye. You will come again soon, will you not?"

"Some day next week, if not sooner. Good-bye, mother."

Douglas left Manchester Square, not to go to his club, where he had no real appointment, but to avoid spending the afternoon with his mother, who, though a little hurt at his leaving her, was also somewhat relieved by being rid of him. They maintained toward one another an attitude which their friends found beautiful and edifying; but, like artists' models, they found the attitude fatiguing, in spite of their practice and its dignity.

At Hyde Park Corner, Douglas heard his name unceremoniously shouted. Turning, he saw Marmaduke Lind, carelessly dressed, walking a little behind him.

"Where are you going to?" said Marmaduke, abruptly.

"Why do you ask?" said Douglas, never disposed to admit the right of another to question him.

"I want to have a talk with you. Come and lunch somewhere, will you?"

"Yes, if you wish."

"Let's go to the South Kensington Museum."

"The South—! My dear fellow, why not suggest Putney, or the Star and Garter? Why do you wish to go westward from Hyde Park in search of luncheon?"

"I have a particular reason. I am to meet someone at the Museum this afternoon; and I want to ask your advice first. You might as well come; it's only a matter of a few minutes if we drive."

"Well, as you please. I have not been to the Museum for years."

"All right. Come al—oh, damn! There's Lady Carbury and Constance coming out of the Park. Dont look at them. Come on."

But Constance, sitting a little more uprightly than her mother, who was supine upon the carriage cushions, had seen the two gentlemen as they stood talking.

"Mamma," she said, "there's Marmaduke and Sholto Douglas."

"Where???" said the Countess, lifting her head quickly. "Josephs, drive slowly. Where are they, Constance?"

"They are going away. I believe Marmaduke saw us. There he is, passing the hospital."

"We must go and speak to them. Look pleasant, child; and dont make a fool of yourself."

"Surely youll not speak to him, mamma! You dont expect me—"

"Nonsense. I heard a great deal about him the other day. He has moved from where he was living, and is quite reformed. His father is very ill. Do as I tell you. Josephs, stop half way to the hotel."

"I say," said Marmaduke, finding himself out-manoeuvred: "come back. There they are right ahead, confound them. What are they up to?"

"It cannot be helped," said Douglas. "There is no escape. You must not cross: it would be pointedly rude."

Marmaduke went on grumbling. When he attempted to pass,

the Countess called his name, and greeted him with smiles.

"We want to know how your father is," she said. "We have had such alarming accounts of him. I hope he is better."

"They havnt told me much about him," said Marmaduke. "There was deuced little the matter with the governor when I saw him last."

"Wicked prodigal! What shall we do to reform him, Mr. Douglas? He has not been to see us for three years past, and during that time we have had the worst reports of him."

"You never asked me to go and see you."

"Silly fellow! Did you expect me to send you invitations and leave cards on you, who are one of ourselves? Come to-morrow to dinner. Your uncle the Bishop will be there; and you will see nearly all the family besides. You cannot plead that you have not been invited now. Will you come?"

"No. I cant stand the Bishop. Besides, I have taken to dining in the middle of the day."

"Come after dinner, then?"

"Mamma," said Constance, peevishly, "can't you see that he does not want to come at all? What is the use of persecuting him?"

"No, I assure you," said Marmaduke. "It's only the Bishop I object to. I'll come after dinner, if I can."

"And pray what is likely to prevent you?" said the Countess.

"Devilment of some sort, perhaps," he replied. "Since you have all given me a bad name, I dont see why I should make any secret of earning it."

George Bernard Shaw

The Countess smiled slyly at him, implying that she was amused, but must not laugh at such a sentiment in Constance's presence. Then, turning so as to give the rest of the conversation an air of privacy, she whispered, "I must tell you that you no longer have a bad name. It is said that your wild oats are all sown, and I will answer for it that even the Bishop will receive you with open arms."

"And dry my repentant tears on his apron, the old hypocrite," said Marmaduke, speaking rather more loudly than before. "Well, we must be trotting. We are going to the South Kensington Museum—to improve our minds."

"Why, that is where we are going; at least, Constance is. She is going to work at her painting while I pay a round of visits. Wont you come with us?"

"Thank you: I'd rather walk. A man should have gloves and a proper hat for your sort of travelling."

"Nonsense! you look very nice. Besides, it is only down the Brompton Road."

"The worst neighborhood in London to be seen in with me. I know all sorts of queer people down Brompton way. I should have to bow to them if we met; and that wouldnt do before *her*,"—indicating Constance, who was conversing with Douglas.

"You are incorrigible: I give you up. Good-bye, and dont forget to-morrow evening."

"I wonder," said Marmaduke, as the carriage drove off, "what she's saying about me to Constance now."

"That you are the rudest man in London, perhaps."

"Serve her right! I hate her. I have got so now that I can't stand that sort of woman. You see her game, dont you; she can't get

Constance off her hands; and she thinks there's a chance of me still. How well she knows about the governor's state of health! And Conny, too, grinning at me as if we were the best friends in the world. If that girl had an ounce of spirit she would not look on the same side of the street with me."

Douglas, without replying, called a cab. Marmaduke's loud conversation was irksome in the street, and it was now clear that he was unusually excited. At the museum they alighted, and passed through the courts into the grill-room, where they sat down together at a vacant table, and ordered luncheon.

"You were good enough to ask my advice about something," said Douglas. "What is the matter?"

"Well," said Marmaduke, "I am in a fix. Affairs have become so uncomfortable at home that I have had to take up my quarters elsewhere."

"I did not know that you had been living at home. I thought your father and you were on the usual terms."

"My father! Look here: I mean home—*my* home. My place at Hammersmith, not down at the governor's."

"Oh! I beg your pardon."

"Of course, you know all about my establishment there with Lalage Virtue? her real name is Susanna Conolly."

"Is it true, then, that she is a cousin of Marian's husband?"

"Cousin! She's his sister, and Marian's sister-in-law."

"I never believed it."

"It's true enough. But thats not the mischief. Douglas: I tell you she's the cleverest woman in London. She can do anything she likes. She can manage a conversation with any foreigner in

George Bernard Shaw

his own language, whether she knows it or not. She gabbles Italian like a native. She can learn off her part in a new piece, music and all, between breakfast and luncheon, any day. She can cook: she can make a new bonnet out of the lining of an old coat: she can drive a bargain with a Jew. She says she never learns a thing at all unless she can learn it in ten minutes. She can fence, and shoot. She can dance anything in the world. I never knew such a mimic as she is. If you saw her take off the Bones at the Christy Minstrels, you'd say she was the lowest of the low. Next minute she will give herself the airs of a duchess, or do the ingenuous in a style that would make Conny burst with envy. To see her preaching like George would make you laugh for a week. There's nothing she couldnt do if she chose. And now, what do you think she has taken to? Liquor. Champagne by the gallon. She used to drink it by the bottle: now she drinks it by the dozen—by the case. She wanted it to keep up her spirits. That was the way it began. If she felt down, a glass of champagne would set her up. Then she was always feeling down, and always setting herself up. At last feeling down came to mean the same thing as being sober. You dont know what a drunken woman is, Douglas, unless youve lived in the same house with one." Douglas recoiled, and looked very sternly at Marmaduke, who proceeded more vehemently. "She's nothing but a downright beast. She's either screaming at you in a fit of rage, or clawing at you in a fit of fondness that makes you sick. When she falls asleep, there she is, a besotted heap tumbled anyhow into bed, snoring and grunting like a pig. When she wakes, she begins planning how to get more liquor. Think of what you or I would feel if we saw our mothers tipsy. By God, that child of mine wouldnt believe its eyes if it saw its mother sober. Only for Lucy, I'd have pitched her over long ago. I did all I could when I first saw that she was overdoing the champagne. I swore I'd break the neck of any man I caught bringing wine into the house. I sacked the whole staff of servants twice because I found a lot of fresh corks swept into the dustpan. I stopped drinking at home myself: I got in doctors to frighten her: I tried bribing, coaxing, threatening: I knocked her down once when I caught her with a bottle in her hand; and she fell with her head against the fender, and frightened me a good deal more than she hurt herself. It was no use. Sometimes she used to defy me, and say she *would* drink, she didnt care whether she was killing herself or not. Other times she cried; implored me to save her from destroying herself; asked me why I didnt thrash the life out of her whenever I caught her drunk; promised on her oath never to touch another drop. The same evening she would be drunk again, and, when I taxed her with it, say that she wasn't drunk, that she was sick, and that she prayed the Almighty on her knees to strike her dead if she had a bottle in the house. Aye, and the very stool she knelt on would be a wine case with a red cloth stuck to it with a few gilt-headed nails to make it look like a piece of furniture. Next day she would laugh at me for believing her, and ask me what use I supposed there was in talking to her. How she managed to hold on at the theatre, I dont know. She wouldnt learn new parts, and stuck to old ones that she could do in her sleep, she knew them so well. She would go on the stage and get through a long part when she couldnt walk straight from the wing to her dressing-room. Of course, her voice went to the dogs long ago; but by dint of screeching and croaking she pulls through. She says she darent go on sober now; that she knows she should break down. The theatre has fallen off, too. The actors got out of the place one by one—they didnt like playing with her—and were replaced by a third-rate lot. The audiences used to be very decent: now they are all cads and fast women. The game is up for her in London. She has been offered an engagement in America on the strength of her old reputation; but what is the use of it if she continues drinking."

"That is very sad," said Douglas, with cold disgust, perfunctorily veiled by a conventional air of sympathy. "But if she is irreclaimable, why not leave her?"

"So I would, only for the child. I *have* left her—at least, I've taken lodgings in town; but I am always running out to Laurel Grove. I darent trust Lucy to her; and she knows it; for she wouldnt let me take the poor little creature away, although she doesnt care two straws for it. She knows that it gives her a grip over me. Well, I have not seen her for a week past. I have tried the trick of only going out in the evening when she has to be at the theatre. And now she has sent me a long letter; and I dont exactly know what to do about it. She swears she has given up drinking—not touched a spoonful since I saw her last. She's as superstitious as an old woman; and yet she will swear to that lie with oaths that make *me* uncomfortable, although I am pretty thick-skinned in religious matters. Then she goes drivelling on about me having encouraged her to drink at first, and then turned upon her and deserted her when I found out the mischief I had done. I used to stand plenty of champagne, but I am sure I never thought what would come of it. Then she says she gave up every friend in the world for me: broke with her brother, and lost her place in society. *Her* place in society, mind you, Douglas! Thats not bad, is it? Then, of course, I am leaving her to die alone with her helpless child: I might have borne with her a little longer: she will not trouble me nor anyone else much more; and so on. The upshot is that she wants me to come back. She says I ought to be there to save the child from her, if I dont care to save her from herself; that I was the last restraint on her; and that if I dont come she will make an end of the business by changing her tipple to prussic acid. The whole thing is a string of maudlin rot from beginning to end; and I believe she primed herself with about four bottles of champagne to write it. Still, I dont want to leave her in the lurch. You are a man who stand pretty closely on your honor. Do you think I ought to go back? I may tell you that as regards money she is under no compliment to me. Her earnings were a good half of our income; and she saved nothing out of them. In fact, I owe her some money for two or three old debts she paid for me. We always shared like husband and wife."

"I hardly understand your hesitation, Lind. You can take the little girl out of her hands; allow her something; and be quit of her."

"Thats very easy to say; but I cant drag her child away from her if she insists on keeping it."

"Well, so much the better for you. It would be a burden to you. Pay her for its maintenance: that is probably what she wants."

"No, no," said Marmaduke, impatiently. "You dont understand. Youre talking as if I were a rake living with a loose woman."

Douglas looked at him doubtfully. "I confess I do not understand," he said. "Perhaps you will be good enough to explain."

"It's very simple. I went to live with her because I fell in love with her, and she wouldnt marry me. She had a horror of marriage; and I was naturally not very eager for it myself. Matters must be settled between us as if we were husband and wife. Paying her off is all nonsense. She doesnt want money; and I want the child; so she has the advantage of me. Only for the drink I would go back to her to-morrow; but I cant stand her when she is not sober. I bore with it long enough; and now all I want is to get Lucy out of her hands and be quit of her, as you say—although it seems mean to leave her."

"She must certainly be a very extraordinary woman if she refused to marry you. Are you sure she is not married already?"

"Bosh! Not she. She likes to be independent; and she has a sort of self-respect—not like Constance and the old Countess, who hunted me long enough in the hope of running me down at last in a church."

"If you offered her marriage, that certainly frees you from the least obligation to stay with her. She reserved liberty to leave you; and, of course, the same privilege was implied on your part. If you have no sentimental wish to return to her, you are most decidedly not bound in honor to."

"I'm fond enough of her when she is sober; but I loathe her when she is fuddled. If she would only give up drinking, we might make a fresh start. But she wont."

"You must not think of doing that. Get rid of her, my dear fellow. This marriage of Marian's has put the affair on a new footing altogether. I tell you candidly, I think that under the circumstances your connexion with Conolly's sister is a disgraceful one."

"Hang Conolly! Everybody thinks of Marian, and nobody of Susanna. I have heard enough of that side of the question. Marian married him with her eyes open."

"Do you mean to say that she knew?"

"Of course she did. Conolly told her, fairly enough. He's an extraordinary card, that fellow."

"Reginald Lind told my mother that the discovery was made by accident after the marriage, and that they were all shocked by it. It was he who said that it was Conolly's *cousin* that you were with."

"Uncle Rej. is an old liar. So are most of the family: I never believe a word they say."

"Marian must have been infatuated. I advise you to break the connexion. She will be glad to give you the child if she sees that you are resolved to leave her. She only holds on because she hopes to make it the means of bringing you back."

"I expect youre about right. She wants me to meet her here to-day at half past three. Thats the reason I came."

"Do you know that it now wants twenty minutes of four?"

"Whew! So it does. I had better go and look for her. I'm very much obliged to you, old fellow, for talking it over with me. I suppose you dont want to meet her."

"I should be in the way at present."

"Then good-bye."

Marmaduke, leaving Douglas in the grill-room, went upstairs to the picture galleries, where several students were more or less busy at their easels. Lady Constance was in the Sheep-shanks gallery, copying "Sterne's Maria," by Charles Landseer, as best she could. She had been annoyed some minutes before by the behavior of a stout woman in a rich costume of black silk, who had stopped for a moment to inspect her drawing. Lady Constance, by a look, had made her aware that she was considered intrusive, whereupon she had first stared Lady Constance out of countenance, and then deliberately scanned her work with an expression which conveyed a low opinion of its merit. Having thus revenged herself, she stood looking uneasily at the door for a minute, and at last wandered away into the adjoining gallery. A few minutes later Marmaduke entered, looking round as if in search of someone.

"Here I am," said Constance to him, playfully.

"So I see," said Marmaduke, recognizing her with rueful astonishment. "You knew I was looking for you, did you?"

"Of course I did, sir."

"Youre clever, so you are. What are you doing here?"

"Dont you see? I am copying a picture."

"Oh! it's very pretty. Which one are you copying?"

"What an impertinent question! You can tell my poor copy well enough, only you pretend not to."

"Yes, now that I look closely at it, I fancy it's a little like Mary the maid of the inn there."

George Bernard Shaw

"It's not Mary: it's Maria—Sterne's Maria."

"Indeed! Do you read Sterne?"

"Certainly not," said Constance, looking very serious.

"Then what do you paint his Maria for? How do you know whether she is a fit subject for you?"

"Hush, sir! You must not interrupt my work."

"I suppose you have lots of fun here over your art studies, eh?"

"Who?"

"You, and all the other girls here."

"Oh, I am sure I dont know any of them."

"Quite right, too, your ladyship. Dont make yourself cheap. I hope none of the low beggars ever have the audacity to speak to you."

"I dont know anything about them," said Lady Constance, pettishly. "All I mean is that they are strangers to me."

"Most likely theyll remain so. You all seem to stick to the little pictures tremendously. Why dont you go in for high art? There's a big picture of Adam and Eve! Why dont you paint that?"

"Will you soon be leaving town?" she replied, looking steadily at her work, and declining to discuss Adam and Eve, who were depicted naked. Receiving no reply, she looked round, and saw Marmaduke leaving the room with the woman in the black silk dress.

"Who is that girl?" said Susanna, as they went out.

"That's Lady Constance, whom I was to have married."

"I guessed as much when I saw you talking to her. She is a true English lady, heaven bless her! I took the liberty of looking at her painting; and she stared at me as if I had bitten her."

"She is a little fool."

"She will not be such a little fool as to try to snub me again, I think. Bob: did you get my letter?"

"Of course I got it, or I shouldnt be here."

"Well?"

"Well, I dont believe a word of it."

"That's plain speaking."

"There is no use mincing matters. You are just as likely to stop drinking as you are to stop breathing."

"Perhaps I shall stop breathing before long."

"Very likely, at your present rate."

"That will be a relief to you."

"It will be a relief to everybody, and a release for yourself. You have made me miserable for a year past; and now you expect me to be frightened at the prospect of being rid of you."

"I dont expect you to be frightened. I expect you to do what all men do: throw me aside as soon as I have served your turn."

"Yes. Of course, *you* are the aggrieved party. Where's Lucy?"

"I dont know, and I dont care."

"Well, I want to know; and I do care. Is she at home?"

"How do I know whether she is at home or not. I left her there. Very likely she is with her Aunt Marian, telling stories about her mother."

"She is better there than with you. What harm has she done you that you should talk about her in that way?"

"No harm. I dont object to her being there. She has very pleasant conversations with Mrs. Ned, which she retails to me at home. 'Aunty Marian: why do you never drink champagne? Mamma is always drinking it.' And then, 'Mamma: why do you drink so much wine? Aunty Marian never drinks any.' Good heavens! the little devil told me this morning by way of consolation that she always takes care not to tell her Aunty that I get drunk."

"What did you do to her for saying it?"

"Dont lose your temper. I didnt strangle her, nor even box her ears. Why should I? She only repeats what you teach her."

"She repeats what her eyes and ears teach her. If she learned the word from me, she learned the meaning from you. A nice lesson for a child hardly three years old."

Susanna sat down on a bench, and looked down at her feet. After a few moments, she tightened her lips; rose; and walked away.

"Hallo! Where are you going to?" said Marmaduke, following her.

"I'm going to get some drink. I have been sober and miserable ever since I wrote to you. I have not got much thanks for it, except to be made more miserable. So I'll get drunk, and be happy."

"No, you shant," said Marmaduke, seizing her arm, and forcibly stopping her.

"What does it matter to you whether I do or not? You say you wont come back. Then leave me to go my own way."

"Here! you sit down," he said, pushing her into a chair. "I know your game well enough. You think you have me safe as long as you have the child."

"Oh, thats it, is it? Why dont you go out; take a cab; and go to Laurel Grove for her? There is nothing to prevent you taking her away."

"I have a good mind to do it."

"Well, *do* it. I wont stop you. Why didnt you do it long ago? Her home is no place for her. I'm not fit to have charge of her. I have no fancy for having her talking about me, and most likely mimicking me to other people."

"Thats exactly what I want to arrange with you to do, if you will only be reasonable. Listen. Let us part friends, Susanna, since there is no use in our going on together. You must give me the child. It would only be a burden to you; and I can have it well taken care of. You can keep the house just as it is: I will pay the rent of it."

"What good is the house to me?"

"Can't you hear me out? It will be good to you to live in, I suppose; or you can set it on fire, and wipe it off the face of the earth, for what I care. I can give you five hundred pounds down—"

"Five hundred pounds! And what will you live on until your October dividends come in? On credit, I suppose. Do you think you can impose on me by flourishing money before me? I will never take a halfpenny from you; no, not if I starve

George Bernard Shaw

for it."

"Thats all nonsense, Susanna. You must."

"Must I? Do you think you can make me take your money as you made me sit down here? by force!"

"I only offer you what I owe you. Those debts—"

"I dont want what you owe me. If you think it mean to leave me, you shant plaster up your conscience with bank notes. You would like to be able to say in your club that you treated me handsomely."

"I dont think it mean to leave you, not a bit of it. Any other man would have left you months ago. If I had married that little fool inside there, and she had taken to drink, I wouldnt have stood it a week. I have stood it from you nearly a year. Can you expect me to stay under the same roof with you, with the very thought of you making me sick and angry? I was looking at some of your old likenesses the other day; and I declare that it is enough to make a man cry to look at your face now and listen to your voice. When you used to lecture me for losing a twenty pound note at billiards, and coming home half screwed—no man shall ever see me drunk again—I little thought which of us would be the first to go to the dogs."

"I shall not trouble you long."

"What is the use of harping on that? I have seen you drunk so often that I should almost be glad to see you dead."

"Stop!" said Susanna, rising. "All right: you need say no more. Talking will not remedy matters; and it makes me feel pretty much as if you were throwing big stones at my heart. Youre in the right, I suppose: I've chosen to make a beast of myself, and I must take the consequences. You can have the child. I will send for my things: you wont see me at Laurel Grove again. Good-bye."

"But—"

"Dont say another word, Bob. Good-bye." He took her hand irresolutely. She drew it quickly away; nodded to him; and went out, whilst he stood wondering whether it would be safe—seeing that he did not desire a reconciliation—to kiss her good-bye.

George Bernard Shaw

CHAPTER XIV

On Sunday afternoon Douglas walked, facing a glorious sunset, along Uxbridge Road to Holland Park, where he found Mrs. Conolly, Miss McQuinch, and Marmaduke. A little girl was playing in the garden. They were all so unconstrained, and so like their old selves, that Douglas at once felt that Conolly was absent.

"I am to make Ned's excuses," said Marian. "He has some pressing family affairs to arrange." She seemed about to explain further; but Marmaduke looked so uneasily at her that she stopped. Then, resuming gaily, she added, "I told Ned that he need not stand on ceremony with you. Fancy my saying that of you, the most punctilious of men!"

"Quite right. I am glad that Mr. Conolly has not suffered me to interfere with his movements," he replied, with a smile, which he suppressed as he turned and greeted Miss McQuinch with his usual cold composure. But to Marmaduke, who seemed much cast down, he gave an encouraging squeeze of the hand. Not that he was moved by the misfortunes of Marmaduke; but he was thawed by the beauty of Marian.

"We shall have a pleasant evening," continued Marian. "Let us fancy ourselves back at Westbourne Terrace again. Reminiscences make one feel so deliciously aged and sad. Let us think that it is one of our old Sunday afternoons. Sholto had better go upstairs and shave, to heighten the illusion."

"Not for me, since I cannot see myself, particularly if I have to call you Mrs. Conolly. If I may call you Marian, as I used to do, I think that our conversation will contain fewer reminders of the lapse of time."

"Of course," said Marian, disregarding an anxious glance from Elinor. "What else should you call me? We were talking about Nelly's fame when you came in. The colonial edition of her book has just appeared. Behold the advertisement!"

There was a newspaper open on the table; and Marian pointed to one of its columns as she spoke. Douglas took it up and read the following:

Now Ready, a New and Cheaper Edition, crown 8vo, 5s.

THE WATERS OF MARAH,

BY ELINOR MCQUINCH.

"Superior to many of the numerous tales which find a ready sale at the railway bookstall." *Athenaeum.*

"There is nothing to fatigue, and something to gratify, the idle reader." *Examiner.*

"There is a ring of solid metal in 'The Waters of Marah.'" *Daily Telegraph.*

"Miss McQuinch has fairly established her claim to be considered the greatest novelist of the age." *Middlingtown Mercury.*

"Replete with thrilling and dramatic incident..... Instinct with passion and pathos." *Ladies' Gazette.*

TABUTEAU & SON, COVENT GARDEN.

"That is very flattering," said Douglas, as he replaced the paper on the table.

"Highly so," said Elinor. "Coriolanus displaying his wounds in the Forum is nothing to it." And she abruptly took the paper, and threw it disgustedly behind the sofa. Just then a message from the kitchen engaged Marian's attention, and Douglas, to relieve her from her guests for the moment, strolled out upon the little terrace, whither Marmaduke had moodily preceded him.

"Still in your difficulties, Lind?" he said, with his perfunctory air of concern, looking at the garden with some interest.

"I'm out of my difficulties clean enough," said Marmaduke. "There's the child among the currant bushes; and I am rid of her mother: for good, I suppose."

"So much the better! I hope it has not cost you too much."

"Not a rap. I met her in the museum after our confab on Wednesday, and told her what you recommended: that I must have the child, and that she must go. She said all right, and shook hands. I havnt seen her since."

"I congratulate you."

"I dont feel comfortable about her."

"Absurd, man! What better could you have done?"

"Thats just what I say. It was her own fault; I did all in my power. I offered her five hundred pounds down. She wouldnt have it, of course; but could I help that? Next day, when she sent her maid for her things, I felt so uneasy that I came to Conolly, and told him the whole affair. He behaved very decently about it, and said that I might as well have left her six months ago for all the good my staying had done or was likely to do. He has gone off to see her to-day—she is in lodgings somewhere near the theatre; and he will let me know in case any money is required. I should like to know what they are saying to one another about me. They're a rum pair."

"Well, let us eat and drink; for to-morrow we die," said Douglas, with an unnatural attempt at humor. "Marian seems happy. We must not spoil her evening."

"Yes: she is always in good spirits when he is away."

"Indeed?"

"It seems to me that they dont pull together. I think she is afraid of him."

"You dont mean to say that he ill-treats her?" said Douglas, fiercely.

"No: I dont mean that he thrashes her, or anything of that sort. And yet he is just that sort of chap that I shouldnt be surprised at anything he might do. As far as ordinary matters go, he seems to treat her particularly well. But Ive noticed that she shuts up and gets anxious when he comes into the room; and he has his own way in everything."

"Is that all? He embarrasses her by his behavior, I suppose. Perhaps she is afraid of his allowing his breeding to peep out."

"Not she. His manners are all right enough. Besides, as he is a genius and a celebrity and all that, people dont expect him to be conventional. He might stand on his head, if he chose."

"Sholto," said Marian, joining them: "have you spoken to little Lucy?"

"No."

"Then you are unacquainted with the most absolute imp on the face of the earth," said Elinor. "You neednt frown, Marma-duke: it is you who have made her so."

"Leave her alone," said Marmaduke to Marian, who was about to call the child. "Petting babies is not in Douglas's line: she will only bore him."

"Not at all," said Douglas.

"It does not matter whether she bores him or not," said Marian. "He must learn to take a proper interest in children. Lucy: come here."

Lucy stopped playing, and said, "What for?"

"Because I ask you to, dear," said Marian, gently.

The child considered for a while, and then resumed her play. Miss McQuinch laughed. Marmaduke muttered impatiently, and went down the garden. Lucy did not perceive him until he was within a few steps of her, when she gave a shrill cry of surprise, and ran to the other side of a flower-bed too wide for him to spring across. He gave chase; but she, with screams of laughter, avoided him by running to and fro so as to keep on the opposite side to him. Feeling that it was undignified to dodge his child thus, he stopped and bade her come to him; but she only laughed the more. He called her in tones of command, entreaty, expostulation, and impatience. At last he shouted to her menacingly. She placed her thumbnail against the tip of her nose; spread her fingers; and made him a curtsy. He uttered an imprecation, and returned angrily to the house, saying, between his teeth:

"Let her stay out, since she chooses to be obstinate."

"She is really too bad to-day," said Marian. "I am quite shocked at her."

"She is quite right not to come in and be handed round for inspection like a doll," said Elinor.

"She is very bold not to come when she is told," said Marian.

"Yes, from your point of view," said Elinor. "I like bold children."

Marmaduke was sulky and Marian serious for some time after this incident. They recovered their spirits at dinner, when Marian related to Douglas how she had become reconciled to his mother. Afterward, Marmaduke suggested a game at whist.

"Oh no, not on Sunday," said Marian. "Whist is too wicked."

"Then what the dickens *may* we do?" said Marmaduke. "May Nelly play *ecarte* with me?"

"Well, please dont play for money. And dont sit close to the front window."

"Come along, then, Nell. You two may sing hymns, if you like."

"I wish you could sing, Sholto," said Marian. "It is an age since we last had a game of chess together. Do you still play?"

"Yes," said Douglas; "I shall be delighted. But I fear you will beat me now, as I suppose you have been practising with Mr. Conolly."

"Playing with Ned! No: he hates chess. He says it is a foolish expedient for making idle people believe they are doing something very clever when they are only wasting their time. He actually grumbled about the price of the table and the pieces; but I insisted on having them, I suppose in remembrance of you."

"It is kind of you to say that, Marian. Will you have black or white?"

"White, please, unless you wish me to be always making moves with your men."

George Bernard Shaw

"Now. Will you move?"

"I think I had rather you began. Remember our old conditions. You are not to checkmate me in three moves; and you are not to take my queen."

"Very well. You may rely upon it I shall think more of my adversary than of my game. Check."

"Oh! You have done it in three moves. That is not fair. I won't play any more unless you take back that."

"No, I assure you it is not checkmate. My bishop should be at the other side for that. There! of course, that will do."

"What a noise Marmaduke makes over his cards! I hope the people next door will not hear him swearing."

"Impossible. You must not move that knight: it exposes your king. Do you know, I think there is a great charm about this house."

"Indeed? Yes, it is a pretty house."

"And this sunset hour makes it additionally so; Besides, it is inexpressibly sad to see you here, a perfectly happy and perfectly beautiful mistress of this romantic foreign home."

"What do you mean, Sholto?"

"I call it a foreign home because, though it is yours, I have no part nor lot in it. Remember, we are only playing at old times to-night. Everything around, from the organ to the ring on your finger, reminds me that I am a stranger here. It seems almost unkind of you to regret nothing whilst I am full of regrets."

"Check," said Marian. "Mind your game, sir."

"Flippant!" exclaimed Douglas, impatiently moving his king. "I verily believe that if your husband were at the bottom of the Thames at this moment, you would fly off unconcernedly to some other nest, and break hearts with as much indifference as ever."

"I wish you would not make suggestions of that sort, Sholto. You make me uncomfortable. Something *might* happen to Ned. I wish he were home. He is very late."

"Happy man. You can be serious when you think about him. I envy him."

"What! Sholto Douglas stoop to envy any mortal! Prodigious!"

"Yes: it has come to that with me. Why should I not envy him? His career has been upward throughout. He has been a successful worker in the world, where I have had nothing real to do. When the good things I had been dreaming of and longing for all my life came in his path, he had them for the mere asking. I valued them so highly that when I fancied I possessed them, I was the proudest of men. I am humble enough now that I am beggared."

"You are really talking the greatest nonsense."

"No doubt I am. Still in love, Marian, you see. There is no harm in telling you so now."

"On the contrary, it is now that there is harm. For shame, Sholto!"

"I am not ashamed. I tell you of my love because now you can listen to me without uneasiness, knowing that it is no longer associated with hope, or desire, or anything but regret. You see that I do not affect the romantic lover. I eat very well; I play chess; I go into society; and you reproach me for growing fat."

Marian bent over the chessboard for a moment to hide her

George Bernard Shaw

face. Then she said in a lower voice, "I have thoroughly convinced myself that there is no such thing as love in the world."

"That means that you have never experienced it."

"I have told you already that I have never been in love, and that I dont believe a bit in it. I mean romantic love, of course."

"I verily believe that you have not. The future has one more pang in store for me; for you will surely love some day."

"I am getting too old for that, I fear. At what age, pray, did you receive the arrow in your heart?"

"When I was a boy, I loved a vision. The happiest hours of my life were those in which I was slowly, tremulously daring to believe that I had found my vision at last in you. And then the dreams that followed! What a career was to have been mine! I remember how you used to reproach me because I was austere with women and proud with men. How could I have been otherwise? I contrasted the gifts of all other women with those of my elect, and the lot of all other men with my own. Can you wonder that, doing so, I carried my head among the clouds? You must remember how unfamiliar failure was to me. At school, at Oxford, in society, I had sought distinction without misgiving, and attained it without difficulty. My one dearest object I deemed secure long before I opened my lips and asked expressly for it. I think I walked through life at that time like a somnambulist; for I have since seen that I must have been piling mistake upon mistake until out of a chaos of meaningless words and smiles I had woven a Paphian love temple. At the first menace of disappointment—a thing as new and horrible to me as death—I fled the country. I came back with only the ruins of the doomed temple. You were not content to destroy a ruin: the feat was too easy to be glorious. So you rebuilt it in one hour to the very dome, and lighted its altars with more than their former radiance. Then, as though it were but a house of cards—as indeed it was nothing else—you gave it one delicate touch and razed it to its foundations. Yet I am afraid those altar lamps were not wholly extinguished. They smoulder beneath the ruins still."

"I wonder why they made you the Newdigate poet at Oxford, Sholto: you mix your metaphors most dreadfully. Dont be angry with me: I understand what you mean; and I am very sorry. I say flippant things because I must. How *can* one meet seriousness in modern society except by chaff?"

"I am not angry. I had rather you did not understand. The more flippant you are, the more you harden my heart; and I want it to be as hard as the nether millstone. Your pity would soften me; and I dread that."

"I believe it does every man good to be softened. If you ever really felt what you describe, you greatly over-estimated me. What can you lose by a little more softness? I often think that men—particularly good men—make their way through the world too much as if it were a solid mass of iron through which they must cut—as if they dared not relax their hardest edge and finest temper for a moment. Surely, that is not the way to enjoy life."

"Perhaps not. Still, it is the way to conquer in life. It may be pleasant to have a soft heart; but then someone is sure to break it."

"I do not believe much in broken hearts. Besides, I do not mean that men should be too soft. For instance, sentimental young men of about twenty are odious. But for a man to get into a fighting attitude at the barest suggestion of sentiment; to believe in nature as something inexorable, and to aim at being as inexorable as nature: is not that almost as bad?"

"Do you know any such man? You must not attribute that sort of hardness to me."

"Oh no; I was not thinking of you. I was not thinking of

George Bernard Shaw

anyone in fact. I only put a case. I sometimes have disputes with Ned on the subject. One of his cardinal principles is that there is no use in crying for spilt milk. I always argue that as irremediable disasters are the only ones that deserve or obtain sympathy, he might as well say that there is no use in crying for anything. Then he slips out of the difficulty by saying that that was just what he meant, and that there is actually no place for regret in a well-regulated scheme of life. In debating with women, men brazen out all the ridiculous conclusions of which they are convicted; and then they say that there is no use in arguing with a woman. Neither is there, because the woman is always right."

"Yes; because she suffers her heart to direct her."

"You are just as bad as the rest of your sex, I see. Where you cannot withold credit from a woman, you give it to her heart and deny it to her head."

"There! I wont play any more," said Miss McQuinch, suddenly, at the other end of the room. "Have you finished your chess, Marian?"

"We are nearly done. Ring for the lamps, please, Nelly. Let us finish, Sholto."

"Whose turn is it to move? I beg your pardon for my inattention."

"Mine—no, yours. Stop! it must be mine. I really dont know."

"Nor do I. I have forgotten my game."

"Then let us put up the board. We can finish some other night."

It had become dark by this time; and the lamps were brought in whilst Douglas was replacing the chessmen in their box.

"Now," said Marian, "let us have some music. Marmaduke: will you sing Uncle Ned for us? We have not heard you sing for ages."

"I believe it is more than three years since that abominable concert at Wandsworth; and I have not heard you sing since," said Elinor.

"I forget all my songs—havnt sung one of them for months. However, here goes! Have you a banjo in the house?"

"No," said Marian. "I will play an accompaniment for you."

"All right. See here: you need only play these three chords. When one sounds wrong, play another. Youll learn it in a moment."

Marmaduke's voice was not so fresh, nor his fun so spontaneous, as at Wandsworth; but they were not critical enough to appreciate the difference: they laughed like children at him. Elinor was asked to play; but she would not: she had renounced that folly, she said. Then, at Douglas's request, Marian sang, in memory of Wandsworth, "Rose, softly blooming." When she had finished, Elinor asked for some old melodies, knowing that Marian liked these best. So she began gaily with The Oak and the Ash and Robin Adair. After that, finding both herself and the others in a more pathetic vein, she sang them The Bailiff's Daughter of Islington, and The Banks of Allan Water, at the end of which Marmaduke's eyes were full of tears, and the rest sat quite still. She paused for a minute, and then broke the silence with Auld Robin Gray, which affected even Douglas, who had no ear. As she sang the last strain, the click of a latchkey was heard from without. Instantly she rose; closed the pianoforte softly; and sat down at some distance from it. Her action was reflected by a change in their behavior. They remembered that they were not at home, and became more or less uneasily self-conscious. Elinor was the least disturbed. Conolly's first glance on entering was at the piano: his next went in search of his wife.

"Ah!" he said, surprised. "I thought somebody was singing."

"Oh dear no!" said Elinor drily. "You must have been mistaken."

"Perhaps so," said he, smiling. "But I have been listening carefully at the window for ten minutes; and I certainly dreamt that I heard Auld Robin Gray."

Marian blushed. Conolly did not seem to have been moved by the song. He was alert and loquacious: before he had finished his greeting and apology to Douglas, they all felt as little sentimental as they had ever done in their lives. Marian, after asking whether he had dined, became silent, and dropped the pretty airs of command which, as hostess, she had worn before.

"Have you any news?" said Marmaduke at last. "Douglas knows the whole business. We are all friends here."

"Only what we expected," said Conolly. "Affairs are exactly as they were. I called to-day at her address—"

"How did you get it?" said Marmaduke.

"I wrote for it to her at the theatre."

"And did she send it?"

"Of course. But she did not give me any encouragement to call on her, and, in fact, evidently did not want to see me. Her appearance has altered very much for the worse. She is a confirmed dipsomaniac; and she knows it. I advised her to abstain in future. She asked me, in her sarcastic, sisterly way, whether I had any other advice to give her. I told her that if she meant to go on, her proper course was to purchase a hogshead of brandy; keep it by her side; and condense the process of killing herself, which may at present take some years, into a few days."

"Oh, Ned, you did not really say that to her!" said Marian.

"I did indeed. The shocking part of the affair is not, as you seem to think, my giving the advice, but that it should be the very best advice I could have given."

"I do not think I would have said so."

"Most likely not," said Conolly, with a smile. "You would have said something much prettier. But dipsomania is not one of the pretty things of life; nor can it by any stretch of benevolent hypocrisy be made to pass as one. When Susanna and I get talking, we do not waste time in trying to spare one another's feelings. If we did, we should both see through the attempt and be very impatient of it."

"Did she tell you what she intends to do?" said Marmaduke.

"She has accepted an American engagement. When that draws to a close, it will, she says, be time enough for her to consider her next step. But she has no intention of leaving the stage until she is compelled."

"Has she any intention of reforming her habits?" said Elinor, bluntly.

"I should say every intention, but no prospect of doing so. Dipsomaniacs are always intending to reform; but they rarely succeed. Has Lucy been put to bed?"

"Lucy is in disgrace," said Elinor. Marian looked at her apprehensively.

"In disgrace!" said Conolly, more seriously. "How so?"

Elinor described what had taken place in the garden. When she told how the child had disregarded Marian's appeal, Conolly laughed.

"Lucy has no sense of how pretty she would have looked toddling in obediently because her aunt asked her to," he said. "She is, like all children, very practical, and will not assist in getting up amiable little scenes without good reason rendered."

Elinor glanced at Marian, and saw that though Douglas was speaking to her in a low voice, she was listening nervously to her husband. So she said sharply, "It is a pity you were not here to tell us what to do."

"Apparently it is," said Conolly, complacently.

"What would you have done?" said Marian suddenly, interrupting Douglas.

"I suppose," said Conolly, looking round at her in surprise, "I should have answered her question—told her what she was wanted for. If I asked you to do anything, and you enquired why, you would be extremely annoyed if I answered, 'because I ask you.'"

"I would not ask why," said Marian. "I would do it."

"That would be very nice of you," said Conolly; "but you cannot: expect such a selfish, mistrustful, and curious animal as a little child to be equally kind and confiding. Lucy is too acute not to have learned long since that grown people systematically impose on the credulity and helplessness of children."

"Thats true," said Elinor, reluctantly. Marian turned away and quietly resumed her conversation with Douglas. After a minute she strolled with him into the garden, whither Marmaduke had already retired to smoke.

"Has the evening been a pleasant one, Miss McQuinch?" said Conolly, left alone with her.

"Yes: we have had a very pleasant evening indeed. We played

chess and *ecarte*; and we all agreed to make old times of it. Marmaduke sang for us; and Marian had us nearly in tears with those old ballads of hers."

"And then I came in and spoiled it all. Eh?"

"Certainly not. Why do you say that?"

"Merely a mischievous impulse to say something true: jealousy, perhaps, because I missed being here earlier. You think, then, that if I had been here, the evening would have been equally pleasant, and Marian equally happy in her singing?"

"Dont you like Marian's singing?"

"Could you not have refrained from that most indiscreet question?"

"I ought to have. It came out unawares. Do not answer it."

"That would make matters worse. And there is no reason whatever why the plain truth should not be told. When I was a child I heard every day better performances than Marian's. She believes there is something pretty and good in music, and patronizes it accordingly to the best of her ability. I do not like to hear music patronized; and when Marian, lovely as she is, gives her pretty renderings of songs which I have heard a hundred times from singers who knew what they were about, then, though I admire her as I must always, my admiration is rather increased than otherwise when she stops; because then I am no longer conscious of a deficiency which even my unfortunate sister could supply."

"Your criticism of her singing sounds more sincere than your admiration of her loveliness. I am not musician enough to judge. All I know is that her singing is good enough for me."

"I know you are displeased because it is not good enough for me; but how can I help myself? Poor Marian—"

"Do hush!" said Elinor. "Here she is."

"You need not be in such a hurry, Duke," said Marian. "What can it matter to you how late you get back?"

"No," said Marmaduke. "I've got to write home. The governor is ill; and my mammy will send me a five-sheet sermon if I neglect writing to-night. You will keep Lucy for another week, wont you? Box her ears if she gives you any cheek. She wants it: she's been spoiled."

"If we find we can do no better than that with her, we shall hand her back to you," said Conolly. Then the visitors took their leave. Marian gently pressed Douglas's hand and looked into his eyes as he bade her farewell. Elinor, seeing this, glanced uneasily at Conolly, and unexpectedly met his eye. There was a gleam of cynical intelligence in it that did not reassure her. A few minutes later she went to bed, leaving the couple alone together. Conolly looked at his wife for a moment with an amused expression; but she closed her lips irresponsively, and went to the table for a book which she wanted to bring upstairs. She would have gone without a word had he not spoken to her.

"Marian: Douglas is in love with you."

She blushed; thought a moment; and said quietly, "Very well. I shall not ask him to come again."

"Why?"

She colored more vividly and suddenly, and said, "I thought you cared. I beg your pardon."

"My dear," he replied, amiably: "if you exclude everybody who falls in love with you, we shall have no one in the house but blind men."

"And do you like men to be in love with me?"

"Yes. It makes the house pleasant for them; it makes them attentive to you; and it gives you great power for good. When I was a romantic boy, any good woman could have made a saint of me. Let them fall in love with you as much as they please. Afterwards they will seek wives according to a higher standard than if they had never known you. But do not return the compliment, or your influence will become an evil one."

"Ned: I had not intended to tell you this; but now I will. Sholto Douglas not only loves me, but he told me so to-day."

"Of course. A man always does tell it, sooner or later."

Marian sat down on the sofa and looked at him for some time gravely and a little wistfully. "I think," she said, "I should feel very angry if any woman made such a confession to you."

"A Christian British lady does not readily forgive a breach of convention; nor a woman an invasion of her privileges, even when they have become a burden to her."

"What do you mean by that?" she said, rising.

"Marian," he said, looking straight at her: "are you dissatisfied?"

"What reason have I to—"

"Never mind the reasons. Are you?"

"No," said she, steadfastly.

He smiled indulgently; pressed her hand for a moment against his cheek; and went out for the short walk he was accustomed to take before retiring.

CHAPTER XV

In October Marian was at Sark, holiday making at the house of Hardy McQuinch's brother, who had recently returned to England with a fortune made in Australia. Conolly, having the house at Holland Park to himself, fitted a spare room as a laboratory, and worked there every night. One evening, returning home alone a little before five o'clock, he shut himself into this laboratory, and had just set to work when Armande, the housemaid, interrupted him.

"Mrs. Leith Fairfax, sir."

Conolly had had little intercourse with Mrs. Fairfax since before his marriage, when he had once shewn her the working of his invention at Queen Victoria Street; and as Marian had since resented her share of Douglas's second proposal by avoiding her society as far as possible without actually discontinuing her acquaintance, this visit was a surprise. Conolly looked darkly at Armande, and went to the drawing-room without a word.

"*How* do you do, Mr. Conolly?" said Mrs. Fairfax, as he entered. "I need not ask: you are looking so well. Have I disturbed you?"

"You have—most agreeably. Pray sit down."

"I know your time is priceless. I should never have ventured to come, but that I felt sure you would like to hear all the news from Sark. I have been there for the last fortnight. Marian told me to call on you the moment I returned."

"Yes," said Conolly, convinced that this was not true. "She promised to do so in her last letter."

Mrs. Fairfax, on the point of publishing a few supplementary fictions, checked herself, and looked suspiciously at him.

"The air of Sark has evidently benefited you," he said, as she paused. "You are looking very well—I had almost said charming."

Mrs. Fairfax glanced archly at him, and said, "Nonsense! but, indeed, the trip was absolutely necessary for me. I should hardly have been alive had I remained at work; and poor Willie McQuinch was bent on having me."

"He has been described to me as an inveterate lion hunter."

"It is not at all pleasant, I assure you, to be persecuted with invitations from people who wish to see a real live novelist. But William McQuinch's place at Sark is really palatial. He is called Sarcophagus on account of his wealth. A great many people whom he knew were staying in the island, besides those in the house with us. Marian was the beauty of the place. How every one admires her! Why do you not go down, Mr. Conolly?"

"I am too busy. Besides, it will do Marian good to be rid of me for a while."

"Absurd, Mr. Conolly! You should not leave her there by herself."

"By herself! Why, is not the place full?"

"Yes; but I do not mean that. There is nobody belonging to her there."

"You forget. Miss McQuinch is her bosom friend. There is Marmaduke, her cousin; and his mother, her Aunt Dora. Then, is there not Mr. Sholto Douglas, one of her oldest and most attached friends?"

"Oh! Is Mr. Douglas in charge of her?"

"No doubt he will take charge of her, if she is overtaken by her second childhood whilst he is there. Meanwhile, she is in charge of herself, is she not? And there is hardly any danger of her feeling lonely."

"No. Sholto Douglas will provide against that."

"Your opinion confirms the accounts I have had from other sources. It appears that Mr. Douglas is very attentive to my wife."

"Very, indeed, Mr. Conolly. You must not think that I am afraid of anything—anything—"

"Anything?"

"Well—Oh, you know what I mean. Anything wrong. At least, not exactly wrong, but—"

"Anything undomestic."

"Yes. You see, Marian's position is a very difficult one. She is so young and so good looking that she is very much observed; and it seems so strange her being without her husband."

"Pretty ladies whose husbands are never seen, often get talked about in the world, do they not?"

"That is just what I mean. How cleverly you get everything out of me, Mr. Conolly! I called here without the faintest idea of alluding to Marian's situation; and now you have made me say all sorts of things. What a fortune you would have made at the bar!"

"I must apologize, I did not mean to cross-examine you. Naturally, of course, you would not like to make me uneasy about Marian."

"It is the very last thing I should desire. But now that it has slipped out, I really think you ought to go to Sark."

"Indeed! I rather infer that I should be very much in the way."

"The more reason for you to go, Mr. Conolly."

"Not at all, Mrs. Leith Fairfax. The attentions of a husband are stale, unsuited to holiday time. Picture to yourself my arrival at Sark with the tender assurance in my mouth, 'Marian, I love you.' She would reply, 'So you ought. Am I not your wife?' The same advance from another—Mr. Douglas, for instance— would affect her quite differently, and much more pleasantly."

"Mr. Conolly; is this indifference, or supreme confidence?"

"Neither of these conjugal claptraps. I merely desire that Marian should enjoy herself as much as possible; and the more a woman is admired, the happier she is. Perhaps you think that, in deference to the general feeling in such matters, I should become jealous."

Mrs. Fairfax again looked doubtfully at him. "I cannot make you out at all, Mr. Conolly," she said submissively. "I hope I have not offended you."

"Not in the least. I take it that having observed certain circumstances which seemed to threaten the welfare of one very dear to you (as, I am aware, Marian is), the trouble they caused you found unpremeditated expression in the course of a conversation with me." Conolly beamed at her, as if he thought this rather neatly turned.

"Exactly so. But I do not wish you to think that I have observed anything particular."

"Certainly not. Still, you think there would be no harm in my writing to Marian to say that her behavior has attracted your notice, and—"

"Good heavens, Mr. Conolly, you must not mention *me* in the matter! You are so innocent—at least so frank, so workman-like, if I may say so, in your way of dealing with things! I would not have Marian know what I have said—I really did not notice anything—for worlds. You had better not write at all, but just go down as if you went merely to enjoy yourself; and dont on any account let Marian suspect that you have heard anything. Goodness knows what mischief you might make, in your—your ingenuousness!"

"But I should have thought that the opinion of an old and valued friend like yourself would have special weight with her."

"You know nothing about it. Clever engineer as you are, you do not understand the little wheels by which our great machine of society is worked."

"True, Mrs. Leith Fairfax," he rejoined, echoing the cadence of her sentence. "Educated as a mere mechanic, I am still a stranger to the elegancies of life. I usually depend on Marian for direction; but since you think that it would be injudicious to appeal to her in the present instance—"

"Out of the question, Mr. Conolly."

"—I must trust to your guidance in the matter. What do you suggest?"

Mrs. Fairfax was about to reply, when the expression which she habitually wore like a mask in society, wavered and broke. Her lip trembled: her eyes filled with tears: she rose with a sniff that was half a sob. When she spoke, her voice was sincere for the first time, and at the sound of it Conolly's steely, hard manner melted, and his inhuman self-possession vanished.

"You think," she said, "that I came here to make mischief. I did not. Marian is nothing to me: she does not even like me; but I dont want to see her ruin herself merely because she is too inexperienced to know when she is well off. I have had to fight my way in London: and I know what it is, and what the world is. She is not fit to take charge of herself. Good-bye, Mr. Conolly: you are a great deal too young yourself to know the danger, for all your cleverness. You may tell her that I came here and gossipped against her, if you like. She will never speak to me again; but if it saves her, I dont care. Good-bye."

"My dear Mrs. Fairfax," he said, with entire frankness, "I am now deeply and sincerely obliged to you." And in proof that he was touched, he kissed her hand with the ease and grace of a man who had been carefully taught how to do it. Mrs. Fairfax recovered herself and almost blushed as he went with her to the door, chatting easily about the weather and the Addison Road trains.

She was not the last visitor that evening. She had hardly been fifteen minutes gone when the Rev. George presented himself, and was conducted to the laboratory, where he found Conolly, with his coat off, surrounded by apparatus. The glowing fire, comfortable chairs, and preparations for an evening meal, gladdened him more than the presence of his brother-in-law, with whom he never felt quite at ease.

"You wont mind my fiddling with these machines while I talk," said Conolly.

"Not at all, not at all. I shall witness your operations with great interest. You must not think that the wonders of science are indifferent to me."

"So you are going on to Sark, you say?"

"Yes. May I ask whether you will be persuaded to come?"

"No, for certain. I have other fish to fry here."

"I think it would renovate your health to come for a few days."

"My health is always right as long as I have work. Did you meet Mrs. Fairfax outside?"

"A—yes. I passed her."

"You spoke to her, I suppose?"

"A few words. Yes."

"Do you know what she came here for?"

"No. But stay. I am wrong. She mentioned that she came for a book she lent you."

"She mentioned what was not true. What did she say to you about Marian?"

"Well, she—She was just saying that it is perhaps as well that I should go down to Sark at once, as Marian is quite alone."

The clergyman looked so guilty as he said this that Conolly laughed outright at him. "You mean," he said, "that Marian is *not* quite alone. Well, very likely Douglas occupies himself a good deal with her. If so, there may be some busybody or another down there fool enough to tell her that people are talking about her. That would spoil her holiday; so it is lucky that you are going down. No one will take it upon themselves to speak to her when you are there; and if they say anything to you, you can let it in at one ear and out at the other."

"That is, of course, unless I should see her really acting indiscreetly."

"I had better tell you beforehand what you will see if you keep your eyes open. You will see very plainly that Douglas is in love with her. Also that she knows that he is in love with her. In fact, she told me so. And you will see she rather likes it. Every married woman requires a holiday from her husband occasionally, even when he suits her perfectly."

The Rev. George stared. "If I follow you aright—I am not sure that I do—you impute to Marian the sin of entertaining feelings which it is her duty to repress."

"I impute no sin to her. You might as well tell a beggar that he has no right to be hungry, as a woman that it is her duty to feel this and not to feel that."

"But Marian has been educated to feel only in accordance with her duty."

"So have you. How does it work? However," continued Conolly, without waiting for an answer, "I dont deny that Marian shews the effects of her education. They are deplorably evident in all her conscientious actions."

"You surprise and distress me. This is the first intimation I have received of your having any cause to complain of Marian."

"Nonsense! I dont complain of her. But what you call her education, as far as I can make it out, appears to have consisted of stuffing her with lies, and making it a point of honor with her to believe them in spite of sense and reason. The sense of duty that rises on that sort of foundation is more mischievous than downright want of principle. I dont dispute your right, you who constitute polite society, to skin over all the ugly facts of life. But to make your daughters believe that the skin covers healthy flesh is a crime. Poor Marian thinks that a room is clean when all the dust is swept out of sight under the furniture; and if honest people rake it out to bring it under the notice of those whose duty it is to remove it, she is disgusted with them, and ten to one accuses them of having made it themselves. She doesnt know what sort of world she is in, thanks to the misrepresentations of those who should have taught her. She will deceive her children in just the same way, if she ever has any. If she had been taught the truth in her own childhood, she would know how to face it, and would be a strong woman as well as an amiable one. But it is too late now. The truth seems natural to a child; but to a grown woman or man, it is a bitter lesson in the learning, though it may be invigorating when it is well mastered. And you know how seldom a hard task forced on an unwilling pupil *is* well mastered."

"What is truth?" said the clergyman, sententiously.

"All that we know, Master Pilate," retorted Conolly with a laugh. "And we know a good deal. It may seem small in comparison with what we dont know; but it is more than any one of us can hold, for all that. We know, for instance, that the world was not planned by a sentimental landscape gardener. If Marian ever learns that—which she may, although I am neither able nor willing to teach it to her—she will not thank those who gave her so much falsehood to unlearn. Until then, she will, I am afraid, do little else than lay up a store of regrets for herself."

"This is very strange. We always looked upon Marian as an exceptionally amiable girl."

"So she is, unfortunately. There is no institution so villainous but she will defend it; no tyranny so oppressive but she will make a virtue of submitting to it; no social cancer so venomous but she will shrink from cutting it out, and plead that it is a comfortable thing, and much better as it is. She knows that she disobeyed her father, and that he deserved to be disobeyed; yet she condemns other women who are disobedient, and stands out against Nelly McQuinch in defence of the unselfishness of parental love. She knows that the increased freedom of move-ment allowed to her as a married woman has been healthy for her; yet she looks coldly at other young women who assert their right to freedom, and are not afraid to walk through the streets without a sheepdog, human or otherwise, at their heels. She knows that marriage is not what she expected it to be, and that it gives me many unfair advantages over her; and she knows also that ours is a happier marriage than most. Nevertheless she will encourage other girls to marry; she will maintain that the chain which galls her own wrists so often is a string of honeysuckles; and if a woman identifies herself with any public movement for the lightening of that chain, she wont allow that that woman is fit to be admitted into decent society. There is not one of these shams to which she clings that I would not like to take by the throat and shake the life out of; and she knows it. Even in that she has not the consistency to believe me wrong, because it is undutiful and out of keeping with the honeysuckles to lack faith in her husband. In order to blind herself to her inconsistencies, she has to live in a rose-colored fog; and what with me constantly, in spite of myself, blowing this fog away on the one side, and the naked facts of her everyday experience as constantly letting in the daylight on the other, she must spend half the time wondering whether she is mad or sane. Between her desire to do right and her discoveries that it generally leads her to do wrong, she passes her life in a wistful melancholy which I cant dispel. I can only pity her. I suppose I could pet her; but I hate treating a woman like a child: it means giving up all hope of her becoming rational. She may turn for relief any day either to love or religion; and for her own sake I hope she will choose the first. Of the two evils, it is the least permanent." And Conolly, having disburdened himself, resumed his work without any pretence of waiting for the clergyman's comments.

"Well," said the Rev. George, cautiously, "I do not think I have quite followed your opinions, which seem to me to be exactly upside down, as if they were projected upon the retina of your mind's eye—to use Shakspear's happy phrase—just as they would be upon your—your real eye, you know. But I can assure you that your view of Marian is an entirely mistaken one. You seem to think that she does not give in her entire adherence to the doctrines of the Establishment. This is a matter which I venture to say you do not understand."

"Admitted," interposed Conolly, hastily. "Here is my workman's tea. Are you fond of scones?"

"I hardly know. Anything—the simplest fare, will satisfy me."

"So it does me, when I can get nothing better. Help yourself, pray."

Conolly did not sit down to the meal, but worked whilst the clergyman ate. Presently the Rev. George, warmed by the fire and cheered by the repast, returned to the subject of his host's domestic affairs.

"Come," he said, "I am sure that a few judicious words would lead to an explanation between you and Marian."

"I also think that a few words might do so. But they would not be judicious words."

"Why not? Can it be injudicious to restore harmony in a household?"

"No; but that would not be the effect of an explanation, because the truth is not likely to reconcile us. If I were to explain the difficulty to a man, he would argue. But Marian would just infer that I despised her, and nothing else."

"Oh no! Oh dear no! A few kind words; an appeal to her good sense; a little concession on both sides—"

"All excellent for a pair estranged by a flash of temper, or a mother-in-law, or a trifle of jealousy, or too many evenings spent at the club on the man's part, or too many dances with a gallant on the woman's; but no good for us. We have never exchanged unkind words: there are no concessions to be made: her good sense is not at fault. Besides, these few kind words that are supposed to be such a sovereign remedy for all sorts of domestic understandings are generally a few kind fibs. If I told them, Marian wouldnt believe them. Fibs dont make lasting truces either. No: the situation is graver than you think. Just suppose, for instance, that you undertake to restore harmony, as you call it! what will you say to her?"

"Well, it would depend on circumstances."

"But you know the circumstances on which it depends. How would you begin?"

"There are little ways of approaching delicate subjects with women. For instance, I might say, casually, that it was a pity that a pair so happily situated as you two should not agree perfectly."

"You would get no further; for Marian would never admit that we do not agree. She does not know what her complaint is, and therefore feels bound in honor to maintain that she has nothing to complain of. She is not the woman to cast reproach on me for a discontent she cannot explain. Or, if she could explain it, how much wiser should you be? *I* have explained; and you confess you cannot understand me. The difference between us is neither her fault nor mine; and all the explanations in the world will not remove it."

"If you would allow me to appeal to her religious duty—"

"Religion! She doesnt believe in it."

"What!" exclaimed the clergyman, unaffectedly shocked. "Surely, surely—"

"Listen. To me, believing in a doctrine doesnt mean holding up your hand and saying, 'Credo.' It means habitually acting on the assumption that the doctrine is true. Marian thinks it wrong not to go to church; and she will hold up her hand and cry 'Credo' to the immortality of her soul, or to any verse in

George Bernard Shaw

the New Testament. The shareholders of our concern in the city will do the same. But do they or she ever act on the assumption that they are immortal, or that riches are dross, or that class prejudice is damnable? Never. They dont believe it. You will find that Marian has been thoroughly trained to separate her practice from her religious professions; and if you allude to the inconsistency she will instinctively feel that you are offending against good taste. In short, her 'Credo' doesnt mean faith: it means church-going, which is practised because it is respectable, and is respectable because it is a habit of the upper caste. But church-going is church-going; and business is business, as Marian will soon let you know if you meddle with *her* business. However, we need not argue about that: we know one another's views and can agree to differ."

"I should be false to my duty as a Christian priest if I made any such agreement."

"Perhaps so; but, at any rate, we cant spend all our lives over the same argument. No, as I was saying, take my advice, and let Marian alone."

"But what do you intend to do, then?"

"What *can* I do but wait? Experience must wear out some of her illusions. She will at least find out that she is no worse off than other women, and better off than some of them. Since the job cannot be undone, we must try how making the best of it will work. I am pretty hopeful myself. How are affairs getting on at your chapel? I am told that the sermons of your *locum tenens* send the congregation asleep."

"He is not at his best in the pulpit. A good fellow! a most loving man but not able to grapple with a large congregation. After all, I am obliged to confess that very few of our cloth are. The power of preaching is quite an exceptional one; and it is a gift as well as a trust. I humbly believe that the power of the tongue comes of a higher ordination than the bishop's."

Nothing further was said about Marian. The clergyman's object in visiting Conolly was, it presently appeared, to borrow a portmanteau. When he was gone, Conolly returned to the laboratory, and wrote the following letter:

"My dear Marian

"I have just had two unexpected visits, one from Mrs. Fairfax, and one from George. Mrs. L.F. said you asked her to call and give me the news. When I told her, without blushing, that you had written to prepare me for her visit, she was rather put out, justly thinking me to mean that I did not believe her. As this is fully the thirty-sixth falsehood in which you have detected good Mrs. F., I fear you will be compelled, in spite of your principle of believing the best of everybody, to regard her in future as a not invariably accurate woman. She came with the object of making me go down to Sark. You were so young and so much admired: Mr. Douglas was so attentive: you should not be left entirely alone, and so forth. You will be angry with her; but she thinks Douglas so irresistible that she is genuinely anxious about you: I believe she really meant well this time. As to our reverend brother, his portmanteau burst in the train coming from Edinburgh; so he came to borrow mine, having apparently resolved to wear out those of all his friends before buying a new one. Unfortunately, he met Mrs. F. down the road; and she urged him to go down to Sark just as she had urged me. Now as George is incapable of holding his tongue when he ought, I feel sure that unless I tell you what Mrs. F. said, he will anticipate me. Otherwise I should not have mentioned it until your return, for fear of annoying you and spoiling your visit. So if his reverence hints or lectures, you will know what he means and not heed him. Mrs. F's confidences have probably not been confined to me; but were I in your place, I should not make the slightest change in my conduct in consequence. At all events, if you feel constrained to display any sudden accession of reserve toward Douglas, tell him the reason; because if you dont, he will ascribe the change to coquetry.

"I have turned the spare room on the first floor into a laboratory, and am sitting in it now. I'm thinking of fitting it up like a studio, and having private views of my inventions, as Scott has of his pictures. Parson's man came with some flowers the other day, and informed me that three balls, to the first of which he was invited, took place in the house while I was away. One or two trifling dilapidations, and the fact that somebody has been tampering with the locks of the organ and piano, dispose me to believe this tale. Parson's man declares that he was too virtuous to come to the two last entertainments after finding out that the first was a clandestine one; but I believe he made himself disagreeable, and was not invited. Probably he quarrelled with some military follower of Armande's; for he was particularly bitter on the subject of a common soldier making free in a gentleman's house. I have not said anything to the two culprits; but I have contrived to make them suspect that I know all; and they now do their duty with trembling diligence. Some man sat on the little walnut table and broke it; but no other damage worth mentioning has been done. The table was absurdly repaired with a piece of twine, and pushed into the recess between the organ and the front window, whence I sometimes amuse myself by the experiment of pulling it into broad daylight. It is always pushed back again before I return in the evening.

"How are you off for money? I have plenty of loose cash just now. Madame called last Monday, and asked Matilda, who opened the door, when you would be back. Thereupon I interviewed her. I must say she is loyal to her clients; for I had great difficulty in extracting her bill, which was, of course, what she called about. She evidently recognizes the necessity of keeping husbands in the dark in such matters. One of the items was for the lace on your maccaroni-colored body, which, as I chanced to remember, you supplied yourself. After a brief struggle she deducted it; so I paid her the balance: only 35L 13s. 9d.

"When are you coming back to me? After Sark I fear you will find home a little dull. Nevertheless, I should like to see you again. Come back before Christmas, at any rate.

"Yours, dear Marian, in solitude,
"NED."

The answer came two days later than return of post, and ran thus:

"Melbourne House, Sark,
"Sunday.

"My dear Ned

"How very provoking about the servants! I do not mind Matilda so much; but I do think it hard that we could not depend on Armande, considering all the kindness we have shewn her. I can scarcely believe that she would have acted so badly unless she were led away by Matilda, whom I will pack off the moment I return. As to Armande, I will give her another chance; but she shall have a sharp talking to. I am quite sure that a great deal more mischief has been done than you noticed. If the carpet was danced on for three nights by men in heavy boots, it must be in ribbons. It is really too bad. I do not want any money. Indeed the twenty pounds you sent me last was quite unnecessary, as I have nearly sixteen left. What a rogue Madame is to try and make you pay for my lace! I am sorry you paid the bill. She had no business to call for her money: she is *never* paid so soon by *anybody*. We have had great fun down here. It has been one continual garden party all through; and the weather is still lovely. Mr. McQuinch is very colonial: but I think his ways make the house pleasanter than if he were still English. Carbury is quite stupid in comparison to this place. I have danced more than I ever did in my life before; and now we are so tired of frivolity that if any one ventures to strum a waltz or propose a game, we all protest. We tried to get up some choral music; but it was a failure. On Friday, George, who is looked on as a great man here, was asked to give us a Shakespeare reading. He was only too glad to be asked; for he had heard Simonton, the actor, read at a bazaar in Scotland, and was full of Richard the Third in consequence. He was not very bad; but his imitation of Simonton was so obvious and so queerly mixed with his own churchy style that he seemed rather monotonous and affected. At least I thought so. I was dreadfully uncomfortable during the reading because of Marmaduke, who behaved scandalously. There were some schoolboys present; and he not only encouraged them to misbehave themselves, but was worse than any of them himself. At last he pretended to be overcome by the heat, and went out of the room, to my great relief; but when the passage about the early village cock came, he crew outside the door, where he had been waiting expressly to do it. Nobody could help laughing; and the boys screamed so that Mr. McQuinch took two of them out by the collar. I believe he was glad of the excuse to go out and laugh himself. George was very angry, and no wonder! He will hardly speak to Marmaduke, who, of course, denies all knowledge of the interruption; but George knows better. All the Hardy McQuinches are down here. Uncle Hardy is rather stooped from rheumatism. Nelly is now the chief personage in the family: Lydia and Jane are nowhere beside her. They are good-humored, bouncing girls; but they are certainly not brilliant. I hope it is not Aunt Dora's walnut table that is broken. Was it not mean of Parson's man to tell on Armande? I think, since you have plenty of loose cash, we might venture on a set of those curtains we saw at Protheroe's, for the drawing-room. I can easily use the ones that are there now for *portieres*.

"You must not think that I have written this all at once. I shall be able to finish to-day, as it is Sunday, and I have made an excuse to stay away from church. George is to preach; and somehow I never feel toward the service as I ought when he officiates. I know you will laugh at this.

"The first part of your letter must have a paragraph all to

itself. I hardly know what to say. I could not have believed that Mrs. Leith Fairfax would have behaved as she has done. I was so angry at first that for fully an hour I felt ill; and I spoke quite wickedly to George the day after he arrived, because he said that Sholto had better not take me down to dinner, although his doing so was quite accidental. I know you will believe me when I tell you that I was quite unconscious that he had been unusually attentive to me; and I was about to write you an indignant denial, only I shewed Nelly your letter, and she crushed me by telling me she had noticed it too. We nearly had a quarrel about it; but she counted up the number of times I had danced with him and sat beside him at dinner; and I suppose an evil-minded woman looking on might think what Mrs. Leith Fairfax thought. But there is no excuse for her. She knows that Sholto and I have been intimate since we were children; and there is something odious in her, of all people, pretending to misunderstand us. What is worse, she was particularly friendly and confidential with me while she was here; and although I tried to keep away from her at first, she persisted in conciliating me, and persuaded me that Douglas had entirely mistaken what she said that other time. Who could have expected her to turn round and calumniate me the moment my back was turned! How can people do such things! I hope we shall not meet her again; for I will never speak to her. I have not said anything to Douglas. How could I? It would only make mischief. I feel that the right course is to come home as soon as I can, and in the meantime to avoid him as much as possible. So you may expect me on Saturday next. Mr. McQuinch is quite dismayed at my departure, which he says will be the signal for a general breaking up; but this I cannot help. I shall be glad to go home, of course. Still, I am sorry to leave this place, where we have all been so jolly. I will write and let you know what train I shall come by; but you need not trouble to meet me, unless you like: I can get home quite well by myself. After all, it is just as well that I am getting away. It *was* pleasant enough; but now I feel utterly disgusted with everything and everybody. I find I must

George Bernard Shaw

stop. They have just come in from church; and I must go down.

"Your affectionate
"MARIAN."

CHAPTER XVI

One Saturday afternoon in December Marian and Elinor sat drinking tea in the drawing-room at Holland Park. Elinor was present as an afternoon caller: she no longer resided with the Conollys. Marian had been lamely excusing herself for not having read Elinor's last book.

"Pray dont apologize," said Elinor. "I remember the time when you would have forced yourself to read it from a sense of duty; and I am too delighted to find that nonsense washing out of you at last to feel the wound to my vanity. Oh, say no more, my dear you can read it still whenever you please. Brother George read it, and was shocked because the heroine loves the villain and tells him so without waiting to be asked. It is odd that long ago, when I believed so devoutly in the tender passion, I never could write a really flaming love story."

"Dont begin to talk like that," said Marian, crossly. "People *do* fall in love, fortunately for them. It may be injudicious; and it may turn out badly; but it fills up life in a way that all the barren philosophy and cynicism on earth cannot. Do you think I would not rather have to regret a lost love than to repine because I had been too cautious to love at all? The disappointments of love warm the heart more than the triumphs of insensibility."

"Thats rather a good sentence," said Elinor. "Your talk is more classical than my writing. But what would the departed Marian Lind have said?"

George Bernard Shaw

"The departed Marian Lind was so desperately wise that she neglected that excellent precept, 'Be not righteous over much, neither make thyself over wise; why shouldest thou destroy thyself?' I took up the Bible last night for the first time since my marriage; and I thought what fools we two used to be when we made up our minds to avoid all the mistakes and follies and feelings of other people, and to be quite superior and rational. 'He that observeth the wind shall not sow; and he that regardeth the clouds shall not reap.' It is all so true, in spite of what Ned says. We were very clever at observing the wind and regarding the clouds; and what are we the better for it? How much irreparable mischief, I wonder, did we do ourselves by letting our little wisdoms stifle all our big instincts! Look at those very other people whom we despised; how happy they are, in spite of their having always done exactly what their hearts told them!"

"I think we are pretty well off as people go. I know I am. Certainly it was part of our wisdom that marriage was a bad thing; and I grant that though you married in obedience to your instincts you are as well off as I. But I dont see that we are the worse for having thought a little."

"I did *not* marry in obedience to my instincts, Nelly; and you know it. I made a disinterested marriage with a man whom I felt I could respect as my superior. I was convinced then that a grand passion was a folly."

"And what do you think now?"

"I think that I did not know what I was talking about."

"I believe you were in love with Ned when you married him, and long enough before that, too."

"Of course I loved him. I love him still."

"Do you, really? To hear you, one would think that you only respected him as a superior."

"You have no right to say that. You dont understand."

"Perhaps not. Would you mind explaining?"

"I do not mean anything particular; but there are two kinds of love. There is a love which one's good sense suggests—a sort of moral approval—"

Elinor laughed. "Go on," she said. "What is the other sort?"

"The other sort has nothing to do with good sense. It is an overpowering impulse—a craving—a faith that defies logic— something to look forward to feeling in your youth, and look back to with a kindling heart in your age."

"Indeed! Isnt the difference between the two sorts much the same as the difference between the old love and the new?"

"What do you mean?"

"I think I will take another cup of tea. You neednt stop flying out at me, though: I dont mind it."

"Excuse me. I did not mean to fly out at you."

"It's rather odd that we so seldom meet now without getting on this subject and having a row. Has that struck you at all?"

Marian turned to the fire, and remained silent.

"Listen to me, Marian. You are in the blues. Why dont you go to Ned, and tell him that he is a cast-iron walking machine, and that you are unhappy, and want the society of a flesh-and-blood man? Have a furious scene with him, and all will come right."

"It is very easy to talk. I could not go to him and make myself ridiculous like that: the words would choke me. Besides, I am not unhappy."

"What a lie! You wicked woman! A moment ago you were contemning all prudence; and now you will not speak your mind because you are afraid of being ridiculous. What is that but observing the wind and regarding the clouds, I should like to know?"

"I wish you would not speak harshly to me, even in jest. It hurts me."

"Serve you right! I am not a bit remorseful. No matter: let us talk of something else. Where did those flowers come from?"

"Douglas sent them. I am going to the theatre to-night; and I wanted a bouquet."

"Very kind of him. I wonder he did not bring it himself. He rarely misses an excuse for coming."

"Why do you say that, Nelly? He comes here very seldom, except on Sunday; and that is a regular thing, just as your coming is."

"He was here on Tuesday; you saw him at Mrs. Saunders's on Wednesday; he was at your at-home on Thursday; and he sends a bouquet on Saturday."

"I cannot help meeting him out; and not to invite him to my at-home would be to cut him. Pray are you growing spiteful, like Mrs. Leith Fairfax?"

"Marian: you got out of bed at the wrong side this morning; and you have made that mistake oftener since your return from Sark than in all your life before. Douglas has become a lazy good-for-nothing; and he comes here a great deal too often. Instead of encouraging him to dangle after you as he does, and to teach you all those finely turned sentiments about love which you were airing a minute ago, you ought to make him get called to the bar, or sent into Parliament, or put to work in some fashion."

"Nelly!"

"Bother Nelly! It is true; and you know it as well as I do."

"If he fancies himself in love with me, I cannot help it."

"You can help his following you about."

"I cannot. He does not follow me about. Why does not Ned object? He knows that Sholto is in love with me; and he does not care."

"Oh, if it is only to make Ned jealous, then I have nothing more to say: you may flirt away as hard as you please. There's a knock at the door, just in time to prevent us from quarrelling. I know whose knock it is, too."

Marian had flushed slightly at the sound; and Elinor, with her feet stretched out before her, lapped the carpet restlessly with her heels, and watched her cousin sourly as Douglas entered. He was in evening dress.

"Good-evening," said Elinor. "So you are going to the theatre, too?"

"Why?" said Douglas. "Is any one coming with us? Shall we have the pleasure of your company?"

"No," replied Elinor, drily. "I thought Mr. Conolly was perhaps going with you."

"I shall be very glad, I am sure, if he will," said Douglas.

"He will not," said Marian. "I doubt if he will come home before we start."

"You got my flowers safely, I see."

"Yes, thank you. They are beautiful."

"They need be, if you are to wear them."

"I think I will go," said Elinor, "if you can spare me. Marian has been far from amiable; and if you are going to pay her compliments, I shall very soon be as bad as she. Good-bye." Douglas gratefully went with her to the door. She looked very hard at him, and almost made a grimace as they parted; but she said nothing.

"I am very glad she went," said Marian, when Douglas returned. "She annoys me. Everything annoys me."

"You are leading an impossible life here, Marian," he said, putting his hand on her chair and bending over her. "Whilst it lasts, everything will annoy you; and I, who would give the last drop of my blood to spare you a moment's pain, shall never experience the delight of seeing you happy."

"What other life can I lead?"

Douglas made an impulsive movement, as though to reply; but he hesitated, and did not speak. Marian was not looking at him. She was gazing into the fire.

"Sholto," she said, after an interval of silence, "you must not come here any more."

"What!"

"You are too idle. You come here too often. Why do you not become a barrister, or go into Parliament, or at least write books? If Nelly can succeed as an author, surely you can."

"I have left all that behind me. I am a failure: you know why. Let us talk no more of it."

"Do not go on like that," said Marian, pettishly. "I dont like it."

"I am afraid to say or do anything, you are so easily distressed."

"Yes, I know I am very cross. Elinor remarked it too. I think you might bear with me, Sholto." Here, most unexpectedly, she rose and burst into tears. "When my whole life is one dreary record of misery, I cannot always be patient. I have been forbearing toward you many times."

Douglas was at first frightened; for he had never seen her cry before. Then, as she sat down again, and covered her face with her handkerchief, he advanced, intending to kneel and put his arm about her; but his courage failed: he only drew a chair to the fire, and bent over, as he sat beside her, till his face was close to hers, saying, "It is all the fault of your mad marriage. You were happy until then. I have been silent hitherto; but now that I see your tears, I can no longer master myself. Listen to me, Marian. You asked me a moment since what other life was open to you. There is a better life. Leave England with me; and—and—" Marian had raised her head; and as she looked steadily at him, he stopped, and his lips became white.

"Go on," she said. "I am not angry. What else?"

"Nothing else except happiness." His voice died away: there was a pause. Then, recovering himself, he went on with something of his characteristic stateliness. "There is no use in prolonging your present life; it is a failure, like mine. Why should you hesitate? You know how seldom the mere letter of duty leads to either happiness or justice. You can rescue me from a wasted existence. You can preserve your own heart from a horrible slow domestic decay. *He* will not care: he cares for nothing: he is morally murdering you. You have no children to think of. I love you; and I offer you your choice of the fairest spots in the wide world to pass our future in, with my protection to ensure your safety and comfort there, wherever it may be. You know what a hollow thing conventional virtue is. Who are the virtuous people about you? Mrs. Leith Fairfax, and her like. If you love me, you must know that you are committing a crime against nature in living as you are with a man who is as far removed from you in every human emotion as his workshop is from heaven. You have striven to do your duty by him in vain. He is none the happier: we are unutterably the more miserable. Let us try a new life. I have lived in society here all my days, and have found its atmosphere most worthless, most selfish, most impure. I want to be free—to shake the dust of London off my feet, and enter on a life made holy by love. You can respond to such an aspiration: you, too, must yearn for a pure and free life. It is within our reach: you have but to stretch out your hand. Say something to me. Are you listening?"

"It seems strange that I should be listening to you quite calmly, as I am; although you are proposing what the world thinks a disgraceful thing."

"Does it matter what the world thinks? I would not, even to save myself from a wasted career, ask you to take a step that would really disgrace you. But I cannot bear to think of you looking back some day over a barren past, and knowing that you sacrificed your happiness to Fashion—an idol. Do you remember last Sunday when we discussed that bitter saying that women who have sacrificed their feelings to the laws of society secretly know that they have been fools for their pains? *He* did not deny it. You could give no good reason for disbelieving it. You know it to be true; and I am only striving to save you from that vain regret. You have shewn that you can obey the world with grace and dignity when the world is right. Shew now that you can defy it fearlessly when it is tyrannical. Trust your heart, Marian—my darling Marian: trust your heart—and mine."

"For what hour have you ordered the carriage?"

"The carriage! Is that what you say to me at such a moment? Are you still flippant as ever?"

"I am quite serious. Say no more now. If I go, I will go deliberately, and not on the spur of your persuasion. I must have time to think. What hour did you say?"

"Seven."

"Then it is time for me to dress. You will not mind waiting here alone?"

"If you would only give me one hopeful word, I think I could wait happily forever."

"What can I say?"

"Say that you love me."

"I am striving to discover whether I have always loved you or not. Surely, if there be such a thing as love, we should be lovers."

He was chilled by her solemn tone; but he made a movement as if to embrace her.

"No," she said, stopping him. "I am his wife still. I have not yet pronounced my own divorce."

She left the room; and he walked uneasily to and fro Until she returned, dressed in white. He gazed at her with quickened breath as she confronted him. Neither heeded the click of her husband's latchkey in the door without.

"When I was a little boy, Marian," he said, gazing at her, "I used to think that Paul Delaroche's Christian martyr was the most exquisite vision of beauty in the world. I have the same feeling as I look at you now."

"Marian reminds me of that picture too," said Conolly. "I remember wondering," he continued, smiling, as they started and turned toward him, "why the young lady—she was such a perfect lady—was martyred in a ball dress, as I took her costume to be. Marian's wreath adds to the force of

George Bernard Shaw

the reminiscence."

"If I recollect aright," said Marian, taking up his bantering tone with a sharper irony, "Delaroche's martyr shewed a fine sense of the necessity of having her wrists gracefully tied. I am about to follow her example by wearing these bracelets, which I can never fasten. Be good enough to assist me, both of you."

She extended a hand to each; and Conolly, after looking at the catch for a moment, closed it dexterously at the first snap. "By the bye," he said, whilst Douglas fumbled at the other bracelet, "I have to run away to Glasgow to-night by the ten train. We shall not see one another again until Monday evening."

Douglas's hand began to shake so that the gold band chafed Marian's arm. "There, there," she said, drawing it away from him, "you do it for me, Ned. Sholto has no mechanical genius." Her hand was quite steady as Conolly shut the clasp. "Why must you go to Glasgow?"

"They have got into a mess at the works there; and the engineer has telegraphed for me to go down and see what is the matter. I shall certainly be back on Monday. Have something for me to eat at half past seven. I am sorry to be away from our Sunday dinner, Douglas; but you know the popular prejudice. If you want a thing done, see to it yourself."

"Sholto has been very eloquent this evening on the subject of popular prejudices," said Marian. "He says that to defy the world is a proof of honesty."

"So it is," said Conolly. "I get on in the world by defying its old notions, and taking nobody's advice but my own. Follow Douglas's precepts by all means. Do you know that it is nearly a quarter to eight?"

"Oh! Let us go. We shall be late."

"I shall not see you to-morrow, Douglas. Good-night."

"Good-night," said Douglas, keeping at some distance; for he did not care to offer Conolly his hand before Marian now. "Pleasant journey."

"Thank you. Hallo! [Marian had impatiently turned back.] What have you forgotten?"

"My opera-glass," said Marian. "No, thanks: you would not know where to look for it: I will go myself."

She went upstairs; and Conolly, after a pause, followed, and found her in their bedroom, closing the drawer from which she had just taken the opera-glass.

"Marian," he said: "you have been crying to-day. Is anything wrong? or is it only nervousness?"

"Only nervousness," said Marian. "How did you find out that I had been crying? it was only for an instant, because Nelly annoyed me. Does my face shew it?"

"It does to me, not to anyone else. Are you more cheerful now?"

"Yes, I am all right. I will go to Glasgow with you, if you like."

Conolly recoiled, disconcerted. "Why?" he said. "Do you wish—?" He recovered himself, and added, "It is too cold, my dear; and I must travel very fast. I shall be busy all the time. Besides, you are forgetting the theatre and Douglas, who, by the bye, is catching cold on the steps."

"Well, I had better go with Douglas, since it will make you happier."

"Go with Douglas, my dear one, if it will make *you* happier," said he, kissing her. To his surprise, she threw her arm round him, held him fast by the shoulder, and looked at him with extraordinary earnestness. He gave a little laugh, and disengaged himself gently, saying, "Dont you think your nervousness is taking a turn rather inconvenient for Douglas?" She let her hands fall; closed her lips; and passed quietly out. He went to the window and watched her as she entered the carriage. Douglas held the door open for her; and Conolly, looking at him with a sort of pity, noted that he was, in his way, a handsome man and that his habit of taking himself very seriously gave him a certain, dignity. The brougham rolled away into the fog. Conolly pulled down the blind, and began to pack his portmanteau to a vigorously whistled accompaniment.

CHAPTER XVII

Conolly returned from Glasgow a little before eight on Monday evening. There was no light in the window when he entered the garden. Miss McQuinch opened the door before he reached it.

"What!" he said. "Going the moment I come in!" Then, seeing her face by the hall lamp, he put down his bag quickly, and asked what the matter was.

"I dont know whether anything is the matter. I am very glad you have returned. Come into the drawing-room: I dont want the servants to hear us talking."

"There is no light here," he said, following her in. "Is it possible you have been waiting in the dark?"

He lit a candle, and was about to light a lamp when she exclaimed impatiently, "Oh, I did not notice it: what does it matter? Do let the lamp alone, and listen to me." He obeyed, much amused at her irritation.

"Where has Marian gone to?" she asked.

"Is she out?" he said, suddenly grave. "You forget that I have come straight from Glasgow."

"I have been here since three o'clock. Marian sent me a note not to come on Sunday—that she should be out and that you

George Bernard Shaw

were away. But they tell me that she was at home all yesterday, except for two hours when she was out with Sholto. She packed her trunks in the evening, and went away with them. She told the cabman to drive to Euston. I dont know what it all means; and I have been half distracted waiting here for you. I thought you would never come. There is a note for you on your dressing-table."

He pursed his lips a little and looked attentively at her, but said nothing.

"Wont you go and open it?" she said anxiously. "It must contain some explanation."

"I am afraid the explanation is obvious."

"You have no right to say that. How do you know? If you are not going to read her letter, you had better say so at once. I dont want to pry into it: I only want to know what is become of Marian."

"You shall read it by all means. Will you excuse me whilst I fetch it?"

She stamped with impatience. He smiled and went for the letter, which, after a brief absence, he placed unopened on the table before her, saying:

"I suppose this is it. I laid my hand on it in the dark."

"Are you going to open it?" she said, hardly able to contain herself.

"No."

He had not raised his voice; but it struck her that he was in a rage. His friendly look and quiet attitude first reassured, then, on second thoughts, exasperated her.

"Why wont you?"

"I really dont know. Somehow, I am not curious. It interests you. Pray open it."

"I will die first. If it lie there until I open it, it will lie there forever."

He opened the envelope neatly with a paper cutter, and handed her the enclosure. She kept down her hands stubbornly. He smiled a little, still presenting it. At last she snatched it, much as she would have liked to snatch a handful of his hair. Having read it, she turned pale, and looked as she had used to in her childhood, when in disgrace and resolute not to cry. "I had rather have had my two hands cut off," she said passionately, after a pause.

"It is very sad for you," said Conolly, sympathetically. "He is an educated man; but I cannot think that he has much in him."

"He is a selfish, lying, conceited hound. Educated, indeed! And what are *you* going to do, may I ask?"

"Eat my supper. I am as hungry as a bear."

"Yes, you had better, I think. Good-evening." He seemed to know that she would not leave; for he made no movement to open the door for her. On her way out, she turned, and so came at him with her fists clenched, that for a moment he was doubtful whether she would not bodily assault him.

"Are you a brute, or a fool, or both?" she said, letting her temper loose. "How long do you intend to stand there, doing nothing?"

"What *can* I do, Miss McQuinch?" he said, gently.

"You can follow her and bring her back before she has made an utter idiot of herself with that miserable blackguard. Are you afraid of him? If you are, I will go with you, and not let him touch you."

"Thank you," he said, good-humoredly. "But you see she does not wish to live with me."

"Good God, man, what woman do you think *could* wish to live with you! I suppose Marian wanted a human being to live with, and not a calculating machine. You would drive any woman away. If you had feeling enough to have kicked him out of the house, and then beaten her black and blue for encouraging him, you would have been more of a man than you are: she would have loved you more. You are not a man: you are a stone full of brains—such as they are! Listen to me, Mr. Conolly. There is one chance left—if you will only make haste. Go after them; overtake them; thrash him within an inch of his life; and bring her back and punish her how you please so long as you shew her that you care. You can do it if you will only make up your mind: he is a coward; and he is afraid of you: I have seen it in his eye. You are worth fifty of him—if you would only not be so cold blooded—if you will only go—*dear* Mr. Conolly—youre not really insensible—you will, wont you?"

This, the first tender tone he had ever heard in her voice, made him look at her curiously. "What does the letter say?" he asked, still quietly, but inexorably.

She snatched it up again. "Here," she said. "'*Our marriage was a mistake. I am going away with Douglas to the other side of the world. It is all I can do to mend matters. Pray forget me.*' That is what her letter says, since you condescend to ask."

"It is too late, then. You felt that as you read it, I think?"

"Yes," she cried, sitting down in a paroxysm of grief, but unable to weep. "It is too late; and it is all your fault. What business had you to go away? You knew what was going to happen. You intended it to happen. You wanted it to happen. You are glad it has happened; and it serves you right. '*Pray forget her.*' Oh, yes, poor girl! she need not trouble about that. I declare there is nothing viler, meaner, cowardlier, selfisher on earth than a man. Oh, if we had only done what we always said we would do—kept free from you!"

"It was a good plan," said Conolly, submissively.

"Was it? How were we to know that you were not made of flesh and blood, pray? There, let me go. [The table was between them; but she rose and shook off an imaginary detaining hand.] I dont want to hear anything more about it. I suppose you are right not to care. Very likely she was right to go, too; so we are all right, and everything is for the best, no doubt. Marian is ruined, of course; but what does that matter to you? She was only in your way. You can console yourself with your—" Here Armande came in; and Elinor turned quickly to the fireplace and stood there, so that the housemaid should not see her face.

"Your dinner, sir," said Armande, with a certain artificiality of manner that was, under the circumstances, significant. "There is a nice fire in the laboratory."

"Thank you," said Conolly. "Presently, Armande."

"The things will spoil if you wait too long, sir. The mistress was very particular with me and cook about it." And Armande, with an air of declining further responsibility, went out.

"What shall I do without Marian?" said Conolly. "Not one woman in a hundred is capable of being a mistress to her servants. She saved me all the friction of housekeeping."

"You are beginning to feel your loss," said Elinor, facing him again. "A pleasant thing for a woman of her talent to be thrown away to save you the friction of housekeeping. If you had paid half the attention to her happiness that she did to

George Bernard Shaw

your dinners you would not be in your present predicament."

"Have you really calculated that it is twice as easy to make a woman happy as to feed a man?"

"Calc—! Yes, I have. I tell you that it is three times as easy—six times as easy: more fool the woman! You can make a woman happy for a week by a word or a kiss. How long do you think it takes to order a week's dinners? I suppose you consider a kiss a weakness?"

"I am afraid—judging by the result—that I am not naturally clever at kissing."

"No, I should think not, indeed. Then you had better go and do what you *are* clever at—eat your dinner."

"Miss McQuinch: did you ever see an unfortunate little child get a severe fall, and then, instead of a little kindly petting, catch a sound whacking from its nurse for daring to startle her and spoil its clothes?"

"Well, what is the point of that?"

"You remind me a little of the nurse. I have had a sort of fall this evening."

"And now you are going to pretend to be hurt, I suppose; because you dont care to be told that it is your own fault. That is a common experience with children, too. I tell you plainly that I dont believe you are hurt at all; though you may not be exactly pleased—just for the moment. However, I did not mean to be uncivil. If you are really sorry, I am at least *as* sorry. I have not said all I think."

"What more?"

"Nothing of any use to say. I see I am wasting my time here—and no doubt wasting yours too."

"Well, I think you have had your turn. If you are not thoroughly satisfied, pray go on for ten minutes longer: your feelings do you credit, as the phrase goes. Still, do not forget that you thought just the same of me a week ago; and that if you had said as much then you might have prevented what has happened. Giving me a piece of your mind now is of no use except as far as it relieves you. To Marian or me or anyone else it does no good. So when you have said your worst, we cannot do better, I think, than set our wits to work about our next move."

Elinor received this for a moment in dudgeon. Then she laughed sourly, and said, "There is some sense in that. I am as much to blame as anybody: I dont deny it—if that is any comfort to you. But as to the next move, you say yourself that it is too late to do anything; and I dont see that you can do much."

"That is so. But there are a few things to be faced. First, I have to set Marian and myself free."

"How?"

"Divorce her."

"Divorce!" Elinor looked at him in dismay. He was unmoved. Then her gaze fell slowly, and she said: "Yes: I suppose you have a right to that."

"She also."

"So that she may marry him—from a sense of duty. That will be so happy for her!"

"She will have time, before she is free to find out whether she likes him or not. There will be a great fuss in the family over the scandal."

"Do you care about that? *I* dont."

"No. However, thats a detail. Marian will perhaps write to you. If so, just point out to her that her five hundred a year belongs to her still, and makes her quite independent of him and of me. That is all, I think. You need take no pains now to conceal what has happened: the servants below know it as well as we: in a week it will be town talk."

Elinor looked wistfully at him, her impetuosity failing her as she felt how little effect it was producing. Yet her temper rather rose than fell at him. There was a much more serious hostility than before in her tone as she said:

"You seem to have been thoroughly prepared for what has happened. I do not want any instructions from you as to what I shall write to Marian about her money affairs: I want to know, in case she takes it into her head to come back when she has found what a fool she has made of herself, whether I may tell her that you are glad to be rid of her, and that there is no use in her humiliating herself by coming to your door and being turned away."

"Shall I explain the situation to you from my point of view?" said he. At the sound of his voice she looked up in alarm. The indulgent, half-playful manner which she had almost lost the sense of because it was so invariable with him in speaking to ladies was suddenly gone. She felt that the real man was coming out now without ceremony. He was quick to perceive the effect he had produced. To soften it, he placed a comfortable chair on the hearthrug, and said, in his ordinary friendly way: "Sit nearer the fire: we can talk more comfortably. Now," he continued, standing with his back to the mantelpiece, "let me tell you, Miss McQuinch, that when you talk of my turning people away from my door you are not talking fair and square sense to me. I dont turn my acquaintances off in that way, much less my friends; and a woman who has lived with me as my wife for eighteen months must always be a rather particular friend. I liked her before I was her husband, and I shall continue to like her when I am no longer her husband. So you need have no fear on that score. But I wont remain her husband. You said just now that I knew what was going to happen; that I intended it to happen, wanted it to happen, and am glad it happened. There is more truth in that than you thought when you said it. For some time past Marian has been staying with me as a matter of custom and convenience only, using me as a cover for her philandering with Douglas, and paying me by keeping the house very nicely for me. I had asked myself once or twice how long this was to last. I was in no hurry for the answer; for although I was wifeless and had no one to live with who really cared for me, I was quite prepared to wait a couple of years if necessary, on the chance of our making it up somehow. But sooner or later I should have insisted on closing our accounts and parting; and I am not sorry now that the end has come, since it was inevitable; though I am right sorry for the way it has come. Instead of eloping in the conventional way, she should have come to an understanding with me. I could easily have taken her for a trip in the States, where we could have stopped a few months in South Dakota and got divorced without any scandal. I have never made any claims on her since she found out that she didnt care for me; and she might have known from that that I was not the man to keep her against her will and play dog in the manger with a fellow like Douglas. However, thats past praying for now. She has had enough of me; and I have had more than enough of her set and her family, except that I should like to remain good friends with you. You are the only one of the whole lot worth your salt. It is understood, of course, that you take Marian's part against me on all issues; but will you be friends as far as is consistent with that?"

"All right," said Nelly, shortly.

"Shake hands on it; and I'll tell you something else that will help you to understand me better," he said, holding out his hand. She gave hers; and when the bargain was struck, he turned to the fire and seated himself on the edge of the table.

"You know that when I married," he resumed, "I was promoted to mix in fashionable society for the first time. Of

George Bernard Shaw

course you do: that was the whole excitement of the affair for the family. You know the impression I made on polite society better, probably, than I do. Now tell me: do you know what impression polite society made on me?"

"Dont understand."

"Perhaps it has never occurred even to you, sharp as you are, that I could have taken society otherwise than at its own valuation of itself, as something much higher, more cultivated and refined than anything that I had been accustomed to. Well, I never believed in that much at any time; but it was not until I had made a *mesalliance* for Marian's sake that I realized how infinitely beneath me and my class was the one I had married into."

"*Mesalliance!*—with Marian! I take back the shake hands."

"*Mesalliance* with her class, for her sake: I made the distinction purposely. Now what am I, Miss McQuinch? A worker. I belonged and belong to the class that keeps up the world by its millions of serviceable hands and serviceable brains. All the pride of caste in me settles on that point. I admit no loafer as my equal. The man who is working at the bench is my equal, whether he can do my day's work or not, provided he is doing the best he can. But the man who does not work anyhow, and the class that does not work, is a class below mine. When I annoyed Marian by refusing to wear a tall hat and cuffs, I did so because I wanted to have it seen as I walked through Piccadilly and St. James's Street that I did not belong there, just as your people walk through a poor street dressed so as to shew that they dont belong there. To me a man like your uncle, Marian's father, or like Marmaduke or Douglas, loafing idly round spending money that has been made by the sweat of men like myself, are little better than thieves. They get on with the queerest makeshifts for self-respect: old Mr. Lind with family pride. Douglas with personal vanity, and Marmaduke with a sort of interest in his own appetites and his own jollity. Everything is a sham with them: they have drill and etiquet instead of manners, fashions instead of tastes, small talk instead of intercourse. Everything that is special to them as distinguished from workers is a sham: when you get down to the real element in them, good or bad, you find that it is something that is common to them and to all civilized mankind. The reason that this isn't as clear to other workmen who come among them as it is to me is that most workmen share their ignorance of the things they affect superiority in. Poor Jackson, whom you all call the Yankee cad, and who is not a cad at all in his proper place among the engineers at our works, believes in the sham refinements he sees around him at the at-homes he is so fond of. He has no art in him—no trained ear for music or for fine diction, no trained eye for pictures and colors and buildings, no cultivated sense of dignified movement, gesture, and manner. But he knows what fashionable London listens to and looks at, and how it talks and behaves; and he makes that his standard, and sets down what is different from it as vulgar. Now the difference between me and him is that I got an artistic training by accident when I was young, and had the natural turn to profit by it. Before I ever saw a West End Londoner I knew beautiful from ugly, rare from common, in music, speech, costume, and gesture; for in my father's operatic and theatrical companies there did come now and then, among the crowd of thirdraters, a dancer, an actor, a scenepainter, a singer, or a bandsman or conductor who was a fine artist. Consequently, I was not to be taken in like Jackson by made-up faces, trashy pictures, drawling and lounging and strutting and tailoring, drawing-room singing and drawing-room dancing, any more than by bad ventilation and unwholesome hours and food, not to mention polite dram drinking, and the round of cruelties they call sport. I found that the moment I refused to accept the habits of the rich as standards of refinement and propriety, the whole illusion of their superiority vanished at once. When I married Marian I was false to my class. I had a sort of idea that my early training had accustomed me to a degree of artistic culture that I could not easily find in a working girl, and that would be quite natural to Marian. I soon found that she had the keenest sense of what was ladylike, and no sense of what was beautiful at all. A

George Bernard Shaw

drawing, a photograph, or an engraving sensibly framed without a white mount round it to spoil it pained her as much as my wrists without cuffs on them. No mill girl could have been less in sympathy with me on the very points for which I had preferred her to the mill girls. The end of it was that I felt that love had made me do a thoroughly vulgar thing—marry beneath me. These aristocratic idle gentlemen will never be shamed out of their laziness and low-mindedness until the democratic working gentlemen refuse to associate with them instead of running after them and licking their boots. I am heartily glad now to be out of their set and rid of them, instead of having to receive them civilly in my house for Marian's sake. The whole business was strangling me: the strain of keeping my feeling to myself was more than you can imagine. Do you know that there have been times when I have been so carried away with the idea that she must be as tired of the artificiality of our life as I was, that I have begun to speak my mind frankly to her; and when she recoiled, hurt and surprised and frightened that I was going to turn coarse at last, I have shut up and sat there apparently silent, but really saying under my breath: 'Why dont you go? Why dont you leave me, vanish, fly away to your own people? You must be a dream: I never married you. You dont know me: you cant be my wife: your lungs were not made to breathe the air I live in.' I have said a thousand things like that, and then wondered whether there was any truth in telepathy—whether she could possibly be having my thoughts transferred to her mind and thinking it only her imagination. I would ask myself whether I despised her or not, calling on myself for the truth as if I did not believe the excuses I made for her out of the fondness I could not get over. I am fond of her still, sometimes. I did not really— practically, I mean—despise her until I gave up thinking about her at all. There was a certain kind of contempt in that indifference, beyond a doubt: there is no use denying it. Besides, it is proved to me now by the new respect I feel for her because she has had the courage and grit to try going away with Douglas. But my love for her is over: nothing short of her being born over again—a thing that sometimes happens—will ever bring her into contact with me after this. To put it philosophically, she made the mistake of avoiding all realities, and yet marrying herself to the hardest of realities, a working man; so it was inevitable that she should go back at last to the region of shadows and mate with that ghostliest of all unrealities, the non-working man. Perhaps, too, the union may be more fruitful than ours: the cross between us was too violent. Now you have the whole story from my point of view. What do you—"

"Hush!" said Elinor, interrupting him. "What is that noise outside?"

The house bell began to ring violently; and they could hear a confused noise of voices and footsteps without.

"Can she have come back?" said Elinor, starting up.

"Impossible!" said Conolly, looking disturbed for the first time. They stood a moment listening, with averted eyes. A second peal from the bell was followed by roars of laughter, amid which a remonstrant voice was audible. Then the house door was hammered with a stick. Conolly ran downstairs at once and opened it. On the step he found Marmaduke reeling in the arms of the Rev. George.

"How are you, ol' fler?" said Marmaduke, plunging into the hall. "The parson is tight. I found him tumbling about High Street, and brought him along."

"Pray excuse this intrusion," whispered the Rev. George. "You see the state he is in. He accosted me near Campden Hill; and I really could not be seen walking with him into town. I wonder he was not arrested."

"He is the worse for drink; but he is sober enough to know how to amuse himself at your expense," said Conolly, aloud. "Come up to the laboratory. Miss McQuinch is there."

"But he is not fit," urged the clergyman. "Look at him trying to hang up his hat. How absurd—I should rather say how deplorable! I assure you he is perfectly tipsy. He has been ringing the bells of the houses, and requesting females to accompany us. Better warn Elinor."

"Nonsense!" said Conolly. "I have some news that will sober him. Here is Miss McQuinch. Are you going?"

"Yes," said Elinor. "I should lose my patience if I had to listen to George's comments; and I am tired. I would rather go."

"Not yet, Nelly. Wont um stay and talk to um's Marmadukes?"

"Let me go," said Elinor, snatching away her hand, which he had seized. "You ought to be at home in bed. You are a sot." At this Marmaduke laughed boisterously. She passed him contemptuously, and left. The three men then went upstairs, Marmaduke dropping his pretence of drunkenness under the influence of Conolly's presence.

"Marian is not in, I presume," said the clergyman, when they were seated.

"No." said Conolly. "She has eloped with Douglas."

They stared at him. Then Marmaduke gave a long whistle; and the clergyman rose, pale. "What do you mean, sir?" he said.

Conolly did not answer; and the Rev. George slowly sat down again.

"Well, I'm damned sorry for it," said Marmaduke, emphatically. "It was a mean thing for Douglas to do, with all his brag about his honor."

The Rev. George covered his face with his handkerchief and sobbed.

"Come, shut up, old fellow; and dont make an ass of yourself," said Marmaduke. "What are you going to do, Conolly?"

"I must simply divorce her."

"Go for heavy damages, Conolly. Knock a few thousand out of him, just to punish him."

"He could easily afford it. Besides, why should I punish him?"

"My dear friend," cried the clergyman, "you must not dream of a divorce. I implore you to abandon such an idea. Consider the disgrace, the impiety! The publicity would kill my father."

Conolly shook his head.

"There is no such thing as divorce known to the Church. 'What God hath joined together, let no man put asunder.'"

"She had no right to bolt," said Marmaduke. "Thats certain."

"I was married by a registrar," said Conolly; "and as there is no such thing as civil marriage known to the Church, our union, from the ecclesiastical point of view, has no existence. We were not joined by God, in fact, in your sense. To deny her the opportunity of remarrying would be to compel her to live as an adulteress in the eye of the law, which, by the bye, would make me the father of Douglas's children. I cannot, merely because your people are afraid of scandal, take such a revenge on Marian as to refuse her the freedom she has sacrificed so much for. After all, since our marriage has proved a childless one, the only reason for our submitting to be handcuffed to one another, now that our hearts are no longer in the arrangement, is gone."

"The game began at Sark," said Marmaduke. "Douglas stuck to her there like a leech. He's been about the house here a good deal since she came back. I often wondered you didnt kick him out. But, of course, it was not my business to say anything. Was she huffed into going? You hadn't any row with her just before, had you?

"We never had rows."

"That was your mistake, Conolly. You should have heard poor Susanna and me fighting. We always ended by swearing we would never speak to one another again. Nothing duller than a smooth life. If you had given Marian something to complain of, she would have been too much taken up with it to bother about Douglas."

"But have you ascertained whither they have gone?" said the clergyman, distractedly. "Will you not follow them?"

"I know nothing of their movements. Probably they are crossing to New York."

"But surely you ought to follow her," said the Rev. George. "You may yet be in time to save her from worse than death."

"Yah!" said Marmaduke. "Drop all that rot, George. Worse than death be hanged! Serves the family right! They are a jolly sight too virtuous: it will do them good to get shewn up a bit."

"If you have no respect for the convictions of a priest," exclaimed the Rev. George, shedding tears, "you might at least be silent in the presence of a heartbroken brother and husband."

"Oh, I dont want to shew any want of consideration for you or Conolly," said Marmaduke, sulkily. "No doubt it's rough on you. But as to the feelings of the family, I tell you flatly that I dont care if the whole crew were brought to the Old Bailey to-morrow and convicted of bigamy. It would take the conceit out of them."

"I know not how to break this wretched news to my father," said the Rev. George, turning disconsolately from his sottish cousin to Conolly.

"It is no such uncommon occurrence. The less fuss made about it the better. She is not to blame, and I shall not be heard crying out misery and disgrace. Your family can very well follow my example. I have nothing to say against her, and I believe she has nothing to say against me. Nothing can prevent such publicity as a petition for divorce must entail. Your father will survive it, never fear."

The clergyman, remembering how vainly he had tried to change Conolly's intention when Marian was to be married, felt that he should succeed no better now that she was to be divorced. Silent and cast down, he sat dangling his handkerchief between his knees and leaning forward on his elbows toward the fire.

"You must excuse me if I see my way straight through to the end. I daresay you would rather realize it gradually, inevitable as it is," added Conolly, looking down with some pity at his drooping figure. "I cannot help my habit of mind. When are you going to be married?" he continued, to Marmaduke.

"I dont know. The Countess is in a hurry. I'm not. But I suppose it will be some time in spring."

"You have made up your mind to it at last?"

"Oh, I never had any particular objection to it, only I dont like to be hunted into a corner. Conny is a good little girl, and will make a steady wife. I dont like her mother; but as for herself, she is fond of me; and after all, I *did* lead her a dance long ago. Besides, old boy, the Earl is forking out handsomely; and as I have some notion of settling down to farm, his dust will come in conveniently as capital."

The clergyman rose, and slowly pulled on his woolen gloves.

"If youre going, I will see you part of the way," said Marmaduke. "I'll cheer you up. You know you neednt tell the governor until to-morrow."

"I had rather go alone, if you intend to behave as you did before."

"Never fear. I'm as sober as a judge now. Come along. Away with melancholy! Youll have Douglas for a brother-in-law before this time next year."

This seemed to have been in the clergyman's mind; for he shook hands with his host more distantly than usual. When they were gone, Conolly went to the laboratory, and rang for his neglected dinner, which he ate with all a traveller's appetite. From the dinner table he went straight to the organ, and played until a little before midnight, when, after a brief turn in the open air, he retired to bed, and was soon quietly asleep.

BOOK IV

CHAPTER XVIII

Miss McQuinch spent Christmas morning in her sitting-room reading; a letter which had come by the morning post. It was dated the 17th December at New York: and the formal beginning and ending were omitted. This was an old custom between Marian and her cousin. In their girlish correspondence they had expressed their affection by such modes of address as "My darling Marian," and "My dearest Nelly." Subsequently they became oppressed by these ceremonies and dropped them. Thereafter their letters contained only the matter to be communicated and the signature.

"You are the only person in England," wrote Marian, "to whom I dare write now. A month ago I had more correspondents than I had time to answer. Do you know, Nelly, I hesitated before commencing this letter, lest you should no longer care to have anything to do with me. That may have been an unworthy thought for a friend: but it was an unavoidable one for a woman.

"And now comes the great vain question: What does everybody say? Oh, if I could only disembody myself; fly back to London for a few hours; and listen invisibly to society talking about me. I know this is mean: but one must fill up life with some mean curiosities. So please tell me what kind of sensation I have caused. Just the usual one. I suppose. Half the people never would have thought it; and the other half knew all along

George Bernard Shaw

what it would come to. Well, I do not care much about the world in general; but I cannot quiet my conscience on the subject of my father and George. It must be very hard on papa that, after being disappointed in my marriage and having suffered long ago from what my mother did, he should now be disgraced by his daughter. For disgraced, alas! is the word. I am afraid poor George's prospects must be spoiled by the scandal, which, I know well, must be terrible. I thought my first duty was to leave Ned free, and to free myself, at all hazards; and so I did not dwell on the feelings and interests of others as much as I perhaps ought to have done. There is one point about which I am especially anxious. It never occurred to me before I went that people might say that my going was Ned's fault, and that he had treated me badly. You must contradict this with all your might and main if you hear it even hinted at.

"There is no use in putting off the confession any longer, Nelly: I have made an utter fool of myself. *I wish I were back with Ned again.* There! what do you think of that? Now for another great confession, and a most humiliating one. Sholto is a—I dont know what epithet is fair. I suppose I have no right to call him an impostor merely because we were foolish enough to overrate him. But I can hardly believe now that we ever really thought that there were great qualities and powers latent beneath his proud reserve. Ned, I know, never believed in Sholto; and I, in my infinite wisdom, set that down to his not understanding him. Ned was right, as usual. If you want to see how selfish people are, and how skin-deep fashionable polite-ness is, take a voyage. Go with a picked company of the nice people you have met for an hour or so at a dinner or an at-home; and see how different they will appear when they have been cooped up in a ship with you day and night for a week. An ocean steamer is the next worst thing to the Palace of Truth. Poor Sholto did not stand the ordeal. He was ridi-culously distant in his manner to the rest of the passengers, and in little matters at table and so forth he was really just as selfish as he could be. He was impatient because I was ill the first two days, and afterwards he seemed to think that I ought not to speak to anyone but himself. The doctor, who was very attentive to me, was his particular aversion; and it was on his account that we had our first quarrel, the upshot of which was a scene between them, which I overheard. One very fine day, when all the passengers were on deck, Sholto met the doctor in the saloon, and offered him a guinea for his attendance on me, telling him in the most offensively polite way that I would not trouble him for any further services. The doctor retorted very promptly and concisely; and though what he said was not dignified, I sympathized with him, and took care to be very friendly with him at dinner. (Meals take place on hoard ship at intervals of ten minutes: it is horrifying to see the quantity of food the elderly people consume.) To prevent further hostilities I took care to be always in the way when the doctor encountered Sholto afterwards. I cannot imagine Ned involving himself in such a paltry squabble. It is odd how things come about. I used to take Sholto's genius for granted, and think a great deal of it. In another sense, I used to take Ned's genius for granted, and think nothing of it. Now I have found out in a single fortnight that we saw all of Sholto that there was to be seen. His reserves of talent existed only in our imagination. He has absolutely no sense of humor; and he is always grumbling. Neither the servants, nor the food, nor the rooms, nor the wine, satisfy him. Imagine how this comes home to me, who, from not having heard grumbling for two years, had forgotten that men ever were guilty of it. I flirted a little, a very little, with the doctor; not because I meant anything serious, but because it amused me and made the trip pleasant. Sholto will not understand this. One day, on board, I was indiscreet enough to ask Sholto the use of a piece of machinery belonging to the ship. Ned would have known, or, if he had not, would very soon have found out. Sholto didnt know, and was weak enough to pretend that he did; so he snubbed me by saying that I could not understand it. This put me on my mettle; and I asked the surgeon that afternoon about it. The surgeon didnt know, and said so; but he appealed to the first officer, who explained it. I intended to revenge myself on Sholto by retailing the explanation to him next day; but unfortunately, whether through the first officer's want of perspicuity or my own stupidity, I was not a bit the

George Bernard Shaw

wiser for the explanation.

"I can tell you nothing as to what we are likely to do next. As Sholto has given up all his prospects for me, I cannot honorably desert him. I know now that I have ruined myself for nothing, and I must at least try to hide from him that he has done likewise. I can see that he is not happy; but he tries so desperately to persuade himself that he is, and clings so to the idea that the world is well lost for me, that I have not the heart to undeceive him. So we are still lovers; and, cynical though it sounds, I make him a great deal happier in my insincerity than I could if I really loved him, because I humor him with a cunning quite incompatible with passion. He, on the other hand, being still sincere, tries my patience terribly with his jealousies and importunities. As he has nothing to do, he is almost always with me; and a man who has no office to go to—I dont care who he is—is a trial of which you can have no conception. So much for our present relations. But I fear—indeed I know—that they will not last long. I dare not look steadily at the future. In spite of all that he has sacrificed for me, I cannot live forever with him. There are times at which he inspires me with such a frenzy of aversion and disgust that I have to put the strongest constraint upon myself to avoid betraying my feelings to him. We intended going to the West Indies direct from here, in search of some idyllic retreat where we could live alone together. He still entertains this project; but as I have totally abandoned it I put him off with some pretext for remaining here whenever he mentions it. I have only one hope of gaining a separation without being open to the reproach of having deserted him. You remember how we disputed that Saturday about the merits of a grand passion, which I so foolishly longed for. Well, I have tried it, and proved it to be a lamentable delusion, selfish, obstinate, blind, intemperate, and transient. As it has evaporated from me, so it will evaporate from Sholto in the course of time. It would have done so already, but that his love was more genuine than mine. When the time comes, he will get rid of me without the least remorse; and so he will have no excuse for reviving his old complaints of my treachery.

"One new and very disagreeable feature in my existence, which I had partly prepared myself for, is the fear of detection. We sailed before our flight had become public; and as there was fortunately no one on board who knew us, I had a nine days' respite, and could fearlessly approach the other women, who, I suppose, would not have spoken to me had they known the truth. But here it is different. Ned's patents are so much more extensively worked here than in England, and the people are so go-ahead, that they take a great interest in him, and are proud of him as an American. The news got into the papers a few days after we arrived. To appreciate the full significance of this, you should know what American newspapers are. One of them actually printed a long account of my going away, with every paragraph headed in large print, 'Domestic Unhappiness,' 'The Serpent in the Laboratory,' 'The Temptation,' 'The Flight,' 'The Pursuit,' and so on, all invented, of course. Other papers give the most outrageous anecdotes. Old jokes are revived and ascribed to us. I am accused of tearing his hair out, and he of coming home late at nights drunk. Two portraits of ferocious old women supposed to be Ned's mother-in-law have been published. The latest version appeared in a Sunday paper, and is quite popular in this hotel. According to it, Ned was in the habit of 'devoting me to science' by trying electrical experiments on me. 'This,' the account says, 'was kind of rough on the poor woman.' The day before I 'scooted,' a new machine appeared before the house, drawn by six horses. 'What are them men foolin' round with, Mr. C.?' said I. 'That's hubby's latest,' replied Ned. 'I guess it's the boss electro-dynamic fixin' in the universe. Full charge that battery with a pint of washing soda, an' youll fetch up a current fit to ravage a cont'nent. You shall have a try t'morro' mornin', Sal. Youre better seasoned to it than most Britishers; but if it dont straighten your hair and lift the sparks outer your eyelashes—!' 'You bet it wont, Mr. C.,' said I. That night (this is only what the paper says, mind) I stole out of bed; arranged the wires on each side of Ned so that if he stirred an inch he would make contact; charged the battery; and gently woke him, saying, 'Mr. C, love, don't stir for your life. Them things that's ticklin' your whiskers is the conductors of that boss fixin' o' yourn. If I was you, I'd lie still

George Bernard Shaw

until the battery runs down.' 'Darn it all,' said Ned, afraid to lift his lips for a shout, and coming out in cold water all over the forehead, 'it wont run down for a week clear.' 'That'll answer me nicely,' I replied. 'Good-bye, Mr. C. Young Douglas from the corner grocery is waitin' for me with a shay down the avenue.' I cannot help laughing at these things, but they drive Sholto frantic. He is always described in them as a young man from some shop or other. He tries hard, out of delicacy, to keep the papers which contain them away from me; but I hear about them at breakfast, and buy them downstairs in the hall for myself. Another grievance of Sholto's is that I will not have meals privately. But my dislike to being always alone with him is greater than my dread that my secret will leak out, and that some morning I shall see in the people's faces that the Mrs. Forster who has so often been regaled with the latest account of the great scandal, is no other than the famous Mrs. Conolly. That evil day will come, sooner or later; but I had rather face it in one of these wonderful hotels than in a boarding-house, which I might be asked to leave. As to taking a house of our own, I shrink from any such permanent arrangement. We are noticed a good deal. Sholto is, of course, handsome and distinguished; and people take a fancy to me just as they used to long ago. I was once proud of this; but now it is a burden to me. For instance, there was a Mrs. Crawford staying here with her husband, a general, who has just built a house here. She was so determined to know me that I found it hard to keep her off without offending her. At last she got ill; and then I felt justified in nursing her. Sholto was very sulky because I did so, and wanted to know what business it was of mine. I did not trouble myself about his anger, and Mrs. Crawford was well in two days. In fact, I think Sholto was right in saying that she had only overeaten herself. After that I could avoid her no longer, and she was exceedingly kind to me. She wanted to introduce me to all her New York friends, and begged me to leave the hotel and go to her new mansion. There was plenty of room for us, she said. I did not know what to say. I could not repay her kindness by going to her house under false colors, and letting her introduce me to her circle; and yet I could make no reasonable excuse. At last, seeing that she attributed my refusals to pride, I told her plainly that if her friends were to learn my history by any accident they might not thank her for the introduction. She was quite confounded; but she did not abate her kindness in the least, although my reservation of confidence in only giving her a hint of the truth, checked her advances. You may think this an insane indis-cretion on my part; but if you knew how often I have longed to stand up before everybody and proclaim who I am, and so get rid of the incubus of a perpetual falsehood, you would not be so much surprised. There is one unspeakable blessing in American law. It is quite easy to obtain a divorce. One can get free without sacrificing everything except bare existence. I do not care what anybody may argue to the contrary, our marriage laws are shameful.

"I shall expect to hear from you very soon. If you desert me, Nelly, there is no such thing as friendship in the world. I want particularly to know what Ned did—as far as you know—when he heard the news. Is papa very angry? And, above all, could you find out how Mrs. Douglas is? I thought that Sholto would be uneasy and remorseful about her; but he does not really care half so much as I do. How selfish I have been! I used to flatter myself that I was thoughtful for others because I made a habit—a detestably self-conscious habit—of being considerate in trifles. And in the end, after being so vain-gloriously attentive to the momentary comfort of all connected with me, I utterly forgot them and thought only of myself when their whole happiness was concerned. I never knew how high I stood in my own estimation until I found how far the discovery of my folly and selfishness made me fall. Tell me everything". I cannot write any more now. My eyes are smarting: I feel as if I had been writing for a whole month instead of two days. Good-bye for three weeks.

"MARIAN."

"P.S. I have just learnt from a very severe criticism in one of the papers that Mdlle. Lalage Virtue has failed here completely.

I fear from the wording that her unfortunate habit was apparent to the audience."

CHAPTER XIX

On a cold afternoon in January, Sholto Douglas entered a hold in New York, and ascended to a room on the first floor. Marian was sitting there, thinking, with a letter in her lap, She only looked up for a moment when he entered; and he plucked off his sealskin gloves and threw aside his overcoat in silence.

"It is an infernal day," he said presently.

Marian sighed, and roused herself. "The rooms look cheerless in winter without the open fireplaces we are accustomed to in England."

"Damn the rooms!" he muttered.

Marian took up her letter again.

"Do you know that he has filed a petition for divorce?" he said, aggressively.

"Yes."

"You might have mentioned it to me. Probably you have known it for days past."

"Yes. I thought it was a matter of course."

"Or rather you did not think at nil. I suppose you would have left me in ignorance forever, if I had not heard from

George Bernard Shaw

London myself."

"Is it of importance, then?"

"Certainly it is—of vital importance."

"Have you any other news? From whom have you heard?"

"I have received some private letters."

"Oh! I beg your pardon."

Five minutes passed in silence. He looked out of the window, frowning. She sat as before.

"How much longer do you intend to stay in this place?" he said, turning upon her suddenly.

"In New York?"

"This is New York, I believe."

"I think we may as well stay here as anywhere else."

"Indeed! On what grounds have you arrived at that cheering conclusion?"

Marian shrugged her shoulders. "I dont know," she said.

"Nor do I. You do not seem happy here. At least, if you are, you fail to communicate your state of mind to those about you."

"So it seems."

"What does that mean?"

"That you do not seem to be happy either."

"How in the devil's name can you expect me to be happy in this city? Do you think it is pleasant to have no alternative to the society of American men except that of a sulky woman?"

"Sholto!" said Marian, rising quickly, and looking at him in surprise.

"Spare me these airs," he said, coldly. "You will have to accustom yourself to hear the truth occasionally."

She sat down again. "I am not giving myself airs," she said, earnestly. "I am astonished. Have I really been sulky?"

"You have been in the sulks for days past: and you are in them at this moment."

"There is some misunderstanding between us then; for you have seemed to me quite cross and out of sorts for the last week; and I thought you were out of temper when you came in just now."

"That is rather an old-fashioned retort."

"Sholto: I do not know whether you intend it or not; but you are speaking very slightingly to me."

He muttered something, and walked across the room and back. "I am quite clear on one point at least," he said. "It was not for this sort of thing that I crossed the Atlantic with you; and you had bettor make our relations more agreeable if you wish me to make them permanent."

"You to make them permanent? I do not understand."

"I shall not shrink from explaining myself. If your husband's suit is undefended, he will obtain a decree which will leave you a single woman in six months. Now, whatever you may think to the contrary, there is not a club in London that would hold me in any way bound to marry you after the manner in which you have behaved. Let me remind you that your future position depends on your present conduct. You have apparently forgotten it."

She looked at him; and he went back to the window.

"My husband's suit cannot be defended," she said. "Doubtless you will act according to the dictates of the London clubs."

"I do not say so," he said, turning angrily. "I shall act according to the dictates of my own common sense. And do not be too sure that the petition will be unopposed. The law recognizes the plea of connivance."

"But it would be a false plea," said Marian, raising her voice.

"I shall not discuss that with you. Whether your husband was blind, or merely kept his eyes shut will not be decided by us. You have been warned. We will drop the subject now, if you please."

"Do you suppose," said Marian, with a bright color in her cheeks, "that after what you have said, anything could induce me to marry you?"

He was startled, and remained for a moment motionless. Then he said, in his usual cold tone, "As you please. You may think better of it. I will leave you for the present. When we meet again, you will be calmer."

"Yes," she said. "Good-bye."

Without answering, he changed his coat for a silk jacket, transferred his cigar-case to a pocket in it, and went out. When he had passed the threshold, he hesitated, and returned.

"Why do you say good-bye?" he said, after clearing his throat uneasily.

"I do not like to leave you without saying it."

"I hope you have not misunderstood me, Marian. I did not mean that we should part."

"I know that. Nevertheless, we shall part. I will never sleep beneath the same roof with you again."

"Come!" he said, shutting the door: "this is nonsense. You are out of temper."

"So you have already told me," she said, becoming pale.

"Well, but—Marian: perhaps I may have spoken rather harshly just now; but I did not mean you to take it so. You must be reasonable."

"Pray let us have no more words about it. I need no apologies, and desire no advances. Good-bye is enough."

"But, Marian," said he, coming nearer, "you must not fancy that I have ceased to love you."

"Above all," said Marian, "let us have no more of that. You say you hate this place and the life we lead here. I am heartily sick of it, and have been so for a long time."

"Let us go elsewhere."

"Yes, but not together. One word," she added resolutely, seeing his expression become fierce. "I will not endure any violence, even of language, from you. I know of old what you are when you lose your temper; and if you insult me I will summon aid, and proclaim who I am."

"Do you think I am going to strike you?"

"No, because you dare not. But I will not listen to oaths or abuse."

"What have you to complain of? What is your grievance?"

"I make no complaint. I exercise the liberty I bought so dearly to go where I please and do what I please."

"And to desert me when I have sacrificed everything for you. I have incurred enormous expenses; alienated my friends; risked my position in society; and broken my mother's heart for your sake."

"But for that I would have left you before. I am very sorry."

"You have heard something in that letter which makes you hope that your husband will take you back. Not a woman in London will speak to you."

"I tell you I am not going back. Oh, Sholto, dont be so mean. Can we not part with dignity? We have made a mistake. Let us acknowledge it quietly, and go our several ways."

"I will not be got rid of so easily as you suppose," he said, his face darkening menacingly. "Do you think I believe in your going out alone from this hotel and living by yourself in a strange city? Come! who is it?"

"Who is—? What do you mean?"

"What new connexion have you formed? You were very anxious about our ship returning the other day—anxious about the mails, of course. Perhaps also about the surgeon."

"I understand. You think I am leaving you to go to some other man. I will tell you now the true reason."

"Do," said he, sarcastically, biting his lip.

"I will. I am leaving you because, instead of loving you, as I foolishly thought I could, I neither respect nor even like you. You are utterly selfish and narrow-minded; and I deserve my disappointment for having deserted for your sake a far better man. I am sorry you have sacrificed so much for me; but if you had been worthy of a woman's regard, you would not have lost me."

Douglas stared at her. "*I* selfish and narrow-minded!" he said, with the calm of stupefaction.

"Yes."

"I may have been narrow-minded in devoting myself so entirely to you," said he slowly, after a pause. "But, though I do not ask for gratitude, I think I have been sufficiently a loser to disregard such a monstrous assertion as that I am selfish."

"You show your selfishness by dwelling on what you have lost. You never think of what I have lost. I make no profession of unselfishness. I am suffering for my folly and egoism; and I deserve to suffer."

"In what way, pray, are you suffering? You came here because you had a wretched home, and a husband who was glad to be rid of you. You do what you like, and have what you like. Name one solitary wish of yours that has not been silently gratified."

"I do not find fault with you. You have been generous in supplying me with luxuries such as money can obtain. But it was not the want of money that made me fancy my home wretched. It is not true that I can do as I like. How many minutes is it since you threatened to cast me off if I did not make myself agreeable to you? Can you boast of your generosity after taunting me with my dependence on you?"

"You misunderstood me, Marian. I neither boasted, nor threatened, nor taunted. I have even apologized for that moment's irritation. If you cannot forgive such a trifle, you yourself can have very little generosity."

"Perhaps not. I do not violently resent things; but I cannot forget them, nor feel as I did before they happened."

"You think so at present. Let us cease this bickering. Lovers' quarrels should not be carried too far."

"I am longing to cease it. It worries me; and it does not alter my determination in the least."

"Do you mean—"

"I do mean. Dont look at me like that: you make me angry instead of frightening me."

"And do you think I will suffer this quietly?"

"You may suffer it as you please," said Marian, stepping quietly to the wall, and pressing a button. "I will never see you again if I can help it. If you follow me, or persecute me in any way, I will appeal to the police for protection as Mrs. Conolly. I despise you more than I do any one on earth."

He turned away, and snatched up his coat and hat. She stood apparently watching him quietly, but really listening with quickened heart to his loud and irregular breathing. As he opened the door to go out, he was confronted on the threshold by a foreign waiter.

"Vas you reeng?" said the waiter doubtfully, retreating a step.

"I will not be accountable for that woman's expenses from this time forth," said Douglas, pointing at her, "You can keep her at your own risk, or turn her into the streets to pursue her profession, as you please."

The waiter, smiting vaguely, looked first at the retreating figure of Douglas, and then at Marian.

"I want another room, if you please," she said. "One on any of the upper floors will do; but I must have my things moved there at once."

Her instructions were carried out after some parley. In the meantime, Douglas's man servant appeared, and said that he had been instructed to remove his master's luggage.

"Is Mr. Forster leaving the hotel?" she asked.

"I dont know his arrangements, madam."

"I guess I do, then," said a sulky man, who was preparing to wheel away Marian's trunk. "He's about to shift his billet to the Gran' Central."

Marian, still in a towering rage, sat down in her new room to consider her situation. To fix her attention, which repeatedly wandered to what had passed between her and Douglas, she counted her money, and found that she had, besides a twenty pound note which she had brought with her from London, only a few loose dollars in her purse. Her practice in house-keeping at Westbourne Terrace and Holland Park had taught her the value of money too well to let her suppose that she could afford to remain at a first rate American hotel with so small a sum in her possession. At home Conolly had made her keep a separate banking account; and there was money to her credit there; but in her ignorance of the law, she was not sure that she had not forfeited all her property by eloping. She resolved to move at once into some cheap lodging, and to live economically until she could ascertain the true state of her affairs, or until she could obtain some employment, to support her. She faced poverty without fear, never having experienced it.

It was still early in the afternoon when she left the hotel and drove to the Crawfords'.

"So you have come at last," cried Mrs. Crawford, who was fifty years of age and stout, but leaner in the face than fat

George Bernard Shaw

Englishwomen of that age usually are.

"I just expected you'd soon git tired of being grand all by yourself in the hotel yonder."

"I fear I shall have to be the reverse of grand all by myself in some very shabby lodging," said Marian. "Dont be surprised Mrs. Crawford. Can one live in New York on ten dollars a week?"

"*You* cant live on ten dollars a week in New York nor on a hundred. You rode here, didnt you?"

"Yes, of course."

"Of course. If you have only ten dollars a week you should have walked. I know the sort you are, Mrs. Forster. You wont be long getting rid of your money, no matter where you live. But whats wrong? Hows your husband?"

"I dont know. I hope he is quite well," said Marian, her voice trembling a little. "Mrs. Crawford: you are the only friend I have in America; and you have been so very kind to me that since I must trouble some one, I have ventured to come to you. The truth is that I have left my husband; and I have only about one hundred dollars in the world. I must live on that until I get some employment, or perhaps some money of my own from England."

"Chut, child! Nawnsnse!" exclaimed Mrs. Crawford, with benevolent intolerance. "You go right back to your husband. I spose youve had a rumpus with him; but you mustnt mind that. All men are a bit selfish; and I should say from what I have seen of him that he is no exception to the rule. But you cant have perfection. He's a fine handsome fellow; and he knows it. And, as for you, I dont know what they reckon you in England; but youre the best-looking woman in Noo York: thats surtn. It's a pity for such a pair to fall out."

"He is not selfish," said Marian. "You never saw him. I am afraid I must shock you, Mrs. Crawford. Mr. Forster is not my husband."

"No! Do! Did you ever tell the General that?"

"General Crawford! Oh, no."

"Think of that man being cuter than me, a woman! He always said so. And the grit you must have, to tell it out as cool as that! Well! I'm sorry to hear it though, Mrs. Forster. It's a bad account—a very bad one. But if I take what you said just now rightly, youre married."

"I am. I have deserted a very good husband."

"It's a pity you didnt find that out a little sooner, isnt it?"

"I know, Mrs. Crawford. I thought I was acting for the best."

"Thought you were acting for the best in running away from a good husband! Well, you British aristocrats are singular. You throw stones at us because our women are so free and our divorces so easy. Yet youre always scandlizing us; and now *you* tell me youve done it on morl grounds! Who educated you, child? And what do you intend to do now?"

"For the present, only to get a lodging. Will you tell me where I should look for one? I dont know the east from the west end of this town; and I am so inexperienced that I might make a mistake easily as to the character of the places. Will you direct me to some street or quarter in which I should he likely to find suitable rooms? I can live very economically."

"I dont know what to do," said Mrs. Crawford, perplexedly, turning her rings on her fingers. "You ought to be ashamed of yourself. And you so pretty!"

"Perhaps you would rather not assist me. You may tell me so

candidly. I shall not be offended."

"You mustnt take me up like that. I must have a talk with the General about you. I dont feel like letting you go into some ordinary place by yourself. But I cant ask you to stay here without consulting—"

"Oh, no, you must not think of any such thing: I must begin to face the world alone at once. I assure you, Mrs. Crawford, I could not come here. I should only keep your friends away."

"But nobody knows you."

"Sooner or later I should meet someone who does. There are hundreds of people who know me by sight, who travel every year. Besides, my case is a very public one, unfortunately. May I take you into my confidence?"

"If you wish, my dear. I dont ask you for it; but I will take it kindly."

"I know you will. You must have heard all about me. Mr. Forster's real name is Douglas."

Mrs. Crawford stifled a whoop of surprise. "And you! Are you—?"

"I am."

"Only think! And that was Douglas! Why, I thought he was a straight-haired, sleeky, canting snake of a man. And you too are not a bit like what I thought. You are quite a person, Mrs.—Mrs. Conolly."

"I have no right to bear that name any longer. Pray call me by my assumed name still, and keep my secret. I hope you do not believe all the newspapers said?"

"No, of course not," said Mrs. Crawford. "But whose fault

was it?"

"Mine. Altogether mine. I wish you would tell people that Mr. Conolly is blameless in the matter."

"He will take care of his own credit, never fear. I am sure you got some provocation: I know what men are. The General is not my first husband."

"No, I got no provocation. Mr. Conolly is not like other men. I got discontented because I had nothing to desire. And now, about the lodgings, Mrs. Crawford. Do not think I am changing the subject from reticence. It is the question of money that makes me anxious. All my resources would be swallowed up at the hotel in less than a week."

"Lodgings? You mean rooms, I guess. People here mostly go to boarding-houses. And as to the cheapness, you dont know what cheapness is. Cant you make some arrangement with your great relations in England? Have you no property of your own?"

"I cannot tell whether my property remains my own or not. You must regard me as a poor woman. I am quite determined to have the lodgings; and I should like to arrange about them at once; for I am rather upset by something that happened this morning."

"Well, if you must, you must, I know a place that might suit you: I lived in it myself when I was not so well off as I am at present. It is a little down-town; but you will have to put up with that for the sake of economy."

Mrs. Crawford, who had read in the papers of her guest's relationship to the Earl of Carbury, then sent for her carriage, and dressed herself handsomely. When they had gone some distance, they entered a wide street, crossed half way along by an avenue and an elevated railway.

"What do you think of this neighborhood?" said Mrs. Crawford.

"It is a fine, wide street," replied Marian; "but it looks as if it needed to be swept and painted."

"The other end is quieter. I'm afraid you wont like living here."

Marian had hitherto thought of such streets as thoroughfares, not as places in which she could dwell. "Beggars cannot be choosers," she said, with affected cheerfulness, looking anxiously ahead for the promised quiet part.

"Boarding-houses are so much the rule here, that it is not easy to get rooms. You will find Mrs. Myers a good soul, and though the house is not much to look at, it is comfortable enough inside."

The appearance of the street improved as they went on; and the house they stopped at, though the windows were dingy and the paint old, was better than Marian had hoped for a minute before. She remained in the carriage whilst her companion conferred with the landlady within. Twenty minutes passed before Mrs. Crawford reappeared, looking much perplexed.

"Mrs. Myers has a couple of rooms that would do you very well; only you would be on the same floor with a woman who is always drunk. She has pawned a heap of clothes, and promises to leave every day; but Mrs. Myers hasnt got rid of her yet. It's very provoking. She's quiet, and doesnt trouble any one; but still, of course—"

"She cannot interfere with me," said Marian. "If that is the only objection, let it pass. I need have nothing to say to her. If she is not violent nor noisy, her habits are her own affair."

"Oh, she wont trouble you. You can keep to yourself,

English fashion."

"Then let us agree at once. I cannot face any more searching and bargaining."

"Youre looking pale. Are you sure you are not ill?"

"No. It is nothing. I am rather tired."

They went in together; and Marian was introduced to Mrs. Myers, a nervous widow of fifty. The rooms were small, and the furniture and carpets old and worn; but all was clean; and there was an open fireplace in the sitting-room.

"They will do very nicely, thank you," said Marian. "I will send for my luggage; and I think I will just telegraph my new address and a few words to a friend in London."

"If you feel played out, I can see after your luggage," said Mrs. Crawford. "But I advise you to come back with me; have a good lunch at Delmonico's; and send your cablegram yourself."

Marian roused herself from a lassitude which was coming upon her, and took Mrs. Crawford's advice. When they returned to the richer quarter of the town, and especially after luncheon, her spirits revived. At the hotel she observed that the clerk was surprised when, arranging for the removal of her luggage and the forwarding of her letters, she mentioned her new address. Douglas, she found, had paid all expenses before leaving. She did not linger in the building; for the hotel staff stared at her curiously. She finished her business by telegraphing to Elinor: "*Separated. Write to new address. Have I forfeited my money?*" This cost her nearly five dollars.

"Only that you must find out about your money, I wouldnt have let you spend all that," said Mrs. Crawford.

"I did not think it would have cost so much," said Marian. "I was horrified when he named the price. However, it cannot be helped."

"We may as well be getting back to Mrs. Myers's now. It's late."

"Yes, I suppose so," said Marian, sighing. "I am sorry I did not ask Nelly to telegraph me. I am afraid my funds will not last so long as I thought."

"Well, we shall see. The General was greatly taken with you for the way you looked after me when I was ill yonder; so you have two friends in Noo York City, at any rate."

"You have proved that to me to-day. I am afraid I shall have to trouble you further if I get bad news. You will have to help me to find some work."

"Yes. Never mind that until the bad news comes. I hope you wont mope at Mrs. Myers's. How does the American air agree with you?"

"Pretty well. I was sick for the first two days of our passage across, and somehow my digestion seems to have got out of order in consequence. Of late I have been a little unwell in the mornings."

"Oh! Thats so, is it? Humph! I see I shall have to come and look after you occasionally."

"Why?"

"Never you mind, my dear. But dont go moping, nor going without food to save money. Take care of yourself."

"It is nothing serious," said Marian, with a smile. "Only a passing indisposition. You need not be uneasy about me. This is the house, is it not? I shall lose myself whenever I go out for a walk here."

"This is it. Now good-bye. I'll see you soon. Meanwhile, you take care of yourself, as youre told."

It was dark when Marian entered her new residence. Mrs. Myers was standing at the open door, remonstrating with a milkman. Marian hastily assured her that she knew the way, and went upstairs alone. She was chilled and weary; her spirits had fallen again during her journey from the telegraph office. As she approached her room, hoping to find a good fire, she heard a flapping noise, which was suddenly interrupted by the rattle of a falling poker, followed by the exclamation, in a woman's voice, "Och, musha, I wouldnt doubt you." Marian, entering, saw a robust young woman kneeling before the grate, trying to improve a dull fire that burnt there. She had taken up the poker and placed it standing against the bars so that it pointed up the chimney; and she was now using her apron fanwise as a bellows. The fire glowed in the draught; and Marian, by its light, noted with displeasure that the young woman's calico dress was soiled, and her hair untidy.

"I think—"

"God bless us!" ejaculated the servant, starting and turning a comely dirty face toward Marian.

"Did I frighten you?" said Marian, herself startled by the exclamation.

"You put the life acrass in me," said the servant, panting, and pressing her hand on her bosom.

"I am sorry for that. I was going to say that I think you need not take any further trouble with the fire. It will light of itself now."

"Very well, miss."

"What is your name?"

"Liza Redmon', miss."

"I should like some light, Eliza, if you please."

"Yis, miss. Would you wish to take your tay now, miss?"

"Yes, thank you."

Eliza went away with alacrity. Marian put off her bonnet and furs, and sat down before the fire to despond over the prospect of living in that shabby room, waited on by that slipshod Irish girl, who roused in her something very like racial antipathy. Presently Eliza returned, carrying a small tray, upon which she had crowded a lighted kerosene lamp, a china tea service, a rolled-up table cloth, a supply of bread and butter, and a copper kettle. When she had placed the lamp on the mantel-piece, and the kettle by the fire, she put the tray on the sofa, and proceeded to lay the cloth, which she shook from its folds and spread like a sail in the air by seizing two of the corners in her hands, and pulling them apart whilst she held the middle fold in her teeth. Then she adroitly wafted it over the table, making a breeze in which the lamp flared and Marian blinked. Her movements were very rapid; and in a few moments she had arranged the tea service, and was ready to withdraw.

"My luggage will be sent here this evening or to-morrow, Eliza. Will you tell me when it comes?"

"Yis, miss."

"You know that my name is *Mrs.* Forster, do you not?"

"Mrs. Forster. Yis, miss."

Marian made no further attempt to get miss changed to maam; and Eliza left the room. As she crossed the landing, she was called by someone on the same floor. Marian started at the sound. It was a woman's voice, disagreeably husky: a voice she felt sure she had heard before, and yet one that was not familiar to her.

"Eliza. Eli-za!" Marian shuddered.

"Yis, yis," said Eliza, impatiently, opening a door.

"Come here, alanna," said the voice, with mock fondness. The door was then closed, and Marian could hear the murmur of the conversation which followed. It was still proceeding when Mrs. Myers came in.

"I didnt ought to have left you to find your way up here alone, Mrs. Forster," she said; "but I do have such worry sometimes that I'm bound to leave either one thing or another undone."

"It does not matter at all, Mrs. Myers. Your servant has been very attentive to me."

"The hired girl? She's smart, she is—does everything right slick away. The only trouble is to keep her out of that room. She's in there now. Unless I am always after her, she is slipping out on errands, pawning and buying drink for that unfortunate young creature."

"For whom?"

"A person that Mrs. Crawford promised to tell you about."

"So she did," said Marian. "But I did not know she was young."

"She's older than you, a deal. I knew her when she was a little girl, and I often forget how old she is. She was the prettiest child! Even now she would talk you into anything. But I cant help her. It's nothing but drink, drink, drink from morning til night. There's Eliza coming out of her room. Eliza."

"Yis, maam," said Eliza, looking in.

"You stay in the house, Eliza, do you hear? I wont have you go out."

"Could I spake a word to you, maam?" said Eliza, lowering her voice.

"No, Eliza. I'm engaged with Mrs. Forster."

"She wants to see you," whispered Eliza.

"Go downrs, Eliza, this minute. I wont see her."

"Mrs. Myers," cried the voice. Marian again shrank from the sound. "Mrs. My-ers. Aunt Sally. Come to your poor Soozy." Mrs. Myers looked perplexedly at Marian. The voice resumed after a pause, with an affected Yankee accent, "I guess I'll raise a shine if you dont come."

"I must go," said Mrs. Myers. "I promise you, Mrs. Forster, she shall not annoy you. She shall go this week. It aint right that you should be disturbed by her."

Mrs. Myers went into the other room. Eliza ran downrs, and Marian heard her open the house door softly and go out. She also heard indistinctly the voices of the landlady and her lodger. After a time these ceased, and she drank her tea in peace. She was glad that Mrs. Myers did not return, although she made no more comfortable use of her solitude than to think of her lost home in Holland Park, comparing it with her dingy apartment, and pressing her handkerchief upon her eyes when they became too full of tears. She had passed more than an hour thus when Eliza roused her by announcing the arrival of the luggage. Thereupon she bestirred herself to superintend its removal to her bedroom, where she unpacked a trunk which contained her writing-case and some books. With these were stowed her dresses, much miscellaneous finery, and some handsomely worked underclothing. Eliza, standing by, could not contain her admiration; and Marian, though she did not permit her to handle the clothes, had not the heart to send her away until she had seen all that the trunk contained. Marian heard her voice afterward in the apartment of the drunken lodger, and suspected from its emphasis that the girl was describing the rare things she had seen.

Marian imparted some interest to her surroundings that evening by describing them in a letter to Elinor. When she had finished, she was weary; and the fire was nearly out. She looked at her watch, and, finding to her surprise that is was two hours after midnight, rose to go to bed. Before leaving the room, she stood for a minute before the old-fashioned pier-glass, with one foot on the fender, and looked at her image, pitying her own weariness, and enjoying the soft beauty of her face and the gentleness of her expression. Her appearance did not always please her; but on this occasion the mirror added so much to the solace she had found in writing to Elinor, that she felt almost happy as she took the lamp to light her to her bedroom.

She had gone no farther than the landing when a sound of unsteady footsteps on the stairs caused her to stop. As she lifted the lamp and looked up, she saw a strange woman descending toward her, holding the balustrade, and moving as though with pains in her limbs. This woman, whose black hair fell nearly to her waist, was dressed in a crimson satin dressing-gown, warmly padded, and much stained and splashed. She had fine dark eyes, and was young, bold-looking, and hand-some; but when she came nearer, the moist pallor of her skin, the slackness of her lower lip and jaw, and an eager and worn expression in her fine eyes, gave her a thirsty, reckless leer that filled Marian with loathing. Her aspect conveyed the same painful suggestion as her voice had done before, but more definitely; for it struck Marian, with a shock, that Conolly, in the grotesque metamorphosis of a nightmare, might appear in some such likeness. The lamp did not seem to attract her attention at first; but when she came within a few steps, she saw some one before her, and, dazzled by the light, peered at Marian, who lost her presence of mind, and stood motionless. Gradually the woman's expression changed to one of astonish-ment. She came down to the landing; stopped, grasping the

George Bernard Shaw

handrail to steady herself; and said in her husky voice:

"Oh, Lord! It's not a woman at all. It's D. Ts." Then, not quite convinced by this explanation, she suddenly stretched out her hand and attempted to grasp Marian's arm. Missing her aim, she touched her on the breast, and immediately cried, "Mrs. Ned!"

Marian shrank from her touch, and recovered her courage.

"Do you know me?" she said.

"I should rather think I do. I have gone off a good deal in my appearance, or you would know me. Youve seen me on the stage, I suppose. I'm your sister-in-law. Perhaps you didnt know you had one."

"Are you Miss Susanna Conolly?"

"Thats who I am. At least I am what is left of Miss Susanna. You don't look overjoyed to make my acquaintance; but I was as good-looking as you once. Take my advice, Mrs. Ned: dont drink champagne. The end of champagne is brandy; and the end of brandy is—" Susanna made a grimace and indicated herself.

"I am afraid we shall disturb the house if we talk here. We had better say good-night."

"No, no. Dont be in such a hurry to get rid of me. Come into my room with me for a while. I'll talk quietly: I'm not drunk. Ive just slept it off; and I was coming down for some more. You may as well keep me from it for a few minutes. I suppose Ned hasnt forbidden you to speak to me."

"Oh, no," said Marian, yielding to a feeling of pity. "Come into my room. There is a scrap of fire there still."

"We used to lodge in this room long ago, in my father's time," said Susanna, following Marian into the room, and reclining with a groan on the sofa. "I'm rather in a fog, you know: I cant make out how the deuce you come to be here. Did Ned send you to look after me? Is he in New York? Is he here?"

"No," said Marian, foreseeing with a bitter pang and a terrible blush what must follow. "He is in England. I am alone here."

"Well, why—? what—? I dont understand."

"Have you not read the papers?" said Marian, in a low voice, turning her head away.

"Papers! No, not since I saw an account of my brilliant *debut* here, of which I suppose you have heard. I never read: I do nothing but drink. What has happened?"

Marian hesitated.

"Is it any secret?" said Susanna.

"No, it is no secret," said Marian, turning, and looking at her steadily. "All the world knows it. I have left your brother; and I do not know whether I am still his wife, or whether I am already divorced."

"You dont mean to say youre on the loose!" cried Susanna.

Marian was silent.

"I always told Ned that no woman could stand him," said Susanna, with sodden vivacity, after a pause, during which Marian had to endure her astonished stare. "He always thought you the very pink of propriety. Of course, there was another man in it. Whats become of him, if I may ask?"

"I have left him," said Marian, sternly. "You need impute no fault to your brother in the matter, Miss Conolly. He is quite blameless."

"Yes," said Susanna, not in the least impressed, "he always is blameless. How is Bob? I mean Marmaduke, your cousin. I call him Bob, short for Cherry Bob."

"He is very well, thank you."

"Now, Bob was not a blameless man, but altogether the reverse; and he was a capital fellow to get on with. Ned was always right, always sure of himself; and there was an end. He has no variety. I wonder will Bob ever get married?"

"He is going to be married in the spring."

"Who to?"

"To Lady Constance Car—"

"Damn that woman!" exclaimed Susanna. "I hate her. She was always throwing herself at his head. Curse her! Damn her! I wish—"

"Miss Conolly," said Marian: "I hope you will not think me rude; but I am very tired, and it is very late. I must go to bed."

"Well, will you come and see me to-morrow? It will be an act of charity. I am dying here all alone. You are a nice woman, and I know what you must feel about me; but you will get used to me. I wont annoy you. I wont swear. I wont say anything about your cousin. I'll keep sober. Do come. You are a good sort: Bob always said so; and you might save me from destroying myself. Say youll come."

"If you particularly wish it, I will," said Marian, not disguising her reluctance.

"Youd rather not, of course," said Susanna, despondently.

"I am afraid I cannot be of any use to you."

"For that matter, no one is likely to be of much use to me. But it's hard to be imprisoned in this den without anyone to speak to but Eliza. However, do as you please. I did as I pleased; and I must take the consequences. Just tell me one thing. Did you find me out by accident?"

"Quite."

"That was odd." Susanna groaned again as she rose from the sofa. "Well, since you wont have anything to do with me, good-bye. Youre quite right."

"I will come and see you. I do not wish to avoid you if you are in trouble."

"Do," said Susanna, eagerly, touching Marian's hand with her moist palm. "We'll get on better than you think. I like you, and I'll make you like me. If I could only keep from it for two days, I shouldnt be a bit disgusting. Good-night."

"Good-night," said Marian, overcoming her repugnance to Susanna's hand, and clasping it. "Remember that my name here is Mrs. Forster."

"All right. Good-night. Thank you. You will never be sorry for having compassion on me."

"Wont you take a light?"

"I dont require one. I can find what I want in the dark."

She went into her apartment. Marian went quickly up to her own bedroom and locked herself in. Her first loathing for Susanna had partly given way to pity; but the humiliation of confessing herself to such a woman as an unfaithful wife was galling. When she went to sleep she dreamed that she was unmarried and at home with her father, and that the household was troubled by Susanna, who lodged in a room upstairs.

CHAPTER XX

Sholto Douglas returned to England in the ship which carried Marian's letter to Elinor. On reaching London he stayed a night in the hotel at Euston, and sent his man next day to take rooms for him at the West End. Early in the afternoon the man reported that he had secured apartments in Charles Street, St. James's. It was a fine wintry day, and Douglas resolved to walk, not without a sense of being about to run the gauntlet.

It proved the most adventurous walk he had ever taken in his life. Everybody he knew seemed to be lying in wait for him. In Portland Place he met Miss McQuinch, who, with the letter fresh in her pocket, looked at him indignantly, and cut him. At the Laugham Hotel he passed a member of his club, who seemed surprised, but nodded coolly. In Regent Street he saw Lady Carbury's carriage waiting before a shop. He hurried past the door, for he had lost courage at his encounter with Elinor. There were, however, two doors; and as he passed the second, the Countess, Lady Constance, and Marmaduke came out just before him.

"Where the devil is the carriage?" said Marmaduke, loudly.

"Hush! Everybody can hear you," said Lady Constance.

"What do I care whether—Hal-lo! Douglas! How are you?"

Marmaduke proffered his hand. Lady Carbury plucked her

daughter by the sleeve and hurried to her carriage, after returning Douglas's stern look with the slightest possible bow. Constance imitated her mother. Douglas haughtily raised his hat.

"How obstinate Marmaduke is!" said the Countess, when she had bidden the coachman drive away at once. "He is going to walk down Regent Street with that man."

"But you didnt cut him, mamma."

"I never dreamed of his coming back so soon; and, of course, I cannot tell whether he will be cut or not. We must wait and see what other people will do. If we meet him again we had better not see him."

"Look here, old fellow," said Marmaduke, as he walked away with Douglas. "Youve come back too soon. It wont do. Take my advice and go away again until matters have blown over. Hang it, it's too flagrant! You have not been away two months."

"I believe you are going to be married," said Douglas. "Allow me to congratulate you."

"Thank you. Fine day, isnt it?"

"Very fine."

Marmaduke walked on in silence. Douglas presently recommenced the conversation.

"I only arrived in London last night. I have come from New York."

"Indeed. Pleasant voyage?"

"Very pleasant."

George Bernard Shaw

Another pause.

"Has anything special happened during my absence?"

"Nothing special."

"Was there much fuss made about my going?"

"Well, there was a great deal of fuss made about it. Excuse my alluding to the subject again. I shouldnt have done so if you hadnt asked me."

"Oh, my dear fellow, you neednt stand on ceremony with me."

"That's all very well, Douglas; but when I alluded to it just now, you as good as told me to mind my own business."

"I told you so!"

"Not in those words, perhaps. However, the matter is easily settled. You bolted with Marian. I know that, and you know it. If the topic is disagreeable, say so, and it is easily avoided. If you want to talk about it, better not change the subject when I mention it."

"You have taken offence needlessly. I changed the subject inadvertently."

"Hm! Well, has she come back with you?"

"No."

"Do you mean that youve thrown her over?"

"I have said nothing of the kind. As a matter of fact, she has thrown me over."

"Thats very strange. You are not going to marry her then, I suppose?"

"How can I? I tell you she has deserted me. Let me remind you, Lind, that I should not be bound to marry her in any case, and I shall certainly not do so now. If I chose to justify myself, I could easily do so by her own conduct."

"I expect you will not be troubled for any justification. People seem to have made up their minds that you were wrong in the first instance, and you ought to keep out of the way until they have forgotten—Oh, confound it, here's Conolly! Now, for God's sake, dont let us have any row."

Douglas whitened, and took a step back into the roadway before he recovered himself; for Conolly had come upon them suddenly as they turned into Charles Street. A group of gentlemen stood on the steps of the clubhouse which stands at that corner.

"Bless me!" said Conolly, with perfect good humor. "Douglas back again! Why on earth did you run away with my wife? and what have you done with her?"

The party on the steps ceased chatting and began to stare.

"This is not the place to call me to account, sir," said Douglas, still on his guard, and very ill at ease. "If you have anything to say to me which cannot be communicated through a friend, it had better be said in private."

"I shall trouble you for a short conversation," said Conolly. "How do you do, Lind? Where can we go? I do not belong to any club."

"My apartments are at hand," said Douglas.

"I suppose I had better leave you," said Marmaduke.

"Your presence will not embarrass me in the least," said Conolly.

"I have not sought this interview," said Douglas. "I therefore prefer Mr. Lind to witness what passes."

Conolly nodded assent; and they went to a house on the doorstep of which Douglas's man was waiting, and ascended to the front drawing-room.

"Now, sir," said Douglas, without inviting his guests to sit down. Conolly alone took off his hat. Marmaduke went aside, and looked out of the window.

"I know the circumstances that have led to your return," said Conolly; "so we need not go into that. I want you, however, to assist me on one point. Do you know what Marian's pecuniary position is at present?'

"I decline to admit that it concerns me in any way."

"Of course not. But it concerns me, as I do not wish that she should be without money in a foreign city. She has telegraphed a question about her property to Miss McQuinch. That by itself is nothing; but her new address, which I first saw on a letter this morning, happens to be known to me as that of a rather shabby lodging-house."

"I know nothing of it."

"I do: it means that she is poor. I can guess at the sum she carried with her to America. Now, if you will be good enough to tell me whether you have ever given her money; if so, how much; and what her expenditure has been, you will enable me to estimate her position at present."

"I do not know that you have any right to ask such questions."

"I do not assert any right to ask them. On the contrary, I have explained their object. I shall not press them, if you think that an answer will in any way compromise you."

"I have no fear of being compromised. None whatever."

Conolly nodded, and waited for an answer.

"I may say that my late trip has cost me a considerable sum. I paid all the expenses; and Miss—Mrs. Conolly did not, to my knowledge, disburse a single fraction. She did not ask me to give her money. Had she done so, I should have complied at once."

"Thank you. Thats all right: she will be able to hold out until she hears from us. Good-afternoon."

"Allow me to add, sir, before you go," said Douglas, asserting himself desperately against Conolly's absolutely sincere disregard of him and preoccupation with Marian, "that Mrs. Conolly has been placed in her present position entirely through her own conduct. I repudiate the insinuation that I have deserted her in a foreign city; and I challenge inquiry on the point."

"Quite so, quite so," assented Conolly, carelessly. "Good-bye, Lind." And he took his hat and went out.

"By George!" said Marmaduke, admiringly, "he did that damned well—*damned* well. Look here, old man: take my advice and clear out for another year or so. You cant stay here. As a looker-on, I see most of the game; and thats my advice to you as a friend."

Douglas, whose face had reddened and reddened with successive rushes of blood until it was now purple, lost all self-control at Marmaduke's commiserating tone. "I will see whether I cannot put him in the wrong," he burst out, in the debased voice of an ignobly angry man. "Do you think I will let him tell the world that I have been thrown over and fooled?"

"Thats your own story, isnt it? At least, I understood you to say so as we came along."

"Let him say so, and I'll thrash him like, a dog in the street. I'll—"

"Whats the use of thrashing a man who will simply hand you over to the police? and quite right, too! What rot!"

"We shall see. We shall see."

"Very well. Do as you like. You may twist one another's heads off for what I care. He has had the satisfaction of putting you into a rage, at all events."

"I am not in a rage."

"Very well. Have it your own way."

"Will you take a challenge to him from me?"

"No. I am not a born fool."

"That is plain speaking."

Marmaduke put his hands into his pockets, and whistled. "I think I will take myself off," he said, presently.

"As you please," replied Douglas, coldly.

"I will look in on you some day next week, when you have cooled down a bit. Good-bye."

Douglas said nothing, and Marmaduke, with a nod, went out. Some minutes later the servant entered and said that Mr. Lind was below.

"What! Back again!" said Douglas, with an oath.

"No, sir. It's old Mr. Lind—Mr. Reginald."

"Did you say I was in?"

"The man belonging to the house did, sir."

"Confound his officiousness! I suppose he must come up."

Reginald Lind entered, and bowed. Douglas placed a chair for him, and waited, mute, and a little put out. Mr. Lind's eyes and voice shewed that he also was not at his ease; but his manner was courtly and his expression grave, as Douglas had, in his boyhood, been accustomed to see them.

"I am sorry, Sholto," said Mr. Lind, "that I cannot for the present meet you with the cordiality which formerly existed between us. However unbearable your disappointment at Marian's marriage may have been, you should not have taken a reprehensible and desperate means of remedying it. I speak to you now as an old friend—as one who knew you when the disparity in our ages was more marked than it is at present."

Douglas bowed.

"I have just heard from Mr. Conolly—whom I met accidentally in Pall Mall—that you have returned from America. He gave me no further account of you, except that he had met you and spoken to you here. I hope nothing unpleasant passed."

"The meeting was not a pleasant one. I shall take steps to make Mr. Conolly understand that."

"Nothing approaching to violence, I trust."

"No. Mr. Conolly's discretion averted it. I am not sure that a second interview between us will end so quietly."

"The interview should not have taken place at all, Sholto. I need not point out to you that prudence and good taste forbid any repetition of it."

George Bernard Shaw

"I did not seek it, Mr. Lind. He forced it upon me. I promise you that if a second meeting takes place, it will be forced upon him by me, and will take place in another country."

"That is a young man's idea, Sholto. The day for such crimes, thank Heaven, is past and gone. Let us say no more of it. I was speaking to your mother on Sunday. Have you seen her yet?"

"No."

"Sholto, you hit us all very hard that Monday before Christmas. I know what I felt about my daughter. But I can only imagine what your mother must have felt about her son."

"I am not insensible to that. I has been rather my misfortune than my fault that I have caused you to suffer. If it will gratify you to know that I have suffered deeply myself, and am now, indeed, a broken man, I can assure you that such is the case."

"It is fortunate for us all that matters are not absolutely irremediable. I will so far take you into my confidence as to tell you that I have never felt any satisfaction in Marian's union with Mr. Conolly. Though he is unquestionably a remarkable man, yet there was a certain degree of incongruity in the match—you will understand me—which placed Marian apart from her family whilst she was with him. I have never entered my daughter's house without a feeling that I was more or less a stranger there. Had she married you in the first instance, the case would have been different: I wish she had. However, that is past regretting now. What I wish to say is that I can still welcome you as Marian's husband, even though she will have a serious error to live down; and I shall be no less liberal to her than if her previous marriage had never taken place."

Douglas cleared his throat, but did not speak.

"Well?" said Mr. Lind after a pause, reddening.

"This is a very painful matter," said Douglas at last. "As a man of the world, Mr. Lind, you must be aware that I am not bound to your daughter in any way."

"I am not speaking to you as a man of the world. I am speaking as a father, and as a gentleman."

"Doubtless your position as a father is an unfortunate one. I can sympathize with your feelings. But as a gentleman—"

"Think of what you are going to say, Sholto. If you speak as a gentleman, you can have only one answer. If you have any other, you will speak as a scoundrel." The last sentence came irrepressibly to Mr. Lind's lips; but the moment he had uttered it, he felt that he had been too precipitate.

"Sir!"

"I repeat, as a scoundrel—if you deny your duty in the matter."

"I decline to continue this conversation with you, Mr. Lind. You know as well as I do that no gentleman is expected or even permitted by society to take as his wife a woman who has lived with him as his mistress."

"No man who betrays a lady and refuses to make her all the reparation in his power can claim to be a gentleman."

"You are dreaming, Mr. Lind. Your daughter was the guardian of her own honor. I made her no promises. It is absurd to speak of a woman of her age and experience being betrayed, as though she were a child."

"I always understood that you prided yourself on acting up to a higher standard of honorable dealing than other men. If this is your boasted—"

"Mr. Lind," said Douglas, interrupting him with determination, "no more of this, if you please. Briefly, I will have nothing whatever to say to Mrs. Conolly in the future. If her reputation were as unstained as your own, I would still refuse to know her. I have suffered from her the utmost refinements of caprice and treachery, and the coarsest tirades of abuse. She left me of her own accord, in spite of my entreaties to her to stay—entreaties which I made her in response to an exhibition of temper which would have justified me in parting from her there and then. It is true that I have moulded my life according to a higher standard of honor than ordinary men; and it is also true that that standard is never higher, never more fastidiously acted up to, than where a woman is concerned. I have only to add that I am perfectly satisfied as to the propriety of my behavior in Marian's case, and that I absolutely refuse to hear another accusation of unworthiness from you, much as I respect you and your sorrow."

Mr. Lind, though he saw that he must change his tone, found it hard to subdue his temper; for though not a strong man, he was unaccustomed to be thwarted. "Sholto," he said: "you are not serious. You are irritated by some lovers' quarrel."

"I am justly estranged from your daughter, and I am resolved never to give her a place in my thoughts again. I have madly wasted my youth on her. Let her be content with that and the other things I have sacrificed for her sake."

"But this is dreadful. Think of the life she must lead if you do not marry her. She will be an outcast. She will not even have a name."

"She would not be advised. She made her choice in defiance of an explicit warning of the inevitable results, and she must abide by it. I challenge the most searching inquiry into my conduct, Mr. Lind. It will be found, if the truth be told, that I spared her no luxury before she left me; and that, far from being the aggressor, it is I who have the right to complain of insult and desertion."

"Still, even granting that her unhappy position may have

rendered her a little sore and impatient at times, do you not owe her some forbearance since she gave up her home and her friends for you?"

"Sacrifice for sacrifice, mine was the greater of the two. Like her, I have lost my friends and my position here—to some extent, at least. Worse, I have let my youth slip by in fruitless pursuit of her. For the home which she hated, I offered her one ten times more splendid. I gave her the devotion of a gentleman to replace the indifference of a blacksmith. What have I not done for her? I freed her from her bondage; I carried her across the globe; I watched her, housed her, fed her, clothed her as a princess. I loved her with a love that taught her a meaning of the word she had never known before. And when I had served her turn—when I had rescued her from her husband and placed her beyond his reach—when she became surfeited with a wealth of chivalrous love which she could not comprehend, and when a new world opened before her a fresh field for intrigue, I was assailed with slanderous lies, and forsaken. Do you think, Mr. Lind, that in addition to this, I will endure the reproaches of any man—even were he my own father?"

"But she suffers more, being a woman. The world will be comparatively lenient toward you. If you and she were married and settled, with no consciousness of being in a false position, and no wearing fear of detection, you would get on together quite differently."

"It may be so, but I shall never put it to the test."

"Listen a moment, Sholto. Just consider the matter calmly and rationally. I am a rich man—at least, I can endow Marian better than you perhaps think. I see that you feel aggrieved, and that you fear being forced into a marriage which you have, as you say—I fully admit it, most fully—a perfect right to decline. But I am urging you to make Marian your legal wife solely because it is the best course for both of you. That, I assure you, is the feeling of society in the matter. Everybody speaks to me of your becoming my son-in-law. The Earl says no other course is possible. I will give you ten thousand pounds down on her wedding-day. You will lose nothing: Conolly will not claim damages. He has contradicted the report that he would. I will pay the costs of the divorce as well. Mind! I do not mean that I will settle the money on her. I will give it to her unconditionally. In other words, it will become your property the moment you become her husband."

"I understand," said Douglas contemptuously. "However, as it is merely a question of making your daughter an honest woman in consideration of so much cash, I have no doubt you will find plenty of poorer men who will be glad to close with you for half the money. You are much in the city now, I believe. Allow me to suggest that you will find a dealer there more easily than in St. James's."

Mr. Lind reddened again. "I do not think you see the matter in the proper light," he said. "You are asked to repair the disgrace you have brought on a lady and upon her family. I offer you a guarantee that you will not lose pecuniarily by doing so. Whatever other loss you may incur, you are bound to bear it as the penalty of your own act. I appeal to you, sir, as one gentleman appeals to another, to remove the dishonor you have brought upon my name."

"To transfer it to my own, you mean. Thank you, Mr. Lind. The public is more accustomed to associate conjugal levity with the name of Lind than with that of Douglas."

"If you refuse me the justice you owe to my daughter, you need not couple that refusal with an insult."

"I have already explained that I owe your daughter nothing. You come here and offer me ten thousand pounds to marry her. I decline the bargain. You then take your stand upon the injury to your name. I merely remind you that your name was somewhat tarnished even before Mrs. Conolly changed it for the less distinguished one which she has really dishonored."

"Douglas," said Mr. Lind, trembling, "I will make you repent this. I will have satisfaction."

"As you remarked when I declared my readiness to give satisfaction in the proper quarter, the practice you allude to is obsolete. Fortunately so, I think, in our case."

"You are a coward, sir." Douglas rang the bell. "I will expose you in every club in London."

"Shew this gentleman out," said Douglas to his servant.

"You have received that order because I told your master that he is a rascal," said Mr. Lind to the man. "I shall say the same thing to every man I meet between this house and the committee-room of his club."

The servant looked grave as Mr. Lind left the room. Soon after, Douglas, whose self-respect, annihilated by Conolly, had at first been thoroughly restored by Mr. Lind, felt upset again by the conclusion of the interview. Finding solitude and idleness intolerable, he went into the streets, though he no longer felt any desire to meet his acquaintances, and twice crossed the Haymarket to avoid them. As he strolled about, thinking of all that had been said to him that afternoon, he grew morose. Twice he calculated his expenditure on the American trip, and the difference that an increment of ten thousand pounds would make in his property. Suddenly, in turning out of Air Street into Piccadilly, he found himself face to face with Lord Carbury.

"How do you do?" said the latter pleasantly, but without the unceremonious fellowship that had formerly existed between them.

"Thank you," said Douglas, "I am quite well."

A pause followed, Jasper not knowing exactly what to say next.

George Bernard Shaw

"I am considering where I shall dine," said Douglas. "Have you dined yet?"

"No. I promised to dine at home this evening. My mother likes to have a family dinner occasionally."

Douglas knew that before the elopement he would have been asked to join the party. "I suppose people have been pleased to talk a good deal about me of late," he said.

"Yes, I fear so. However, I hope it will pass over."

"It shews no sign of passing over as yet, then?"

"Well, it has become a little stale as a topic; but there is undeniably a good deal of feeling about it still. If you will excuse my saying so, I think that perhaps you would do well to keep out of the way a little longer."

"Presuming, of course, that popular feeling is a matter about which I am likely to concern myself."

"That is a question for you to decide. Excuse the hint."

"The question is whether it is not better to be on the spot, so as to strangle calumny at its source, than to hide myself abroad whilst a host of malicious tongues are busy with me."

"As to that, Douglas, I assure you you have been very fairly treated. The chief blame, as usual, has fallen on the weaker sex. Nothing could exceed the moderation of those from whom the loudest complaints might have been expected. Reginald Lind has hardly ever mentioned the subject. Even to me, he only shook his head and said that it was an old attachment. As to Conolly, we have actually reproached him for making excuses for you."

"Aye. A very astute method of bringing me into contempt. Allow me to enlighten you a little, Jasper. Lind, whose daughter I have discovered to be one of the worst of women, has just offered me ten thousand pounds to marry her. That speaks for itself. Conolly, who drove her into my arms by playing the tyrant whilst I played the lover, is only too glad to get rid of her. At the same time, he is afraid to fight me, and ashamed to say so. Therefore, he impudently pretends to pity me for being his gull in the matter. But I will stop that."

"Conolly is a particular friend of mine, Douglas, Let us drop the subject, if you dont mind."

"If he is your friend, of course I have nothing more to say. I think I will turn in here and dine. Good-evening."

They parted without any salutation: and Douglas entered the restaurant and dined alone, he came out an hour later in improved spirits, and began to consider whether he would go to the theatre or venture into his club. He was close to a lamp at a corner of Leicester Square when he stopped to debate the point with himself; and in his preoccupation he did not notice a four-wheeled cab going slowly past him, carrying a lady in an old white opera cloak. This was Mrs. Leith Fairfax, who, recognizing him, called to the cabman to drive a little past the lamp and stop.

"Good heavens!" she said in a half-whisper: "you here! What madness possessed you to come back?"

"I had no further occasion to stay away."

"How coolly you say so! You have iron nerves, all you Douglases. I have heard all, and I know what you have suffered. How soon will you leave London?"

"I have no intention of leaving it at present."

"But you cannot stay here."

"Pray why not? Is not London large enough for any man who does not live by the breath of the world?"

"Out of the question, Mr. Douglas. Absolutely out of the question. You *must* go away for a year at the very least. You must yield something to propriety."

"I shall yield nothing. I can do without any section of society that may feel called upon to do without me."

"Oh, you must subdue that imperious nature of yours for your mother's sake if not for your own. Besides, you have been very wicked and reckless and daring, just like a Douglas. You ought to do penance with a good grace. I may conclude, since you are here, that Elinor McQuinch's story is true as far as the facts go."

"I have not heard her story."

"It is only that you have parted from—you know."

"That is true. Can I gratify your curiosity in any other particular?"

"Strive not to let yourself be soured, Mr. Douglas. I shudder when I think of what you have undergone at the hands of one woman. There! I will not allude to it again."

"You will do wisely, Mrs. Leith Fairfax. What I have suffered, I have suffered. I desire no pity, and will endure none."

"That is so like yourself. I must hurry on to Covent Garden, or I shall be late. Will you come and see me quietly some day before you go? I am never at home to any one on Tuesdays; but if you come at about five, Caroline will let you in. It will be dark: nobody will see you. We can have a chat then."

"Thank you," said Douglas, coldly, stepping back, and raising his hat, "I shall not intrude on you. Good-evening."

She waved her hand at him; and the cab departed. He walked quickly back to Charles Street, and called his servant.

"I suppose no one has called?"

"Yes, sir. Mrs. Douglas came very shortly after you went out. She wishes you to go to the Square this evening, sir."

"This evening? I am afraid—Buckstone."

"Yes, sir."

"Is she looking well?"

"A little tired, sir. But quite well, I have no doubt."

"How much of the luggage have you unpacked?"

"Only your portmanteau, sir. I thought—"

"So much the better. Pack it again. I am going to Brussels to-night. Find out about the trains. I shall want you to take a hansom and take a note to Chester Square; but come back at once without waiting to be spoken to."

"Very good, sir."

Douglas then sat down and wrote the note.

"My dear Mother:

"I am sorry I was out when you called. I did not expect you, as I am only passing through London on my way to Brussels. I am anxious to get clear of this vile city, and so shall start to-night. Buckstone tells me you are looking well; and this assurance must content me for the present, as I find it impossible to go to you. You were quite right in warning me against what has happened; but it is all past and broken off now, and I am still as ever,

"Your affectionate son,
"SHOLTO DOUGLAS."

CHAPTER XXI

One day Eliza, out of patience, came to Mrs. Myers, and said:

"A' thin, maam, will you come up and spake to Miss Conolly. She's rasin ructions above stairs."

"Oh dear, oh dear!" said Mrs. Myers. "Cant you keep her quiet?"

"Arra, how can I kape her quiet, an she cryin an roarin, dyin an desarted?"

"Ask Mrs. Forster to go in and coax her to stop."

"Mrs. Forsther's at dhuddher ind o the town. Whisht! There she is, callin me. Youll have to gup to her, maam. Faith I wont go next or near her."

"There's no use in my going up, Eliza. What can I do?"

Eliza had nothing to suggest. "I'm sure, maam," she pleaded, "if she wont mind you, she wont mind me—bad manners to her!"

Mrs. Myers hesitated. The lodger became noisier.

"I spose Ive got to go," said Mrs. Myers, plaintively. She went upstairs and found Susanna lying on the sofa, groaning, with a dressing-gown and a pair of thick boots on.

George Bernard Shaw

"What *is* the matter with you, Miss Susan? Youre goin on fit to raise the street."

"For God's sake go and get something for me. Make the doctor do something. I'm famishing. I must be poisoned."

"Lord forbid!"

"Look at me. I cant eat anything. Oh! I cant even drink. I tell you I am dying of thirst."

"Well, Miss Susan, thers plenty for you to eat and drink."

"What is the good of that, when I can neither eat nor drink? Nothing will stay inside me. If I could only swallow brandy, I shouldnt care. I thought I could die drunk. Oh! Send Eliza out for some laudanum. I cant stand this: I'll kill myself."

"Be quiet, Miss Susan: youll be better presently. Whats the use of talking-about the doctor? He says youll not be able to drink for days, and that you will get your health back in conesquence. You are doing yourself no good by screeching like that, and you are ruining me and my house."

"Your house is all you care about. Curse you! I hope you may die deserted yourself. Dont go away. *Dear* Aunt Sally, you wont leave me here alone, will you? If you do, I'll scream like a hundred devils."

"I dont know what to do with you," said Mrs. Myers, crying. "Youll drive me as mad as yourself. Why did I ever let you into this house?"

"Oh, bother! Are *you* beginning to howl now? Have you any sardines, or anything spicy? I think I could eat some salted duck. No, I couldnt, though. Go for the doctor. There must be something that will do me good. What use is he if he can't set me right? All I want is something that will make me able to drink a tumbler of brandy."

"The Lord help you! Praise goodness! here's Mrs. Forster coming up. Whatll she think of you if you keep moaning like that? Mrs. Forster: will you step in here and try to quiet her a bit? She's clean mad."

"Come here," cried Susanna, as Marian entered. "Come and sit beside me. You may get out, you old cat: I dont want you any longer."

"Hush, pray," said Marian, putting her bonnet aside and sitting down by the sofa. "What is the matter?"

"The same as last night, only a great deal worse," said Susanna, shutting her eyes and turning her head aside. "It's all up with me this time, Mrs. Ned. I'm dying, not of drink, but of the want of it. Is that fiend of a woman gone?"

"Yes. You ought not to wound her as you did just now. She has been very kind to you."

"I dont care. Oh, dear me, I wonder how long this is going to last?"

"Shall I go for the doctor?"

"No; what can he do? Stay with me. I wish I could sleep or eat."

"You will be better soon. The doctor says that Nature is making an effort to rescue you from your habit by making it impossible for you to drink. Try and be patient. Will you not take off those heavy boots?"

"No, I cant feel my feet without them. I shall never be better," said Susanna, writhing impatiently. "I'm done for. How old are you? You neednt mind telling me. I shall soon be beyond repeating it."

"I was twenty-five in June last"

"I am only twenty-nine. I started at eighteen, and got to the top of the tree in seven years. I came down quicker than I went up. I might have gone on easily for fifteen years more, only for drinking champagne. I wish I had my life to live over again: you wouldnt catch me playing burlesque. If I had got the chance, I know I could have played tragedy or real Italian opera. I had to work hard at first; and they wont fill my place, very readily: thats one comfort. My cleverness was my ruin. Ned was not half so quick. It used to take him months to learn things that I picked up offhand, and yet you see how much better he has done than I."

"Do not disturb yourself with vain regrets. Think of something else. Shall we talk about Marmaduke?"

"No, I dont particularly care to. Somehow, at my pass, one thinks most about one's self, and about things that happened long ago. People that I came to know later on, like Bob, seem to be slipping away from me. There was a baritone in my father's company, a tremendous man, with shining black eyes, and a voice like a great bell—quite pretty at the top, though: he must have been sixty at least; and he was very fat; but he was the most dignified man I ever saw. You should have heard him do the Duke in Lucrezia Borgia, or sing Pro Peccatis from Rossini's Stabat Mater! I was ten years old when he was with us, and my grand ambition was to sing with him when I grew up. He would shake his head if he saw Susanetta now. I would rather hear him sing three bars than have ten visits from Bob. Oh, dear! I thought this cursed pain was getting numbed, but it is worse than ever."

"Try to keep from thinking of it. I have often wondered that you never speak of your child. I have heard from my friend in London that it is very well and happy."

"Oh, you mean Lucy. She was a lively little imp."

"Would you not like to see her again?"

"No, thank you. She is well taken care of, I suppose. I am glad she is out of my hands. She was a nuisance to me, and I am not a very edifying example for her. What on earth should I want to see her for?"

"I wish I had the good fortune to be a mother."

Susanna laughed. "Never say die, Mrs. Ned. You dont know what may happen to you yet. There now! I know, without opening my eyes, that you are shocked, bless your delicacy! How do you think I should have got through life if I'd been thin-skinned? What good does it do you? You are pining away in this hole of a lodging. You squirm when Mrs. Myers tries to be friendly with you; and I sometimes laugh at your expression when Eliza treats you to a little blarney about your looks. Now I would just as soon gossip and swear at her as go to tea with the Queen."

"I am not shocked at all. You see as badly as other people when your eyes are shut."

"They will soon shut up forever. I half wish they would do it at once, I wonder whether I will get any ease before there is an end of me."

"Perhaps the end of you on earth will be a good beginning for you somewhere else, Susanna."

"Thank you. Now the conversation has taken a nice, cheerful turn, hasn't it? Well, I cant be much worse off than I am at present. Anyhow, I must take my chance."

"Would you like to see a clergyman? I dont want to alarm you: I am sure you will get better: the doctor told me so; but I will go for one if you like."

"No: I dont want to be bothered—at least not yet. Besides, I hate clergymen, all except your brother, the doctor, who fell in love with me."

"Very well. I only suggested it in case you should feel uneasy."

"I dont feel quite easy; but I dont care sufficiently about it to make a fuss. It will be time enough when I am actually at death's door. All I know is that if there is a place of punishment in the next world, it is very unfair, considering what we suffer in this. I didnt make myself or my circumstances. I think I will try to sleep. I am half dead as it is with pain and weariness. Dont go until I am asleep."

"I will not. Let me get you another pillow."

"No," said Susanna, drowsily: "dont touch me."

Marian sat listening to her moaning respiration for nearly half an hour. Then, having some letters to write, she went to her own room to fetch her desk. Whilst she was looking for her pen, which was mislaid, she heard Susanna stirring. The floor creaked, and there was a clink as of a bottle. A moment later, Marian, listening with awakened suspicion, was startled by the sound of a heavy fall mingled with a crash of breaking glass. She ran back into the next room just in time to see Susanna, on her hands and knees near the stove, lift her white face for a moment, displaying a bleeding wound on her temple, and then stumble forward and fall prone on the carpet. Marian saw this; saw the walls of the room revolve before her; and fainted upon the sofa, which she had reached without knowing how.

When she recovered the doctor was standing by her; and Eliza was picking up fragments of the broken bottle. The smell of the spilled brandy reminded her of what had happened.

"Where is Miss Conolly?" she said, trying to collect her wits. "I am afraid I fainted at the very moment when I was most wanted."

"All right," said the doctor. "Keep quiet; youll be well presently. Don't be in a hurry to talk."

Marian obeyed; and the doctor, whose manner was kind, though different to that of the London physicians to whom she was accustomed, presently left the room and went upstairs. Eliza was howling like an animal. The sound irritated Marian even at that pass: she despised the whole Irish race on its account. She could hardly keep her temper as she said:

"Is Miss Conolly seriously hurt?"

"Oa, blessed hour! she's kilt. Her head's dhreepin wid blood."

Marian shuddered and felt faint again.

"Lord Almighty save use, I doa knoa how she done it at all, at all. She must ha fell agin the stoave. It's the dhrink, dhrink, dhrink, that brought her to it. It's little I knew what that wairy bottle o brandy would do to her, or sorra bit o me would ha got it."

"You did very wrong in getting it, Eliza."

"What could I do, miss, when she axed me?"

"There is no use in crying over it now. It would have been kinder to have kept it from her."

"Sure I know. Many's the time I tould her so. But she could talk the birds off the bushes, and it wint to me heart to refuse her. God send her well out of her throuble!"

Here the doctor returned. "How are you now?" he said.

"I think I am better. Pray dont think of me. How is she?"

"It's all over. Hallo! Come, Miss Biddy! you go and cry in the kitchen," he added, pushing Eliza, who had set up an intolerable lamentation, out of the room.

"How awful!" said Marian, stunned. "Are you quite sure? She

seemed better this morning."

"Quite sure," said the doctor, smiling grimly at the question. "She was practically dead when they carried her upstairs, poor girl. It's easier to kill a person than you think, Mrs. Forster, although she tried so long and so hard without succeeding. But she'd have done it. She'd have been starved into health only to drink herself back into starvation, and the end would have been a very bad one. Better as it is, by far!"

"Doctor: I must go out and telegraph the news to London. I know one of her relatives there."

The doctor shook his head. "I will telegraph if you like, but you must stay here. Youre not yet fit to go out."

"I am afraid I have not been well lately," said Marian. "I want to consult you about myself—not now, of course, after what has happened, but some day when you have leisure to call."

"You can put off consulting me just as long as you please; but this accident is no reason why you shouldnt do it at once. If there is anything wrong, the sooner you have advice—you neednt have it from me if you prefer some other doctor—the better."

Upon this encouragement Marian described to him her state of health. He seemed a little amused, asked her a few questions, and finally told her coolly that she might expect to become a mother next fall. She was so utterly dismayed that he began to look stern in anticipation of an appeal to him to avert this; an appeal which he had often had to refuse without ever having succeeded in persuading a woman that it was futile, or convincing her that it was immoral. But Marian spared him this: she was overwhelmed by the new certainty that a reconciliation with her husband was no longer possible. Her despair at the discovery shewed her for the first time how homesick she really was.

When the doctor left, Mrs. Myers came. She exclaimed; wept; and gossiped until two police officers arrived. Marian related to them what she had seen of the accident, and became indignant at the apparent incredulity with which they questioned her and examined the room. After their departure Eliza came to her, and invited her to go upstairs and see the body of Susanna. She refused with a shudder; but when she saw that the girl was hurt as well as astonished, it occurred to her that avoidance of the dead might, if it came to Conolly's knowledge, be taken by him to indicate a lack of kind feeling toward his sister. So she overcame her repugnance, and went with Eliza. The window-shades were drawn down, and the dressing-table had been covered with a white cloth, on which stood a plaster statuet of the Virgin and Child, with two lighted candles before it. To please Eliza, who had evidently made these arrangements, Marian whispered a few words of approval, and turned curiously to the bed. The sight made her uncomfortable. The body was decently laid out, its wounded forehead covered with a bandage, and Eliza's rosary and crucifix on its breast; but it did not, as Marian had hoped, suggest peace or sleep. It was not Susanna, but a vacant thing that had always underlain her, and which, apart from her, was ghastly.

"She died a good Catholic anyhow: the light o Heaven to her sowl!" said Eliza, whimpering, but speaking as though she expected and defied Marian to contradict her.

"Amen," said Marian.

"It's sure and sartin. There never was a Conolly a Prodestan yet."

Marian left the room, resolving to avoid such sights in future. Mrs. Myers was below, anxious to resume the conversation which the visit of the police had interrupted. Marian could not bear this. To escape, she left the house, and went to her only friend in New York, Mrs. Crawford, whose frequent visits she had never before ventured to return. To her she narrated the events of the day.

"This business of the poor girl killing herself is real shocking," said Mrs. Crawford. "Perhaps your husband will come over here now, and give you a chance of making up with him."

"If he does, I must leave New York, Mrs. Crawford."

"What are you frightened of? If he is as good a man as you say, you ought to be glad to see him. I'm sure he would have you back. Depend on it, he has been longing for you all this time; and when he sees you again as pretty as ever, he will open his arms to you. He wont like you any the worse for being a little bashful with him after such an escapade."

"I would not meet him for any earthly consideration. After what the doctor told me to-day, I should throw myself out of the window, I think, if I heard him coming upstairs. I should like to see him, if I were placed where he could not see me; but face him I *could* not."

"Well, my dear, I think it's right silly of you, though the little stranger—it will be a regular stranger—is a difficulty: there's no two ways about that."

"Besides, I have been thinking over things alone in my room; and I see that it is better for him to be free. I know he was disappointed in me. He is not the sort of man to be tied down to such an ignorant woman as I."

"What does he expect from a woman? If youre not good enough for him, he must be very hard to please."

Marian shook her head. "He is capable of pitying and being considerate with me," she said: "I know that. But I am not sure that it is a good thing to be pitied and forborne with. There is something humiliating in it. I suppose I am proud, as you often tell me; but I should like to be amongst women what he is amongst men, supported by my own strength. Even within the last three weeks I have felt myself becoming more independent in my isolation. I was afraid to go about the streets by myself at first. Now I am getting quite brave. That unfortunate woman did me good. Taking care of her, and being relied on so much by her, has made me rely on myself more. Thanks to you, I have not much loneliness to complain of. And yet I have been utterly cast down sometimes. I cannot tell what is best. Sometimes I think that independence is worth all the solitary struggling it costs. Then again I remember how free from real care I was at home, and yearn to be back there. It is so hard to know what one ought to do."

"You have been more lively since you got such a pleasant answer to your telegram. I wish the General would offer to let me keep my own money and as much more as I wanted. Not that he is close-fisted, poor man! That reminds me to tell you that you must stay the evening. He wants to see you as bad as can be—never stops asking me to bring you up some time when he's at home. You mustnt excuse yourself: the General will see you safe back to your place."

"But if visitors come, Mrs. Crawford?"

"Nobody will come. If they do, they will be glad to see you. What do they know about you? You cant live like a hermit all your life."

Marian, sooner than go back to Mrs. Myers's, stayed; and the evening passed pleasantly enough, although three visitors came: a gentleman, with his wife and brother. The lady, besides eating, and replying to the remarks with which Mrs. Crawford occasionally endeavored to entertain her, did nothing but admire Marian's dress and listen to her conversation. Her husband was polite; but Marian, comparing him with the English gentlemen of her acquaintance, thought him rather oppressively respectful, and too much given to conversing in little speeches. He had been in London; and he described, in a correct narrative style, his impressions of St. Paul's, the Tower, and Westminster Palace. His brother fell in love with Mrs. Forster at first sight, and sat silent until she remarked to him how strangely the hotel omnibuses resembled old English stage coaches, when he became recklessly talkative and soon convinced her that American society produced quite as choice a compound of off-handedness and folly as London could. But all this was amusing after her long seclusion; and once or twice, when the thought of dead Susanna came back to her, she was ashamed to be so gay.

No one was stirring at Mrs. Myers's when she returned. They had left her lamp in the entry; and she took it upstairs with her, going softly lest she should disturb the household. Susanna's usual call and petition for a few minutes talk was no longer to be feared, for Susanna was now only a memory. Marian tried not to think of the body in the room above. Though she was free from the dread which was just then making Eliza tremble, cry, and cross herself to sleep, she disliked the body all the more as she distinguished it from the no-longer existent woman: a feat quite beyond the Irish peasant girl. She sat down and began to think. The Crawfords and their friends had been very nice to her: no doubt the lady would not have been civil had she known all; but, then, the lady was a silly person. They were not exactly what Marian considered the best sort of people; but New York was not London. She would not stay at Mrs. Myers's: her income would enable her to lodge more luxuriously. If she could afford to furnish some rooms for herself, she would get some curtains she had seen one day lately when shopping with Mrs. Crawford. They would go well with—

A noise in the room overhead: Susanna's death chamber. Marian gave a great start, and understood what Eliza meant by having "the life put across in her." She listened, painfully conscious of the beats of her heart. The noise came again: a footstep, or a chair pushed back, or—she was not certain what. Could Mrs. Myers be watching at the bedside? It was not unlikely. Could Susanna be recovering—finding herself laid out for dead, and making a struggle for life up there alone? That would be inconvenient, undesirable: even Marian forgot just then to consider that obvious view wrong and unfeeling; but, anyhow, she must go and see, and, if necessary, help. She wished there were some one to keep her company; but was ashamed to call Eliza; and she felt that she would be as well by herself as with Mrs. Myers. There was nothing for it but to take a candle and go alone. No repetition of the noise occurred to daunt her afresh; and she reached the landing above almost reassured, and thinking how odd it was that the idea of finding somebody—Susanna—there, though it had come as a fear, was fading out as a disappointed hope.

Finding herself loth to open the door, she at last set her teeth and did it swiftly, as if to surprise someone within. She did surprise some one: her husband, sitting by his sister's body. He started violently on seeing her, and rose; whilst she, mechanically shutting the door without turning, leaned back against it with her hand behind her, and looked at him open-mouthed.

"Marian," he said, in a quite unexpectedly apprehensive tone, putting up his hand deprecatingly: "remember, here"— indicating the figure on the bed—"is an end of hypocrisy! No unrealities now: I cannot bear them. Let us have no trash of magnanimous injured husband, erring but repentant wife. We are man and woman, nothing less and nothing more. After our marriage you declined intercourse on those terms; and I accepted your conventions to please you. Now I refuse all conventions: you have broken them yourself. If you will not have the truth between us, avoid me until I have subsided into the old groove again. There!" he added, wincing, "dont blush. What have you to blush for? It was the only honest thing you ever did."

"I dont understand."

"No," he said gently, but with a gesture of despair; "how could you? You never did, and you never will."

"If you mean to accuse me of having deceived you," said Marian, greatly relieved and encouraged by a sense of being

George Bernard Shaw

now the injured party, "you are most unjust. I dont excuse myself for behaving wickedly, but I *never* deceived you or told you a falsehood. Never. When he first spoke wrongly to me, I told you at once; and you did not care."

"Not a straw. It was nothing to me that he loved you: the point was, did you love him? If not, then all was well: if so, our marriage was already at an end. But you mistake my drift. Falsehood is something more than fibbing. You never told fibs—except the two or three dozen a week that mere politeness required and which you never thought of counting; but you never told me the truth, Marian, because you never told your self the truth. You told me what you told yourself, I grant you; and so you were not conscious of deceit. I dont reproach you. Surely you can bear to be told what every honest man tells himself almost daily."

"I suppose I have deserved it," said Marian; "but unkind words from you are a new experience. You are very unlike yourself to-night."

He repressed, with visible effort, an explosion of impatience. "On the contrary, I am like myself—I actually am myself to-night, I hope." Then the explosion came. "Is it utterly impossible for you to say something real to me? Only learn to do that, and you may have ten love romances every year with other men, if you like. Be anything rather than a ladylike slave and liar. There! as usual, the truth makes you shrink from me. As I said before, I refuse further intercourse on such terms. They have proved unkind in the long run."

"You spoke plainly enough to her," said Marian, glancing at the bed, "but in the long run it did her no good."

"She would have laughed me to scorn if I had minced matters, for she never deceived herself. Society, by the power of the purse, set her to nautch-girl's work, and forbade her the higher work that was equally within her power. Being enslaved and debauched in this fashion, how could she be happy except when she was not sober? It was her own immediate interest to drink; it was her tradesman's interest that she should drink; it was her servants' interest that she should be pleased with them for getting drink for her. She was clever, good-natured, more constant to her home and her man than you, a living fountain of innocent pleasure as a dancer, singer, and actress; and here she lies, after mischievously spending her talent in a series of entertainments too dull for hell and too debased for any better place, dead of a preventable disease, chiefly because most of the people she came in contact with had a direct pecuniary interest in depraving and poisoning her. Aye, look at her! with the cross on her breast, the virgin mother in plaster looking on from where she kept her mirror when she was alive, and the people outside complacently saying 'Serve her right!'"

Marian feared for a moment that he would demolish Eliza's altar by hurling the chair through it. "Dont, Ned," she said, timidly, putting her hand on his arm.

"Dont what?" he said, taken aback. She drew her hand away and retreated a step, coloring at the wifely liberty she had permitted herself to take. "I beg your pardon. I thought—I thought you were going to take the cross away. No," she added quickly, seeing him about to speak, and anticipating a burst of scepticism: "it is not that; but the servant is an Irish girl—a Roman Catholic. She put it there; and she meant well, and will be hurt if it is thrown aside."

"And you think it better that she should remain in ignorance of what educated people think about her superstition than that she should suffer the mortification of learning that her opinions are not those of all the world! However, I had no such intention. Eliza's idol is a respectable one as idols go."

There was a pause. Then Marian said: "It must have been a great shock to you when you came and found what had happened. I am very sorry. But had we not better go downrs? It seems so unfeeling, somehow, to talk without minding her. I suppose you consider that foolish; but I think you are upset by it yourself."

"You see a change in me, then?"

"You are not quite yourself, I think."

"I tell you again that I *am* myself at last. You do not seem to like the real man any better than the unreal: I am afraid you will not have me on any terms. Well, let us go downstairs, since you prefer it."

"Oh, not unless you wish it too," said Marian, a little bewildered.

He took her candle and led the way out without another word or a look at the bed. Marian, as he stood aside to let her go downstairs before him, was suddenly seized with a fantastic fear that he was going to kill her. She did not condescend to hurry or look back; but she only felt safe when they were in her room, and he no longer behind her.

"Sit down," he said, placing the candle on the mantelpiece. She sat down at the table, and he stood on the hearthrug. "Now," said he, "about the future. Are you coming back? Will you give the life at Holland Park another trial?"

"I cannot," she said, bending her head almost on her hands. "I should disgrace you. And there is another reason."

"It is not in your power, nor in that of all London, to disgrace me if I do not feel disgraced. It is useless to say that you cannot. If you say 'I will not,' then that will settle it. What is the other reason?"

"It is not yet born. But it will be."

"That is no reason to me. Do you think I shall be a worse father to it than he would have been?"

"No, indeed. But it would be unfair to you." He made an impatient gesture. "I dont understand you, Ned. Would you not rather be free?"

"Freedom is a fool's dream. I am free. I can divorce you if I please: if I live with you again it will be by my own choice. You are free too: you have burnt your boats, and are rid of fashionable society, of your family, your position, your principles, and all the rest of your chains forever. You are declassed by your own act; and if you can frankly give a sigh of relief and respect yourself for breaking loose from what is called your duty, then you are the very woman I want for a wife. I may not be the very man you want for a husband; but at all events you are free to choose, free to change after you choose if you choose me, free anyhow; for I will divorce you if you refuse; and then you will be—independent—your own mistress—absolute proprietor of your own child—everything that married women and girls envy. You have a foretaste of that freedom now. What is it worth? One or two conditions more or less to comply with, that is all: nature and society still have you hard and fast; the main rules of the game are inviolable."

"I think it is a good thing to be free," said Marian, timidly.

"That means 'I will not.'"

"Not 'will not'; but I think I had better not."

"A characteristic distinction, Marian. I once thought, like you, that freedom was the one condition to be gained at all cost and hazard. My favorite psalm was that nonsense of John Hay's:

'For always in thine eyes, O Liberty,
Shines that high light whereby the world is saved;
And though thou slay us, we will trust in thee.'

And she does slay us. Now I am for the fullest attainable life. That involves the least endurable liberty. You dont see that yet.

Very well: you have liberty—liberty to hurt as well as help yourself; and you are right to try whether it will not make you happier than wedlock has done."

"It was not your fault; and it is very good of you to offer to take me back, I know. Will my refusing disappoint you at all, Ned?"

"I am prepared for it. You may refuse or accept: I foresee how I shall adapt myself to either set of circumstances."

"Yes, I forgot. You foresee everything," said Marian, with some bitterness.

"No: I only face what I see. That is why you do not like living with me. Good-bye. Do not look troubled: we shall meet again to-morrow and often afterward, I hope; but to-night makes an end of the irrational knot."

"Good-night," said Marian rather forlornly, after a pause, proffering her hand.

"One folly more," he said, taking her in his arms and kissing her. She made no resistance. "If such a moment could be eternal, we should never say good-bye," he added. "As it is, we are wise not to tempt Fortune by asking her for such another."

"You are too wise, Ned," she said, suffering him to replace her gently in the chair.

"It is impossible to be too wise, dearest," he said, and unhesitatingly turned and left her.

ABOUT THE AUTHOR

(**George**) **Bernard Shaw** (born Dublin, 26 July 1856 – died 2 November 1950 in Hertfordshire) was an Irish playwright based in England. He uniquely had the honor of being awarded both the Nobel Prize in Literature (in 1925) and an Academy Award for Writing Adapted Screenplay (in 1938 for Pygmalion).

Shaw's career started with frustration and near poverty. Neither music criticism (written under the name of a family friend) nor a telephone company job lasted very long, and only two of the five novels Shaw wrote between 1879 and 1883 found publishers: Cashel Byron's Profession (1882), a novel about prizefighting as an occupation that anticipates the theme of prostitution as an antisocial profession in the play Mrs. Warren's Profession (1893), and An Unsocial Socialist (1883). By the mid-1880s Shaw discovered the writings of Karl Marx and turned to socialist polemics and critical journalism. He also became a firm (and lifelong) believer in vegetarianism, a spellbinding orator, and tentatively, a playwright. He was the force behind the newly founded (1884) Fabian Society, a middle-class socialist group that aimed at the transformation of English government and society. In 1887, Shaw spoke and marched in the Bloody Sunday demonstrations that ended up as a riot in Trafalgar Square.

Choose from Thousands of 1stWorldLibrary Classics By

A. M. Barnard
Ada Leverson
Adolphus William Ward
Aesop
Agatha Christie
Alexander Aaronsohn
Alexander Kielland
Alexandre Dumas
Alfred Gatty
Alfred Ollivant
Alice Duer Miller
Alice Turner Curtis
Alice Dunbar
Allen Chapman
Alleyne Ireland
Ambrose Bierce
Amelia E. Barr
Amory H. Bradford
Andrew Lang
Andrew McFarland Davis
Andy Adams
Angela Brazil
Anna Alice Chapin
Anna Sewell
Annie Besant
Annie Hamilton Donnell
Annie Payson Call
Annie Roe Carr
Annonaymous
Anton Chekhov
Archibald Lee Fletcher
Arnold Bennett
Arthur C. Benson
Arthur Conan Doyle
Arthur M. Winfield
Arthur Ransome
Arthur Schnitzler
Arthur Train
Atticus
B.H. Baden-Powell
B. M. Bower
B. C. Chatterjee
Baroness Emmuska Orczy
Baroness Orczy
Basil King
Bayard Taylor
Ben Macomber
Bertha Muzzy Bower
Bjornstjerne Bjornson

Booth Tarkington
Boyd Cable
Bram Stoker
C. Collodi
C. E. Orr
C. M. Ingleby
Carolyn Wells
Catherine Parr Traill
Charles A. Eastman
Charles Amory Beach
Charles Dickens
Charles Dudley Warner
Charles Farrar Browne
Charles Ives
Charles Kingsley
Charles Klein
Charles Hanson Towne
Charles Lathrop Pack
Charles Romyn Dake
Charles Whibley
Charles Willing Beale
Charlotte M. Braeme
Charlotte M. Yonge
Charlotte Perkins Stetson
Clair W. Hayes
Clarence Day Jr.
Clarence E. Mulford
Clemence Housman
Confucius
Coningsby Dawson
Cornelis DeWitt Wilcox
Cyril Burleigh
D. H. Lawrence
Daniel Defoe
David Garnett
Dinah Craik
Don Carlos Janes
Donald Keyhoe
Dorothy Kilner
Dougan Clark
Douglas Fairbanks
E. Nesbit
E. P. Roe
E. Phillips Oppenheim
E. S. Brooks
Earl Barnes
Edgar Rice Burroughs
Edith Van Dyne
Edith Wharton

Edward Everett Hale
Edward J. O'Biren
Edward S. Ellis
Edwin L. Arnold
Eleanor Atkins
Eleanor Hallowell Abbott
Eliot Gregory
Elizabeth Gaskell
Elizabeth McCracken
Elizabeth Von Arnim
Ellem Key
Emerson Hough
Emilie F. Carlen
Emily Bronte
Emily Dickinson
Enid Bagnold
Enilor Macartney Lane
Erasmus W. Jones
Ernie Howard Pie
Ethel May Dell
Ethel Turner
Ethel Watts Mumford
Eugene Sue
Eugenie Foa
Eugene Wood
Eustace Hale Ball
Evelyn Everett-green
Everard Cotes
F. H. Cheley
F. J. Cross
F. Marion Crawford
Fannie E. Newberry
Federick Austin Ogg
Ferdinand Ossendowski
Fergus Hume
Florence A. Kilpatrick
Fremont B. Deering
Francis Bacon
Francis Darwin
Frances Hodgson Burnett
Frances Parkinson Keyes
Frank Gee Patchin
Frank Harris
Frank Jewett Mather
Frank L. Packard
Frank V. Webster
Frederic Stewart Isham
Frederick Trevor Hill
Frederick Winslow Taylor

Friedrich Kerst
Friedrich Nietzsche
Fyodor Dostoyevsky
G.A. Henty
G.K. Chesterton
Gabrielle E. Jackson
Garrett P. Serviss
Gaston Leroux
George A. Warren
George Ade
Geroge Bernard Shaw
George Cary Eggleston
George Durston
George Ebers
George Eliot
George Gissing
George MacDonald
George Meredith
George Orwell
George Sylvester Viereck
George Tucker
George W. Cable
George Wharton James
Gertrude Atherton
Gordon Casserly
Grace E. King
Grace Gallatin
Grace Greenwood
Grant Allen
Guillermo A. Sherwell
Gulielma Zollinger
Gustav Flaubert
H. A. Cody
H. B. Irving
H.C. Bailey
H. G. Wells
H. H. Munro
H. Irving Hancock
H. R. Naylor
H. Rider Haggard
H. W. C. Davis
Haldeman Julius
Hall Caine
Hamilton Wright Mabie
Hans Christian Andersen
Harold Avery
Harold McGrath
Harriet Beecher Stowe
Harry Castlemon
Harry Coghill
Harry Houidini

Hayden Carruth
Helent Hunt Jackson
Helen Nicolay
Hendrik Conscience
Hendy David Thoreau
Henri Barbusse
Henrik Ibsen
Henry Adams
Henry Ford
Henry Frost
Henry James
Henry Jones Ford
Henry Seton Merriman
Henry W Longfellow
Herbert A. Giles
Herbert Carter
Herbert N. Casson
Herman Hesse
Hildegard G. Frey
Homer
Honore De Balzac
Horace B. Day
Horace Walpole
Horatio Alger Jr.
Howard Pyle
Howard R. Garis
Hugh Lofting
Hugh Walpole
Humphry Ward
Ian Maclaren
Inez Haynes Gillmore
Irving Bacheller
Isabel Cecilia Williams
Isabel Hornibrook
Israel Abrahams
Ivan Turgenev
J.G.Austin
J. Henri Fabre
J. M. Barrie
J. M. Walsh
J. Macdonald Oxley
J. R. Miller
J. S. Fletcher
J. S. Knowles
J. Storer Clouston
J. W. Duffield
Jack London
Jacob Abbott
James Allen
James Andrews
James Baldwin

James Branch Cabell
James DeMille
James Joyce
James Lane Allen
James Lane Allen
James Oliver Curwood
James Oppenheim
James Otis
James R. Driscoll
Jane Abbott
Jane Austen
Jane L. Stewart
Janet Aldridge
Jens Peter Jacobsen
Jerome K. Jerome
Jessie Graham Flower
John Buchan
John Burroughs
John Cournos
John F. Kennedy
John Gay
John Glasworthy
John Habberton
John Joy Bell
John Kendrick Bangs
John Milton
John Philip Sousa
John Taintor Foote
Jonas Lauritz Idemil Lie
Jonathan Swift
Joseph A. Altsheler
Joseph Carey
Joseph Conrad
Joseph E. Badger Jr
Joseph Hergesheimer
Joseph Jacobs
Jules Vernes
Julian Hawthrone
Julie A Lippmann
Justin Huntly McCarthy
Kakuzo Okakura
Karle Wilson Baker
Kate Chopin
Kenneth Grahame
Kenneth McGaffey
Kate Langley Bosher
Kate Langley Bosher
Katherine Cecil Thurston
Katherine Stokes
L. A. Abbot
L. T. Meade

L. Frank Baum
Latta Griswold
Laura Dent Crane
Laura Lee Hope
Laurence Housman
Lawrence Beasley
Leo Tolstoy
Leonid Andreyev
Lewis Carroll
Lewis Sperry Chafer
Lilian Bell
Lloyd Osbourne
Louis Hughes
Louis Joseph Vance
Louis Tracy
Louisa May Alcott
Lucy Fitch Perkins
Lucy Maud Montgomery
Luther Benson
Lydia Miller Middleton
Lyndon Orr
M. Corvus
M. H. Adams
Margaret E. Sangster
Margret Howth
Margaret Vandercook
Margaret W. Hungerford
Margret Penrose
Maria Edgeworth
Maria Thompson Daviess
Mariano Azuela
Marion Polk Angellotti
Mark Overton
Mark Twain
Mary Austin
Mary Catherine Crowley
Mary Cole
Mary Hastings Bradley
Mary Roberts Rinehart
Mary Rowlandson
M. Wollstonecraft Shelley
Maud Lindsay
Max Beerbohm
Myra Kelly
Nathaniel Hawthrone
Nicolo Machiavelli
O. F. Walton
Oscar Wilde

Owen Johnson
P.G. Wodehouse
Paul and Mabel Thorne
Paul G. Tomlinson
Paul Severing
Percy Brebner
Percy Keese Fitzhugh
Peter B. Kyne
Plato
Quincy Allen
R. Derby Holmes
R. L. Stevenson
R. S. Ball
Rabindranath Tagore
Rahul Alvares
Ralph Bonehill
Ralph Henry Barbour
Ralph Victor
Ralph Waldo Emmerson
Rene Descartes
Ray Cummings
Rex Beach
Rex E. Beach
Richard Harding Davis
Richard Jefferies
Richard Le Gallienne
Robert Barr
Robert Frost
Robert Gordon Anderson
Robert L. Drake
Robert Lansing
Robert Lynd
Robert Michael Ballantyne
Robert W. Chambers
Rosa Nouchette Carey
Rudyard Kipling
Saint Augustine
Samuel B. Allison
Samuel Hopkins Adams
Sarah Bernhardt
Sarah C. Hallowell
Selma Lagerlof
Sherwood Anderson
Sigmund Freud
Standish O'Grady
Stanley Weyman
Stella Benson
Stella M. Francis

Stephen Crane
Stewart Edward White
Stijn Streuvels
Swami Abhedananda
Swami Parmananda
T. S. Ackland
T. S. Arthur
The Princess Der Ling
Thomas A. Janvier
Thomas A Kempis
Thomas Anderton
Thomas Bailey Aldrich
Thomas Bulfinch
Thomas De Quincey
Thomas Dixon
Thomas H. Huxley
Thomas Hardy
Thomas More
Thornton W. Burgess
U. S. Grant
Upton Sinclair
Valentine Williams
Various Authors
Vaughan Kester
Victor Appleton
Victor G. Durham
Victoria Cross
Virginia Woolf
Wadsworth Camp
Walter Camp
Walter Scott
Washington Irving
Wilbur Lawton
Wilkie Collins
Willa Cather
Willard F. Baker
William Dean Howells
William le Queux
W. Makepeace Thackeray
William W. Walter
William Shakespeare
Winston Churchill
Yei Theodora Ozaki
Yogi Ramacharaka
Young E. Allison
Zane Grey

www.ingramcontent.com/pod-product-compliance
Lightning Source LLC
Chambersburg PA
CBHW020831030726
47496CB00001B/187